Leading for Learning

Leading for Learning

HOW TO TRANSFORM
SCHOOLS INTO LEARNING
ORGANIZATIONS

Phillip C. Schlechty

JOSSEY-BASS
A Wiley Imprint
www.josseybass.com

Published by Jossey-Bass
A Wiley Imprint
989 Market Street, San Francisco, CA 94103-1741—www.josseybass.com

Library of Congress Cataloging-in-Publication Data

Schlechty, Phillip C., 1937-
  Leading for learning: how to transform schools into learning organizations / Phillip C. Schlechty.
    p. cm.
  Includes bibliographical references and index.
  ISBN 978-0-7879-9434-1 (pbk.)
  1. School improvement programs—United States.   2. School management and organization—United States.   3. Educational change—United States. I. Title.
  LB2822.82.S337 2009
  371.2'070973—dc22

                                        2008051694

Printed in the United States of America
FIRST EDITION

PB Printing   10 9 8 7 6 5 4 3 2 1

CONTENTS

PREFACE

This book is about differences between and among schools—differences that make a difference in the lives of teachers, students, parents, and communities. It is not about *why* schools do not get results. It is about why schools get the results they do.

My intent is to help teachers and other school leaders better understand why their jobs are so hard—and what it will take to make their work more manageable and satisfying. It is also my intention to help local community leaders, especially school board members and state legislators, to better understand what is happening to their schools and why.

GUIDING QUESTIONS

Three questions have guided my thinking in writing this book:

- Is it possible to pursue high standards and attach consequences to performance without resorting to the tools of bureaucracy?

- Is it possible to organize schools so that they reflect concern for the unique circumstance of each child—without giving up the notion that all children should learn some of the same things at high levels?

- Can local school districts develop the capacity to sustain improvement efforts in response to national priorities as well as to local circumstances—without the active intervention of state and federal agencies?

I think that it is possible to answer these questions affirmatively, but only when we shift our images of schools from those that grow out of bureaucratic assumptions to those that grow out of assumptions that schools can become learning organizations. Once this shift is made, the principles on which schools are built will necessarily be quite different from those on which most schools and school districts are now based.

The primary purpose of this book is to make the nature of these principles very clear and to show how they might be applied to create the new system of education America needs. For example, I argue that rather than viewing standards as a means of enforcing bureaucratic authority, standards might better be used as a source of direction for school and communities. This would mean that rather than assigning the authority to establish and enforce standards to state agencies, legislators might require that local communities establish clear standards that their leaders can defend in the public forum and then develop processes to assess the effectiveness of their schools in meeting these standards. The role of the state would be to specify standards for setting standards rather than specifying the standards themselves. Similarly, I argue that local school boards should become much more active as educators of the community about educational matters and much less oriented toward advancing the causes of special interest groups. This will undoubtedly require new thinking regarding the way school boards are elected and held accountable. Much of this book has to do with strategies for bringing such transformations about.

ASSUMPTIONS

As the reader will quickly recognize, what I write is informed by a bias. I am on the side of teachers, principals, and superintendents who must deal every day with the realities of an education system that encourages mindlessness and the docile acceptance of bureaucratically oriented policy decisions that are too often harmful to the cause of good education for children. I proceed from the belief that if the public schools are to work as they must work in the twenty-first century, they must be supported by all citizens—young and old, rich and poor, liberal and conservative. Moreover, they must serve all citizens, not just the students and parents who, at any given time, are involved in the schools or the interest groups and political factions that want to bend the schools to their will. Schools are about the future and posterity more than they are about the present and prosperity.

It is certainly true that in their present bureaucratic form, many schools are not sufficiently responsive to parents and the diverse needs of students. Indeed, it is the failure of locally controlled bureaucracies to respond to the needs of all the children of all the citizens that has led to moving bureaucratic control from local board offices to even more bureaucratic offices in state capitols and in Washington, D.C.

Those who advocate more state and federal control of schools seem oblivious to the fact that such a reform does not solve the problem of America's schools. Rather, it moves the means of solving the problem further from the reach of precisely the people who must solve it if it is to be solved at all: the local educational leaders and the citizens of the local communities the schools are intended to serve.

It is also my view that the link between the quality of schools and the quality of community life is so deep and profound that it makes no sense to work to improve the schools outside the context of improving communities as well. It is not possible to have strong schools in unhealthy communities. School improvement and community building go hand in hand. It is therefore a grave mistake to turn schools into government agencies and to remove control of the schools from local communities, especially at a time when one of the greatest crises facing the nation is the breakdown of communities and the loss of sources of community identity and feelings of belonging on which communities depend.

Education in America will not be helped by making the schools more bureaucratic and by driving in fear. What we need are policies that put joy back into teaching and common sense back into the way schools are led. This book is an effort to assist in such a transformation.

My hope is that this book will provide local educational and civic leaders with ideas and tools that will help them build initiatives to save our schools from the creeping paralysis that is now being foisted on them by those who believe that government experts know better what the people want and need than do the people themselves. My faith in public education is a traditional American faith, based on the Jeffersonian belief that the people, if they are well informed, are the best judges of what they need. I also believe that in the long run, citizens will trust only leaders who trust them in return.

Learning organizations, as we shall see, are based on such trust. Bureaucracies are not. Bureaucracies are based on fear and distrust, and they depend on punishments and extrinsic rewards to gain what leaders want and intend.

THE CONTEXT OF TEACHING AND SCHOOL LEADERSHIP

Not all schools perform well, and some teachers are ineffective. It is also the case that these schools and these teachers are more likely to serve poor children, especially poor minority children, than affluent children.

In my view, low-performing schools function something like canaries did in coal mines. Because the students they serve are more often poor and from places where strong community support is lacking, these schools are the first to reveal the presence of harmful elements in the environment. These elements are, however, likely to be present in other schools as well, though those affected may not be aware of it because the teachers and students have enough external support to survive in spite of what might be happening to them inside the school.

Certainly I believe that highly qualified teachers and good principal leadership are necessary for good schools. It is my view, however, that in the long run, high-performing teachers are either suppressed by bad schools or they flee from them—to other schools or out of education altogether. In fact, one of the reasons poorly performing schools often seem to have a disproportionate number of poorly performing teachers may be that teaching well in these schools is just too hard and too often there are no supports for those who really try. Introducing good teachers into bad schools without working on the schools and the systems in which the schools are embedded seems to me to be a wasted effort and generates cynicism regarding the prospects of improving schools. It also discourages too many gifted teachers.

Certainly I am concerned about low-performing schools, but my attention is not fastened on them. Rather, my quest is for excellence in all schools and for all children. Indeed, I learned long ago that the words *excellence* and *equity* should never be separated, for to honor one without attending to the other is to do harm to both.

A MATTER OF STYLE

This book is the product of a lifetime working in and around schools and learning from educators; it is not my doctoral dissertation. Where I know I have a heavy intellectual debt, I use footnotes to honor that debt, and where I quote specific content from other works I use footnotes as well. I do not, however, try to document every point I make, and I don't cite every possible contrary opinion. Let the contrarians write their own book.

THE AUDIENCE FOR THIS BOOK

This book is written for the men and women who live out their lives in schools and school districts and for the local community leaders, including school board members, whose support for schools is essential for the survival of schools as well as the health of the communities in which they live. I hope that members of the scholarly community will read it and enjoy what they read, but it is not my intention to add to the research related to schooling. Rather, it is my purpose to take what research, theory, and a good deal of practice have taught me about schooling and efforts to improve schools and make what I have learned available to others.

THE ORGANIZATION OF THIS BOOK

This book is organized into three major parts.

The five chapters in Part One make the case for transformation as contrasted with reform and present some of the basic concepts and frameworks essential to understanding the distinctions made between bureaucracies and learning organizations. For those unfamiliar with the literature in sociology and organizational theory, I provide a broad introduction to some of the concepts and issues that I believe are most useful when trying to figure out what is going on in schools and why.

In Chapter One, I make a distinction between reformation and transformation and present an argument for transformation. Chapter Two discusses systems and systemic change. In this chapter, I examine how critical social systems affect the way innovations are introduced in schools and how these systems affect the prospects of survival of innovations once they are introduced. In Chapter Three I make some fundamental distinctions between bureaucracies and learning organizations. Chapter Four presents a series of metaphors intended to help illuminate the nature of bureaucratic practice in schools. Chapter Five presents an alternative set of metaphors to help describe the operation of a school or school system organized as a learning organization.

By the time readers have finished reading these first five chapters, they should have a clear notion of how I distinguish between schools as learning organizations and schools as bureaucracies. It should also be clear how these different conceptions of schooling shape and mold the way those who live out their lives in school view themselves and their work and why so much that happens in school that seems so mindless in fact has a logic; but the logic is a sociologic embedded in the structure of organizational life rather than in the structure of personalities.

Part Two contains three chapters, each addressing a different topic, that should be of concern to those who would lead school transformation. Chapter Six explores the rising power of an emerging education policy elite and the drive toward the bureaucratization of schools. Chapter Seven examines the impact of the standards-based school reform movement on the increasing bureaucratization of the schools and moves toward distinguishing between forms of accountability that are intended to lead to improvement of performance and forms that are intended primarily as a means of exercising external control. Chapter Eight presents a discussion of the ideas of civic capacity and social capital. My intent is to make the case that meaningful efforts to improve schools require attention to community building and political action at the same time that they require attention to the internal operation of schools.

The four chapters in Part Three address a set of topics that must be addressed in an action agenda. Chapter Nine deals with the idea of mental models and the use of metaphors in inspiring transformation initiatives. Chapter Ten examines the idea of capacity building. In this chapter, I set forth specific suggestions of ways to go about building capacity, especially the capacity to support and sustain the introduction of innovations that in the context of bureaucracies are likely to be rejected or domesticated. (*Domestication* is a term I use to refer to the tendency of bureaucracies to alter an innovation to fit the existing system rather than changing the system to accommodate the innovation.) Chapter Eleven presents a discussion of standards as sources of direction and suggests some strategies for using standards to ensure quality without allowing the standards to inhibit creativity and imagination in schools and classrooms. Chapter Twelve presents a theory of action that in effect summarizes much that precedes it, especially much that is contained in Chapters Nine through Twelve.

In the final chapter, I give additional attention to issues related to leadership and community building, and relate these issues to the notion of marketing ideas and persuading publics.

The book also has two appendixes. Both are in fact an integral part of this book and should be read along with Chapters Three through Five. Appendix A presents a detailed description of the differences between and among critical social systems in a bureaucracy and in a learning organization that are outlined in Chapter Three. Many of the school leaders who have read this appendix—and there have now been literally hundreds of such readers—have found it to be extremely useful, especially as a tool for serious discussions about the condition of their schools and what action steps they need to take to move toward the transformation into a learning organization.

Appendix B presents a thumbnail sketch of each of the role descriptions presented in Chapters Four and Five. These sketches have proven most useful to educators who use the charts presented in Chapter Four as a tool to help them assess the culture of their school, especially as that culture is reflected in the rules and roles that typify social relationships in the schoolhouse and between the schoolhouse and the school district.

ACKNOWLEDGMENTS

This book has been a long time in the making. I really don't know when I started it, but some of the framing ideas go back to 1975 or before. Clearly I cannot remember all those who contributed to this book, and I will not try. I simply thank everyone who had a part in this.

Nevertheless, there are a number of individuals whose thoughts and reactions I want to acknowledge. I especially thank Bob Nolte for an early and intensive effort to help me clean up some ugly prose and clarify my thinking as well. My daughter, Jennifer Schlechty, and Kim Vidrine, editor for the Schlechty Center, went above and beyond the call of duty as editors on various drafts of this book. I also owe a clear debt to all the other members of the Schlechty Center staff, not only for their willingness to react to chapters and ideas but also for their tolerance of my tendency to become so fastened on this book that I forgot other matters I should have been attending to.

As has become my custom, once I have completed what I think is a final version of a book, I invite a panel of educators I respect to spend a couple of days with me reviewing the manuscript and helping me to better understand what those for whom the book is written might think about what I have written. This time I invited eight superintendents, all of whom I have worked with in the past and respect. I learned much from them—so much that I revised most of what I thought I had finished. The book is better because of them. The remaining weaknesses are, of course, still mine to own. Specifically, I thank Randy Bridges, superintendent, Alamance-Burlington, North Carolina, School District; Jim Hawkins, superintendent, Killeen, Texas, Independent School District (ISD); James Hutto, superintendent, Petal, Mississippi, School District; J. D. Kennedy, superintendent, Midlothian, Texas, ISD; Rodney Lafon, superintendent, St. Charles Parish, Louisiana, School District; Pam Lannon, consultant; Elizabeth Saenz, superintendent, Cotulla, Texas, ISD; and Steve Waddell, superintendent, Birdville, Texas, ISD. Without them and many of their colleagues, I would have little confidence that what I propose in the pages that follow is possible. It is because of these educators and others like them that I keep hope alive in my heart as well as my head.

I would also like to thank Susan Geraghty who served as production editor. She kept everything on time and on track, and was flexible enough to make it possible to deal with life's emergencies. In addition Bev Miller, the copyeditor for Jossey-Bass, did a masterful job and I thank her as well. Finally, I give a special thanks to Lesley Iura, educational director of K–12 Education for Jossey-Bass. This is the fifth book she has helped me bring to completion. I continue to be impressed with her patience, good humor, and skill. She is also a special friend.

A PERSONAL NOTE

I dedicate this book to my two grandchildren, Lilly Flannigan and Daniel Rademaker, who serve as living inspirations for me to keep on working to improve America's schools. They are in the first grade, early in the great school adventure. I hope the schools get better each year they attend. I hope even more that the schools do not deteriorate because of misguided efforts to improve them. I want my grandchildren and all other children to find meaning in school and to experience the joy of learning and disciplined inquiry. I do not want them to come away from school feeling as Albert Einstein said he felt when he looked back on his experiences in German schools:

> One had to cram all this stuff into one's mind, whether one liked it or not. This coercion had such a deterring effect that, after I had passed the final examination, I found the consideration of any scientific problems distasteful to me for an entire year. . . . It is in fact nothing short of a miracle that the modern methods of instruction have not yet entirely strangled the holy curiosity of inquiry; for this delicate little plant, aside from stimulation, stands mainly in need of freedom; without this it goes to wrack and ruin without fail. It is a very grave mistake to think that the enjoyment of seeing and searching can be promoted by means of coercion and a sense of duty.

Much of the bureaucratic form of America's schools was imported from Germany in the nineteenth century. It is this basic structure that must be changed.

I believe that the future of America depends on the ability of the current generation of American educators to find new ways of linking the cause of public education to the building of democratic communities where they live. Education and America have been good to me and my family. My hope is that what I have written will give back to the community a small down payment on what I have received.

February 2009

Phillip C. Schlechty
Louisville, Kentucky

THE AUTHOR

Phillip Schlechty is the founder and chief executive officer of the Schlechty Center for Leadership in School Reform. He has been a teacher and public school administrator, as well as a university professor and associate dean. He established the Center for Leadership in School Reform in 1988; through this organization, he has developed a staff of experienced educators who are committed to transforming schools from bureaucracies into learning organizations. Schlechty and the center staff work with thousands of teachers, principals, central office staff, superintendents, and school boards, as well as with parents, civic leaders, business leaders, and others interested in the continuing health of public education in America. The center works with school districts across the United States.

Over the past forty years, Schlechty has written seven books and many journal articles dealing with issues related to the transformation of schools and school leadership. He has received awards from such diverse organizations as the American Federation of Teachers, the American Educational Research Association, and the National Staff Development Council. Most recently, his alma mater, The Ohio State University, honored him by inducting him into the School of Education and Human Ecology Faculty and Alumni Hall of Fame.

Schlechty and his wife, Shelia, live in Louisville, Kentucky. They have two daughters and two grandchildren. His grandchildren attend public schools in Kentucky and Colorado.

Leading for Learning

PART ONE

Making the Case for Transformation

The Case for Transformation

There is general agreement that the schools of America must be improved. There is, however less agreement about what needs to be done to improve them. Most who say schools need to be improved want to reform them in some way. The position taken in this book, however, is that reform is not enough. What is needed is transformation.

In the context of recent efforts to improve schools, *reform* usually means changing procedures, processes, and technologies with the intent of improving the performance of existing operating systems. The aim is to make existing systems more effective at doing what they have always been intended to do.

Transformation is intended to make it possible to do things that have never been done by the organization undergoing the transformation. It involves metamorphosis: changing from one form to another form entirely. In organizational terms, transformation almost always involves repositioning and reorienting action by putting the organization into a new business or adopting a radically different means of doing the work it has traditionally done. Transformation by necessity includes altering the beliefs, values, and meanings—the culture—in which programs are embedded, as well as changing the current system of rules, roles, and relationships—social structure—so that the innovations needed will be supported. Reform, in contrast, means only installing innovations that will work within the context of the existing structure and culture of schools.

Transformation is a difficult and risky enterprise, its dimensions uncertain and difficult to define. It requires men and women to do things they have never done before—not just to get better at what they have always done.

Because it is so risky, transformation requires strong leaders who understand that they are dealing with values as well as technique, meaning as well as skills. Most of all, transformation requires leaders who have a deep understanding of both the reasons transformation is necessary and why an easier course cannot be taken. It requires leaders who are themselves passionately committed to the new organization they are trying to create.

Without such leaders, it will not be possible to mobilize the energy required to make the changes that must be made to transform the schools and stick with the task when things go wrong. Without such leaders, the future of public education in the United States, and even the future of democracy in this country, are at great risk.

WHY REFORMATION IS NOT ENOUGH

The drive for reform in public schools has usually been linked to some perceived threat from the outside. In the 1870s the American high school movement was motivated in part by the need to make American boys competitive with the graduates of European trade schools. In the 1960s the threat was the system of education in the Soviet Union, which was said to be responsible for a Soviet advantage in the so-called space race. In the 1980s, the apparent ascendance of Japanese over American manufacturers was attributed to a rising tide of mediocrity that was said to be besetting America's schools. Today engineers from China and India are the perceived threats, and our declining competitive edge relative to these countries—whether real or not—is attributed to a deficient education system that stands in need of repair.

I have no doubt that the U.S. position in the world is linked to the quality of education our schools provide, and I am concerned about these matters. These are not, however, the primary reasons I am committed to transforming America's schools. My rationale for changing schools flows from a very different and more fundamental source than concern about international competitiveness.

Just as I believe that there is a link between education and the economy, I believe there is a link between the schools and the communities in which they are embedded, and through these communities, there is a link to the civic and moral health of the nation and the democratic order that defines that nation. Over the past fifty years, the nature of these links has changed. In addition, the relationships between children and those traditional institutions that have historically stood between the young and the larger society until they were judged to have reached maturity have changed as well. These changes are affecting what the young need to learn as well as the way children are learning what they come to know.

Today there is an increasing sense of community estrangement from the schools, and the depth of this estrangement is well documented.[1] Moreover, the relationships between the young and the institutions that have traditionally been charged with their education—the family, religious institutions, and schools— are being altered in ways that are immutable. It is these changes, more than the needs of the economy, that for me are the driving forces behind the need to transform our schools. It is these changes that lead me to assert that reform is not enough.

THE NEED FOR TRANSFORMATION

It is time reformers quit "tinkering toward utopia," grafting one reform after another onto a tree that is planted in soil deficient of the proper nutrients.[2] It is time to acknowledge that the education of children in America is now rooted in infertile soil and to recognize that if education is to be improved, schools must be transplanted into a more nourishing environment. Schools must be transformed from platforms for instruction to platforms for learning, from bureaucracies bent on control to learning organizations aimed at encouraging disciplined inquiry and creativity.

The purpose of schools today is to ensure that all students have access to a uniform quality of instruction. The difficulty, of course, is in defining *quality instruction.* In today's reform atmosphere, it is defined as that form of instruction that has the most immediate impact on standardized test scores and by testing only those things that can be standardized.

---

[1]See, for example, David Mathews, *Reclaiming Public Education by Reclaiming Our Democracy* (Dayton, Ohio: Kettering Foundation Press, 2006).
[2]Tyack and Cuban use the ideas of "tinkering toward utopia" and "grafting" to help them explain the history of school reform in America. I think they are right in their analysis. I also think the pattern they describe must be disrupted if public education is to survive as a vital force in American life. See David Tyack and Larry Cuban, *Tinkering Toward Utopia: A Century of Public School Reform* (Cambridge, Mass.: Harvard University Press, 1995).

The problem is that the type of instruction that is adequate to ensure that students can write on a standardized form a brief descriptive paragraphs about a poem may not be the same type of instruction that will inspire students to *write* a poem—or to create a novel experiment to test or verify some proposition of concern to them.[3] It is certainly not the type of instruction that will inspire the development of the skills, attitudes, and habits of mind that appear in listings of the skills needed for the workforce of the twenty-first century. It is not the type of instruction that will prepare students to learn in an increasingly digitized environment. And it is not the type that will teach young people how to function as effective citizens in a democracy where men and women are overwhelmed with information and purported facts.

It's Not "Merely Academic"

Certainly some students learn a great deal in schools. One of the primary reasons that this is so is that the backgrounds, experiences, and interests of some students lead them to find academic work inherently engaging. For many other students, however, academic work as it is usually designed holds little inherent interest or value to them.

The work of academics is often of much more interest to members of the academy than it is to most adults and most children. Indeed, many Americans, including many of America's leaders, have a certain antipathy toward academic work.[4] That is why one so often hears highly schooled, if not well-educated, leaders say that this or that proposition is "merely academic."

In the world of schools, however, lack of interest in doing the work that academics do, and doing this work in the way academics do it, is often seen as an absence of intelligence. Sir Ken Robinson, an internationally recognized leader in the development of creativity, has observed:

> The rationalist tradition has driven a wedge between intellect and emotion in human psychology; between the arts and sciences in society at large. It has distorted the idea of creativity in education and unbalanced the development of millions of people. The result

[3]This argument was suggested to me in Linda Perlstein, *Tested: One American School Struggles to Make the Grade* (New York: Holt, 2007).
[4]The idea that there is a deep anti-intellectual strain in American culture is well documented. See, for example, Richard Hofstadter, *Anti-Intellectualism in American Life* (New York: Knopf, 1963).

is that other equally important abilities are overlooked or marginalized. This neglect affects everyone. Children with strong academic abilities often fail to discover their other abilities. Those of lower academic ability may have other powerful abilities that lie dormant. They can pass through the whole of their education never knowing what their real abilities are. They can become disaffected, resentful of their "failure'" and conclude that they are simply not very bright. Some of these educational failures have gone on to have great success in adult life. How many do not?[5]

Academic subjects are important, but there are many ways to learn them and many ways to demonstrate such learning in addition to the ways academics have contrived. Unfortunately, too many of our national leaders, journalists, and pundits cannot imagine a system that will push everyone ahead—a system in which multiple standards of excellence might be applied. Excellence in schools is still seen as the property of the relative few who are academically inclined, and inclined as well to share the values that academics hold most dear.

Academic ability and interest in matters academic are not equally distributed, any more than are athletic ability or artistic ability. This does not mean that race, poverty, or other genetic or cultural features should be considered a source of variance in these abilities. What it does mean is that abilities of all kinds vary within groups, even more than between groups.

Because schools fasten attention on only one of the many abilities possessed by humankind (and define that ability so narrowly that only a relatively few can be demonstrated to possess it), schools have become as much about identifying failure as about promoting success. Indeed, if by some magic every child in America were suddenly to achieve academically at the level of the present top 10 percent of students, and if the schools should honor this achievement by giving all children A's, there would be a national clamor about schools lowering standards even more. "Every child a success" is a great slogan, but one that has fewer believers than some sloganeers believe.

In spite of slogans to the contrary, most Americans cannot imagine a system of schooling in which all children achieve at high levels. Our system assumes that the success of some children is dependent on the failure of others. As one wag has

[5]Ken Robinson, *Out of Our Minds: Learning to Be Creative* (Mankato, Minn.: Capstone Publishing, 2001), pp. 8–9.

said, "It takes a bottom half to hold the top half up." Until schools are designed to capture each child's full potential, rather than simply develop one dimension of it, and until the word *standards* refers to more than a narrowly defined notion of academic standards, there is little chance that most children will be educated in the way democracy requires, the economy demands, and children deserve.

A long line of research demonstrates that time on task alone is adequate to improve test scores, and some research supports the notion that highly structured and prescriptive teaching techniques produce relatively quick improvements in test scores (especially among students whose test score history is on the sorry side). But this research does not speak to the quality of the learning measured, and it is the quality of learning that should be of concern.

Transformation of our schools will require leaders who are prepared to repurpose and reimagine schools rather than simply reform them. The strategies that are most efficient in increasing test scores, at least within the context of our bureaucratically organized schools, have little to do with increasing student engagement, and without engagement, the quality of student learning is likely to be low.

We need to accept the fact that efforts to increase engagement may be less productive of quick gains in test scores than some of the drill, review, and test preparation techniques being employed in many of America's schools. The lasting effects of learning that result from engagement will, however, be profound and will show up in ways that can be observed, measured, and evaluated. Unfortunately, the tests needed to accomplish this end are not easily administered on a mass basis. Moreover, they do not meet the requirements of those who would use tests as a control mechanism as opposed to a tool for continuous assessment of direction and goal attainment. Indeed, the challenge that should be confronted by those who want schools to focus on twenty-first-century skills has to do with finding ways to assess in ways that are believable by ordinary citizens such things as creativity, the ability to collaborate, the ability to synthesize data from many sources, and to critically evaluate that data rather than depending on standardized tests to do their assessment for them.

Twenty-First-Century Realities

Three relatively recent changes are already affecting what happens in schools and the relationships between and among parents, teachers, students, and schools:

- The availability of digital learning opportunities

- The creation of the idea of adolescents as a demographic category and the increasing significance of peer groups among the young
- Direct marketing to children and adolescents

These new realities present both challenges and opportunities—challenges to the educational status quo but also opportunities for innovation and transformation.

The Digital Imperative   No single development has done as much to break down the protective boundaries that the family, religious institutions, and the school have traditionally maintained around the young as has the advent of electronic information transmittal, storage, retrieval, and processing technologies, commonly referred to as *information technology* (IT). It is telling, however, that in schools, IT often means *instructional* technology rather than *information* technology. This is so because schools are organized to support and control instruction, and instruction is the defining characteristic of the work of teachers. Indeed, *instructing* and *teaching* are often used as synonyms. Therefore, new technologies are almost always examined in terms of their potential for supporting and improving the work of teachers rather than in terms of their capacity to support the work of students.

The revolution created by the application of digital technologies to the organization, management, processing, and presentation of information, images, data, and all manner of human expression cannot be appreciated as long as these technologies are viewed as tools for instructors. These technologies are in themselves instructive. What is most powerful about them is that they place instruction under the direct control of the person being instructed: the learner. In the digital world, the learner, not the instructor, is in charge of what will be learned, as well as how and when that learning will occur.

Educators are acutely aware of the digital revolution. Unfortunately, too few value the potential of the new tools as tools for learners. Indeed, the common reaction is to try to bring the new technologies under the control of the instructional system. The following comment from an experienced Indiana educator is illustrative of this view:

> It is my belief from experience, practice, and conversations that many educators still believe technology is either the enemy, because it is our number one competition for the attention and time of our

students, or additional baggage, because technology-related skills are something extra that must be added to the myriad content-related learning objectives which students must master. Another school of thought views technology solely as teacher management tools—instruments that will make for better presentations, easier record-keeping, and/or greater access to student data. Until a shift occurs with this thinking, technologies of all kinds will never be effectively used in the schools to make the greatest impact on learning.

The dimensions of the changes that will be required in schooling are enormous. The following statement by a Texas educator who is struggling with these issues gives an indication of just how dramatic these changes are going to be:

> As a result [of new technologies] students are empowered to take on a more active role in the classroom, which becomes a shared space where teachers and students learn together and from each other. These newer technologies also give students a voice, where traditionally they had none, and provide an authentic audience of potentially millions. Increasingly, students will direct their own learning and learning will happen in conversations, as opposed to structured lesson plans. And just as in life, learning will be connected rather than happening in isolation.
>
> All of this forces us to rethink how we do school. So much of learning can and does happen outside the four walls of the classroom and with so many more people than the teacher. Learning doesn't just happen between the hours of eight and three. It's a continuous process for both teachers and students. We can no longer artificially filter what students are exposed to and instead have to help them learn to filter on their own. The lines between teacher and learner have to be blurred and the very idea of what is considered content has to be reconsidered.

The questions are whether schools have the kinds of leaders needed to bring about such a fundamental transformation in the authority relationship between students and teachers, and whether the boundaries of the schools can be made sufficiently permeable to safely admit the information that the digital world makes available. Without such leaders, the transformation of rules, roles, and relationships that is required will not occur. And without transformation, about all that can be expected from school applications of new developments in the IT world is the digitization of past practices. More important is the fact that without the needed transformation, schools will play a less and less vital role in what the young learn and will be less and less important in shaping the worldviews the young develop.

In the future, students will have increasing choice concerning the form their instruction will take and considerable control of the time and place that instruction will occur. This means that if schools are to continue to be central in the educational lives of the young, teachers must be more than designers of engaging work for students; they will need to learn to be guides to alternative forms of instruction. Rather than be nearly exclusive sources of instruction for students, as they now are, they will need to be prepared to help students locate the sources of information and instruction that are most appropriate to their learning styles.

When this change occurs, students, especially older students, will be encouraged by teachers to seek instruction wherever it is available and wherever the style of instruction meets the learning style of the student. Schools will be places where intellectual work is designed that cause students to want to be instructed and will become platforms that support students in making wise choices among a wide range of sources of instruction available rather than platforms that control and limit the instruction available to them.

For this transformation to occur, digital technologies must be viewed as learning aids rather than tools that instructors use to do only slightly better what instructors have done for the past two hundred years. The survival of the American culture and way of life may well depend on the ability of the today's educators to find ways to encourage the young to become engaged in digitized tasks and activities that will call on them to learn those things the wisdom of elders suggests they need to learn.

The Impact of Peer Groups   Up through the 1940s, adults were much more significant in the lives of adolescents than was the peer group. This is no longer true. Adults, especially parents, continue to play a dominant role in the lives of the young, but the peer group, especially the adolescent peer group, is more influential than was the case at the time that America's system of schooling was designed.

This is not to say that peer groups did not exist in the past or that peer group pressure was not important. Rather, since about 1950, the young have become increasingly independent of their elders, especially in terms of the information they can access and the ways they can process that information. Indeed, one of the earliest major efforts to link the idea of a distinct adolescent subculture to schools can be found in James Coleman's 1961 book, *The Adolescent Society.*[6] Since that time, a plethora of books and articles has been published on this theme.[7]

There are at least two sources for the rise of the influence of peer groups. The more commonly cited are changes in traditional family structures. Increasing numbers of children are living in homes where the presence of adults is much less ubiquitous than it was in earlier generations. For example, the presence of grandparents and large numbers of older siblings in the home is less common than in the past. In addition, the number of children in one-parent families or families in which both parents spend much of their time in a workplace far removed from where their children are located is increasing. In fact, nearly a third of all children live in homes with only one parent, and in 62 percent of two-parent families, both parents work outside the home.[8]

These changes occurred at the same time that the young have gained greater access to information from independent sources, not filtered through the adults who have traditionally controlled it: parents, grandparents, clerics, and teachers. Portable record players and portable radios became commercially available in the 1950s, making it possible for adolescents to hear music and other forms of entertainment free of adult censorship. The car radio and the automobile itself provided similar independence. The paperback revolution and the explosion in niche-marketed magazines, with adolescents being a market niche, occurred largely after World War II. For many years *Boys' Life,* the official publication of the Boy Scouts, was about the only periodical available that was aimed at adolescent boys, and there were virtually none for girls. *Seventeen,* a magazine for young girls, began publication in 1944. Nowadays many children have their own television and their own computer in their bedroom, seldom frequented by parents. All of these converging forces reinforce the relative power of the peer group

[6]James S. Coleman, *The Adolescent Society: The Social Life of the Teenager and Its Impact on Education* (New York: Free Press, 1961).

[7]See, for example, Patricia Hersch, *A Tribe Apart: A Journey into the Heart of American Adolescence* (New York: Fawcett-Columbine, 1998), or Linda Perlstein, *Not Much Just Chillin': The Hidden Lives of Middle Schoolers* (New York: Ballantine Books, 2003).

[8]U.S. Bureau of Labor Statistics, "Employment Characteristics of Families Summary," May 20, 2008. Accessed June 10, 2008, at http:///www.bls.gov/news.release/famee.nr0.htm.

and diminish the power of traditional authority to serve as a meaningful base for controlling the activity of the young.

In the face of this reality, schools must be organized in ways that take advantage of the power of peer groups and the networking that these groups suggest. Educators must learn to take into account and exploit for positive ends the social networking available on the Internet. Educators must not allow fear of the harm that can be done by these developments to divert attention from their efforts to invent ways to exploit the good.[9]

If educators fail in this regard, other developments in American society, especially in the world of the Internet, make it likely that most of what students learn will be outside the direction of the school (and even outside the direction of parents) and will be increasingly under the control of peer groups and commercially oriented marketers. Such a "curriculum" will clearly not be as likely to result in a more civil society and a more thoughtful citizenry, as would be the case if the curriculum were an expression of a clear set of community values and beliefs regarding what it means to be an educated person.

Young people have more control of their own learning today than in the past, whether adults like that or not. Adults must find ways to engage the young in activity that causes them to exercise this control in personally and socially desirable ways.

Marketing to Children   Prior to the 1940s, to the extent that marketers were aware of the youth market, they aimed their efforts at parents rather than the young themselves. But radio began to provide marketers with direct access to the young. This access was later expanded through television, youth-oriented magazines, comic books, and now the Internet.

Marketing to children today is a far cry from what was used in the early days of radio. For example, the first memory I have of being directly "marketed to"

---

[9]The situation suggested here roughly parallels one found by researchers studying efforts to apply scientific management techniques to production work in a factory. They discovered that the peer group had more to do with controlling the performance of workers than did the rational system of incentives provided by management. The studies that demonstrated this point, known as the Hawthorne Studies, are classics in the management literature, and numerous other studies have replicated the findings. For many years, managers tried to fight against peer group influence. Today wise business leaders understand that peer influence can also serve as a powerful source of positive motivation.

is when, as a child in the 1940s, I listened to *Captain Midnight* on the radio and was invited to send in an Ovaltine wrapper in exchange for a "secret decoder."

The marketing aimed at my six-year-old grandchildren is much more sophisticated and more ubiquitous than these early efforts. And modern marketing is not limited to cereal, soft drinks, and clothing. Indeed, the fastest-growing market for the young, including sometimes the very young, is the world of electronics: electronic games, iPhones, iPods, and so on. These items are clearly much more relevant to the way children can and will be educated than was Ovaltine.[10]

What I find most interesting and important about this development—in addition to the possibilities that it might suggest for direct applications in school—is the fact that those who engage in marketing to the young and designing games for the young seem to understand better than do most religious leaders, teachers, or even parents the fundamental fact that the power relationship between the relatively young and the relatively old has changed in immutable ways: parents, teachers, and religious leaders no longer control young people's access to information and knowledge. Moreover, marketers understand that if they are to gain access to the attention and commitment of the young, they must be willing to compete for that attention and vie for their commitment.

Commercial marketers understand that they must design products and campaigns in ways that appeal to the values of the young. Many educators have yet to discover this fact. Rather than seeing themselves as marketers who try to discover and appeal to the motives of their customers, educators are more likely to see themselves as salespeople who try, by providing incentives, to induce students to buy what they have to offer. Sometimes these inducements involve such extrinsic rewards as grades and free passes to concerts, and sometimes they involve reducing the effort that must be expended to receive the reward—something akin to lowering the price. Some teachers frame the problem as one of needing to compete with professional entertainers. Most teachers, however, do not feel they can compete in this world. Such a framing of the problem can do little other than to increase despair.

Even more interesting is that many marketers have turned to some classic educational thinkers for guidance in how to proceed. For example, the work of Jean Piaget, the famous developmental psychologist, is often used as a basis for differentiating the market so that campaigns and products are geared to appeal

[10]For a powerful discussion of many of the issues suggested here, see Kathryn C. Montgomery, *Generation Digital: Politics, Commerce and Childhood in the Age of the Internet* (Cambridge, Mass.: MIT Press, 2007).

appropriately to different age groups.[11] It is perhaps time that educators consider the lessons these observations by marketers might suggest and then begin to organize their schools and classrooms in ways that take these lessons into account.

The Democratic Imperative

Democracy is based on the belief that ordinary citizens can be trusted to make civic and political decisions that will affect their own lives and the lives of others. In nondemocratic states, these rights are reserved for the elite.

There is, of course, always the fear that the masses will prove too ignorant and too ruled by runaway passions to be trusted with such matters. This is why public education is so central to democratic life. It is through education that the ability to make disciplined and discerning judgments and to create new options is developed, and it is this ability on which democracy depends.

In a world where ordinary citizens are increasingly bombarded with facts and information, high-quality mass education is more important than ever before. Moreover, it is no longer simply facts that citizens need. They need disciplined ideas that they can use as tools to organize these facts. Without ideas to organize facts, citizens will be overwhelmed by information, and in their confusion, they may be easily deceived. Critical thinking skills, skills in collaboration, and skills for working in groups are not only work skills; they are, as they have always been, essential citizenship skills as well.

In a democracy, all citizens must develop a taste for excellence so that the judgments they make will lead to excellence rather than mediocrity.[12] Assurance that this will be so can be granted only by a strong public education system that provides all students with the opportunity to learn to think and to reason and to use their minds well.[13] Simply put, modern democracy requires an elite education for nearly every student. This is a tall order. It assumes that nearly everyone is capable of learning at high levels and that they will learn at high levels if given the right opportunity to do so.

[11]Ibid.

[12]Alexis de Tocqueville, the famous French observer of American democracy, as well as many others who have commented on the consequences of democracy, believed and believe that democracy inherently leads to mediocrity. It is my view that this thinking is flawed, but the only thing that makes it so is the assurance that all citizens can be, and are, well educated at public expense.

[13]Those who are familiar with the literature of education will know that I have been influenced by Theodore Sizer. See for example, Theodore Sizer, *Horace's Compromise: The Dilemma of the American High School* (Boston: Houghton Mifflin, 1984).

Many Americans fear that an inadequate system of education will compromise America's ability to compete in the global economy. In fact, they have more to fear from the possibility that young people who graduate will lack the skills and understandings needed to function well as citizens in a democracy. Americans have more to fear from the prospect that the IT revolution will so overwhelm citizens with competing facts and competing opinions that they will give up their freedom in order to gain some degree of certainty than they have to fear from economic competition from around the world. Leaders should be more concerned that Americans will cease to know enough to preserve freedom and value liberty, equity, and excellence than they are with how well American students compare on international tests. As numerous scholars have shown, authoritarian leaders and charlatans thrive in a world where ordinary citizens are overwhelmed with facts and competing opinions and lack the ideas and tools to discipline their thinking without appealing to some authority figure for direction and support.[14]

All students must have a sufficient educational acquaintance with the academic disciplines to enable them to distinguish sense from nonsense, an ancient notion that dates back to Aristotle. In a multiethnic, multicultural society characterized by religious pluralism, it is also essential that attitudes of tolerance and empathetic understanding be fostered, for without these attitudes, balkanization is almost certain to occur. Indeed, even now the fabric of American society is being strained more than ever in the past, at least in part because differences have become more important than the common good.

The continued vitality of American democracy, as well as the nation's economy, may well depend on the ability of educational leaders to transform schools. Surely what students need to know and be able to do to live well in a democracy will also serve well as a basis for their becoming the scientists and engineers our society needs to maintain its standing in the world of commerce. At the

---

[14]Studies of the rise of authoritarian states are not as popular today as they once were, but those who care about the future of this nation could do worse than to read, or reread, authors like Hannah Arendt and Eric Hofer. In this age of information overload and extreme commercialization of nearly every aspect of life, America may have as much to fear from what Arendt called the "banality of evil" as from the many other evils Americans are being encouraged to fear. (By "banality of evil" Arendt is talking about the tendency of ordinary citizens to blindly follow political and cultural leaders without exercising independent judgment and critical faculties.) See Hannah Arendt, *Eichmann in Jerusalem: A Report on the Banality of Evil* (New York: Penguin, 1994). See also Eric Hofer *The True Believer: Thoughts on the Nature of Mass Movements* (New York: HarperCollins, 2002).

same time, the education students are provided might serve as a basis for some becoming the artists, historians, novelists, journalists, and musicians needed to make living worthwhile. More important, such an education might increase the prospect that the young will learn what they need to know to more fully appreciate the quality of life that democracy makes possible for all citizens. Finally, it might enhance the attachment of the young to each other, to their elders, and to their sense of the common good.

The Moral Imperative

One need not be a proponent of censorship to acknowledge that some elements of the entertainment industry and the mass media expose America's young people to forms of art and music that coarsen the culture and the individual. Try as they might, however, neither parents nor religious leaders can protect the young from these forces. Neither can schools, but a well-rounded education can help ensure that students become more discerning in their tastes. Education can sensitize their judgments regarding what is beautiful, honest, elegant, and refined.

Knowledge may not be power, but ignorance certainly does not bestow bliss. There are differences among joy, delight, arousal, and titillation. There are differences between art and pornography, and between music and sheer noise. Opinions supported by and consistent with facts are better than opinions that are at variance with facts and have no support other than the passions of the person expressing the opinion.

If all graduates left high school with sufficient understanding of the academic disciplines to distinguish sense from nonsense and with enough understanding of the arts to appreciate the impact of feeling and emotion on the human spirit and thought processes, they would also be well equipped to function as members of a world-class workforce in an information economy. Properly educated, they would also be in a better position to evaluate the art and music they are exposed to in the mass media, as well as to evaluate the claims of marketers and politicians. More than that, they would be prepared to assume roles as responsible citizens and enjoy the benefits that accrue to men and women who have discovered how to learn independent of teachers and schools. The necessity of providing such an education is yet another piece of the argument that schools must be transformed rather than merely reformed, for without transformation, the education that schools provide most students will become increasingly formulaic, uninspired, and superficial.

Learning to Exploit New Opportunities

Teachers lament the fact that peer group loyalties distract students, especially young adolescents, from their schoolwork. Parents and teachers alike complain that television advertising and some of the cartoon programming that goes with these ads are harmful to the physical and mental health of children. School boards spend countless hours figuring out how to formulate policies limiting the use of cell phones, iPods, and Internet access in school buildings.

These concerns are legitimate, but they cannot be dealt with by denial, outrage, or the wish that the world were somehow different. For teachers, parents, and other adults to properly understand and appreciate the changes that are occurring in the lives of the young, they must stop seeing these changes as threats and instead identify the opportunities they present.

What must be acknowledged is that the traditional authority principles that have defined relationships between children and adults have been altered in immutable ways. Not only do students now often have access to information before their teachers or their parents do, but they are often the first to learn the newest techniques for gaining access to information and of creating content and processing information. There are indeed parallels between intergenerational relationships affected by information technology and the relationships between natives and immigrants. Marc Prensky, a digital guru, has in fact used the terms *digital immigrants* and *digital natives* to describe this phenomenon.[15] And in the digital world, the young are often the natives and the adults the immigrants, whereas in the not-so-distant past, this relationship was reversed.

Peer groups supported by new technologies present a serious challenge to traditional authority relationships in school. To deal productively with this situation, teachers and school administrators have to learn how to turn the power of peer group loyalty into a mechanism for fastening student attention on useful educational ends. Rather than fight electronic networking, educators need to learn how to exploit these innovations for positive educational ends.

Finally, although direct marketing to the young has its unsettling dimensions, what the work of marketers and the designers of games for the young might teach educators is loaded with potential. As a quick Google search using the key words *marketing* and *children* will reveal, much of the research done by marketers is just as available to educators as it is to the marketers themselves. Educators

[15]Marc Prensky, "Digital Native, Digital Immigrants," *On the Horizon,* 2001, 9, 1–2.

and those who educate educators need to become at least as familiar with this literature as they are with the more classic education literature dealing with student motivation.

Moreover, those who design games for the young are astutely aware of the motives and values the young bring to their products. Many understand, for example, that electronic networking and the building of virtual communities is as important to some forms of gaming as is the activity of the game itself. Game designers also understand that the ability to fail without punishment is an important part of the appeal of games, as are the clarity of standards and the access to multiple ways of meeting those standards. School reformers can learn much from studying the work of those who some consider to be the competition.

WHY WE TINKER: THE PROBLEM DEFINED

As I noted above, Tyack and Cuban have rightly observed that most efforts to improve America's schools have involved tinkering. These efforts have not been radical. They have barely scratched the surface of the problems that confront public schools and certainly have not gone to the root of the problems. When tinkering has exceeded the limits of the existing systems, as was the case with many of the curriculum reforms of the 1960s, such as flexible scheduling, non-graded classrooms, and open classrooms, rejection or domestication have been the predictable results.

Those who occupy power positions in the education bureaucracy, and many of those who advise such people, assume that the test of the merit and worth of an innovation is its ability to deliver within the context of the existing bureaucratic arrangements. This assumption clearly limits the types of innovations that can be installed and made eligible for comparative tests. Moreover, it ensures that the existing system will be maintained pretty much in its present form, because it does not allow the implementation of the systemic changes that would be required before the disruptive innovation might produce the effects it promises.

Such a scenario almost certainly dooms public schools to the ash heap of history. Knowledge and information are at the heart of the educational enterprise. The knowledge development and transmission system assumed by bureaucratic schools is a linear system that requires the physical presence of a person or a book, magazine, or some other form of print for instruction to occur. It provides a platform for systematizing instruction.

The major innovations of our time have had to do with storing, retrieving, processing, and communicating knowledge, information, images, and voice communications by electronic means. It is now possible to store and access knowledge and information in a random, nonlinear fashion. Educational systems that can draw on the new capacities provided by random access are more likely to thrive than are educational systems that can use them only if they are domesticated and adapted to existing linear assumptions. For example, content no longer needs to be preorganized into textbook chapters. Students can create their own "chapters" once they have determined what questions they want the chapter to answer. Schools must therefore become platforms for optimizing learning opportunities for students (and adults as well).

In the digital world, print- and person-dependent learning is not the rule. And as businesses are beginning to learn and religious leaders are beginning to discover, these new technologies threaten existing boundaries and existing arrangements of power and authority in fundamental ways. Organizations that are change adept—that is, organizations that can learn as well as encourage learning—will survive and thrive in this new world.[16] Organizations that require stability, tranquility, and predictability will perish. And bureaucracies absolutely require stability, tranquility, and predictability if they are to function in optimal ways, a topic explored in the following chapters.

If the limitations of bureaucracies continue to be imposed on or accepted in schools, the only alternative available to those who desire a high-quality education will be to create a new system of education outside the range of the state and federal bureaucracies that now dominate public schools. Indeed, such a system is likely to function outside schools more generally, as most private schools are structured on the same organizational premises that guide public schools, and thus are based on assumptions that are not valid in a world where digital learning opportunities abound.

If schools both public and private cannot become more adept than they now are at absorbing and supporting disruptive technologies—and it is clear that digital technologies, properly exploited, will be disruptive in bureaucratically organized schools—then customized, commercially provided education is likely to replace both public and private schools, at least for most students. Those left

---

[16]See Rosabeth Moss Kanter, *On the Frontiers of Management* (Boston: Harvard Business School Press, 1997), for a discussion of the ideal of change-adept organizations.

behind will be the children of the poor, who will be trained in state-run bureaucracies rather than educated in outstanding schools, making even more real the social class divisions that are tearing at America's social fabric.

The problems with America's public schools do not reside in the quality of teachers or school leaders. Nevertheless, as they now are organized, public schools too often encourage teachers and school leaders to value passive compliance over active involvement and to value the amount of time spent on tasks over the quality of the energy invested in the task. Rather than fostering a sound grasp of the fundamental tools needed to pursue a vigorous intellectual life, schools too often encourage teachers to settle for students' passing a state-mandated test whose primary virtue is ease of scoring in large numbers and in a relatively short period of time. Schools focused in this way are more likely to encourage teachers to value docility and compliance in students above creativity and intellectual curiosity. Those who work in such environments are likely to confuse rigor with rigor mortis and submission with discipline. Indeed, given the circumstances that now exist, most teachers are already accomplishing more than the schools were designed for them to accomplish. Indeed, America is fortunate to have so many teachers who are as successful as they are in spite of the systems in which they work rather than because of them.

If we are to provide every child with the best education possible, we need schools that give a central place to creativity and imagination and enforce standards of excellence through shared commitments, collegial reinforcement, and collaborative agendas rather than through bureaucratically managed external controls, extrinsic rewards, and threats of punishment. The chapters that follow point the way toward the creation of such schools.

Systems and Technological Change

The relationship between social systems and the introduction of new technologies has been of interest to me most of my life. Indeed, the first book I authored, in 1976, was one in which I tried to explain the reasons for the failure of school reform initiatives to take hold in schools by reference to a body of sociological theory that dealt with the relationship between structure and technology. I wrote:

> One of the basic hypotheses of this book is that when administrative or curricular innovations are introduced that are compatible with the existing social structures of the schools, they are likely to have some measurable effects. If, however, administrative or curricular innovations are introduced that are not compatible with the existing social arrangements in the school or classroom, one of three results seems likely. (1) The innovation will be modified to fit existing patterns of behavior and thus not affect student learning. This, for example, is what has apparently happened with many efforts to introduce integrated language arts—social studies programs. Teachers simply took larger blocks of time and rescheduled their activities to conform to the traditional breakdown of history, geography, grammar, and literature. In many cases, the only "innovation" combined language arts–social studies programs produce is that in grading social studies papers, teachers are a bit more sensitive to spelling, grammar, and

punctuation. (2) A second possible result of introducing innovation into incompatible structures is that the innovation will meet resistance and will eventually be abandoned because it is thought to be "inappropriate to the local situation." Indeed, unless there is a conscious effort to change that structure, this conclusion may appear to be the only logical one. Apparently this is what is happening with some efforts at adapting the British infant school to the American school system. (3) A final consequence of lack of structural support for innovation could be that the tensions created by the innovation will cause the social structure of the school or classroom to shift in ways that will accommodate the change. This, of course, is the desirable circumstance, assuming it is intended that administrative or curricular changes will have a measurable impact, but unfortunately it is not what usually happens. Indeed, because most educators have an inadequate view of the social structure of the school, they are apt to view the tensions or conflicts resulting from an innovation as evidence that the change will not work in their school. The result is that innovations are adopted and abandoned for reasons that have little to do with their potential benefit to children. Rather, they are adopted and abandoned on the basis of their fit with the existing structure of the school.[1]

Over the intervening thirty years I have refined my views on these matters considerably. I am now convinced, for example, that the primary barrier to the introduction of major innovations in schools is that schools are organized as bureaucracies, which are by and large change-inept organizations.[2] Until schools can be transformed into a different type of organization—what I refer to in this book as learning organizations—there is little prospect that they can support innovations required to improve the schools. Thus, the transformation of schools is a precondition to the improvement of school performance. Transformation will not in itself improve the performance of schools. It will,

[1]Phillip C. Schlechty, *Teaching and Social Behavior: Toward an Organizational Theory of Instruction* (Needham Heights, Mass.: Allyn and Bacon, 1976), pp. 231–232.
[2]The idea of change-adept and change-inept organizations was brought to my attention in Rosabeth Moss Kanter's book, *On the Frontiers of Management* (Boston: Harvard Business School Press, 1997). I have used this idea extensively in much that I have written.

however, make it possible to introduce innovations that would not be accepted in a bureaucratic structure that can improve that performance.

Without transformation, such innovations will likely be rejected or modified to fit the existing system, which will compromise the effects the innovation might produce if introduced with fidelity. (I refer to the process of altering an innovation to fit the existing system as *domestication*. I chose this term because the image I have of the process is that of "taming" a technology to make it fit a circumstance that is not natural to it.)

UNDERSTANDING SCHOOLS AS COMPLEX SOCIAL ORGANIZATIONS

Much that happens in schools can be understood only by understanding how the social systems that comprise the schools operate. This is why systems thinking is so important to educational leaders.[3]

Unfortunately, too few educators have a clear-eyed view of the social systems within which they operate. Robert S. Dreeben, a preeminent sociologist, wrote many years ago:

> There is an ironical association between our familiarity with schools and our ignorance about them. It is fair to say that no adequate description or formulation of their structural characteristics currently exists, perhaps because the schooling process so obviously involves psychological change that the most reasonable way to study it—or so it would seem—is to look for those psychological changes that appear related to the main business of the school, which is instruction.[4]

The understanding that scholars have of schools as formal organizations has made some advances. Nevertheless, it remains the case that we lack a formulation of the structural characteristics of schools that would allow meaningful comparisons to be made between and among schools or permit changes within schools to be tracked. Without the understandings that such a formulation would suggest, the cause of school transformation is seriously compromised.

[3]See Peter Senge, *The Fifth Discipline: The Art and Practice of the Learning Organization* (New York: Doubleday, 1990).
[4]Robert S. Dreeben, *On What Is Learned in School* (Reading, Mass.: Addison-Wesley, 1968), p. vii.

One of my purposes in writing this book is to arm educational leaders with a deeper understanding of the social systems that shape behavior in schools. The intent is to place these leaders in a better position to transform America's public schools into the kinds of organizations they must become if public education is to survive and thrive. My belief is that until these systems are changed in fundamental ways, the performance of schools will not be much improved. And it is also my belief that unless the performance of public schools is improved dramatically, the existence of the public schools and the democratic order in which they are embedded are threatened.

THE NATURE OF SYSTEMIC CHANGE

A system is a set of interrelated elements organized around a common function. In the context of school improvement, two kinds of systems are of concern: operating systems and social systems. *Operating systems* are interrelated processes, procedures, programs, and technologies that define the way tasks are carried out and the way technical functions are fulfilled. *Social systems* are a relatively permanent and predictable set of relationships between and among rules (social norms) and roles (position-related configurations of norms) that define behavior within a group. A social system also includes the set of beliefs, values, and shared commitments that give meaning to these rules and roles and on which the rules and roles are based.

Operating systems contain the technologies that are employed and the processes and procedures by which these technologies are employed in fulfilling designated functions.[5] Examples are instructional systems, accounting systems, finance systems, human resource development systems, measurement systems, and personnel management systems.

Social systems define the cultural and structural context within which operating systems must carry out their tasks. Operating systems define how work is done; social systems define the meaning of the work, the values that are attached to the work and its outcomes, the ends toward which the work is aimed, the manner in which authority is assigned, the knowledge that is honored, and so on.

---

[5]According to Dreeben, *technology* should be defined as "the means of doing the job, whatever the means and the job may be." This is the meaning I attach to this word; I do not limit the meaning of *technology* to computers or other electronic devices. A textbook is a form of technology just as a lecture is. See Robert S. Dreeben, *The Nature of Teaching and Schools: Schools and the Work of Teachers* (Upper Saddle River, N.J.: Pearson, 1970), p. 83.

Most efforts to improve schools center on changing operating systems. When one speaks of introducing "innovations," those innovations are usually manifested as changes in one or more technological enhancements being introduced into an operating system or changes in the procedures and processes associated with the existing technologies. Pedagogical innovations are innovations in the system of instruction, just as the introduction of a new computer program might be an innovation in the finance system. Both the instructional system and the finance system are operating systems that define how work is to be done and tasks are to be accomplished.

DISRUPTIVE AND SUSTAINING INNOVATIONS

When educational leaders speak of *systemic reform,* the systems to which they usually refer are the operating systems that define the work flow of the organization: finance, information management, purchasing, human resources, instruction, and so on. They seldom think in terms of the social systems that provide the context within which all of these other systems operate—or fail to operate.

Clayton Christensen, a business school professor, has studied the impact of technological innovations on markets and the operation of established businesses. His research suggests that technological innovations fall into two types:

- *Sustaining innovations,* meaning innovations that are congruent with existing social systems and therefore require little in the way of change in these systems to support their successful implementation

- *Disruptive innovations,* meaning innovations that are incongruent with existing social systems and therefore require fundamental changes in these systems if the innovation is to be properly installed and sustained.[6]

Christensen's basic argument, like mine, is that existing organizations seldom successfully adopt truly disruptive innovations. Viewing the world from the perspective of business, he argues that typically, new enterprises arise around the disruptive technologies—enterprises that can be structured in such a way as to take full advantage of the new technology. Over time, these new enterprises replace the old providers, or the old providers absorb the new organizations and adopt their new mode of organization as their own.

[6]Clayton Christensen developed the concepts of sustaining and disruptive innovations, and I am indebted to him for these ideas. See Clayton M. Christensen, *The Innovator's Dilemma* (Boston: Harvard Business School Press, 1997).

Recently Christensen joined with two colleagues from the field of education to apply his theories to the problems of school reform.[7] For these authors, digital learning technologies are the disruptive technologies that should be of concern to educators, for these are the technologies that are now transforming the way the world learns. Moreover, there is ample evidence that to date, and in spite of massive investments, these new technologies have not been successfully exploited by the public schools.

Christensen's work has done much to help me clarify my own thinking regarding issues related to school reform and transformation. The major point on which I think we might have a fundamental disagreement is the confidence he and his coauthors have in the role of vouchers, charter schools, and unregulated markets to solve problems that beset the schools of America. To point to Merrill Lynch as an example of solutions in the public interest, or to suggest that Southwest Airlines has improved the way Delta, United, and other airlines do their business is something of a stretch.

Privatization may have a place in education, but I am not convinced the introduction of competition in an area of social and political life that is intended to serve the common good is always wise. I am struck by the fact that the U.S. Postal Service too has had its problems and the introduction of competition from UPS and Federal Express has probably had some positive impact on postal service generally. Unfortunately, one of the effects is that UPS and FedEx now deliver much high-priority business mail and commercial packages, while the government-based postal service continues to deliver the low-priority bulk mail that floods our mail boxes each day.

In the epilogue to one of my earlier books, *Shaking Up the School House*, I constructed a different scenario from the one Christensen, Horn, and Johnson presented in *Disrupting Class*, a scenario that was not so happy or uplifting.[8] In this epilogue I wrote a piece entitled "Looking Backward 20-20" in which I projected into the future what I saw—and now see even more—as the direction in which school reform is taking us. In this piece, I saw the world unfolding pretty much as Christensen, Horn, and Johnson would have it unfold. I envisioned about 50 percent of all students in some form of charter school, homeschool, or virtual school or some privately managed collaborative or cooperative arrangement.

[7]Clayton M. Christensen, Michael B. Horn, and Curtis W. Johnson, *Disrupting Class: How Disruptive Innovation Will Change the Way the World Learns* (New York: McGraw-Hill, 2008).
[8]Phillip C. Schlechty, *Shaking Up the Schoolhouse* (San Francisco: Jossey-Bass, 2001).

The difference is that the students who were left behind in the public schools—about 50 percent—did not enjoy such a happy fate. Rather than being in schools that were improved and liberated by force of competition, the schools deteriorated even more and became increasingly bureaucratized.

My more pessimistic view is informed by the fact that even now, we have considerable evidence that government-sponsored efforts to empower schools and teachers through the process of strengthening centralized evaluations and decreasing regulations seldom work out the way designers intended.[9] Rather than liberating local schools, state-sponsored decentralization has had the effect of diminishing the authority of local school districts. When charter school leaders misbehave, as some have already done, states will intervene, and when they intervene, the policies they promulgate will limit the actions of all schools, not simply those that are out of line.

So long as schools are forced to be accountable to government bureaucrats rather than to local publics, this inevitably will be the case. The transformation of the schools involves transforming the way the schools are governed as well as the way they operate on a day-to-day basis. Some means must be found to hold schools accountable to all the citizens in the communities where they exist without introducing the heavy hand of state or federal bureaucracies.

CRITICAL SOCIAL SYSTEMS

All formal organizations must make provision for a variety of basic functions: getting new members; assigning measures of merit and worth; assigning status and ensuring conformance with standards and expectations; coordinating activity; establishing direction and assigning goals; importing, creating, and transmitting knowledge; and defining what is inside and outside the organization—and defending such definitions.[10]

The rules, roles, and relationships, together with the values, commitments, beliefs, and traditions, that shape behavior in human groups gain expression in what sociologists and anthropologists refer to as *norms*. Norms are expressions of patterns of behavior that are preferred or required of members of the group.

[9]See Bruce Fuller, Melissa Henne, and Emily Hannum, *Strong States, Weak Schools: The Benefits and Dilemmas of Centralized Accountability* (Bingley, U.K.: Emerald Group Publishing, 2008).
[10]This section is based in part on a discussion I presented in an earlier book: Phillip C. Schlechty, *Creating Great Schools: Six Critical Systems at the Heart of Educational Innovation* (San Francisco: Jossey-Bass, 2005).

They are also expressions of the values, traditions, lore, and beliefs that guide group action—that is, the culture and the means by which the culture is defined.

In complex social organizations like schools, norms become organized in systemic ways. These norms are expressions of the culture of the organization, and it is these structures and cultural expressions that are referred to as *social systems.* Formal organizations like schools have at least six critical systems:

- *Directional systems.* Systems through which goals are set, priorities are determined, and, when things go awry, corrective actions are initiated.

- *Knowledge development and transmission systems.* Formal and informal systems that define how knowledge related to the moral, aesthetic, and technical norms that shape behavior in schools and school districts is developed, imported, evaluated, and transmitted.

- *Recruitment and induction systems.* Systems that define the way new members are identified and attracted to the organization and brought to understand and embrace the norms and values they must understand and embrace to be full members of the organization. Such systems also include those through which existing members are reoriented when a system is undergoing transition or when role changes are occurring.

- *Boundary systems.* Systems that define who and what are inside the organization and therefore subject to the control of the organization, and who and what are outside the organization and therefore beyond the reach of the systems that comprise the organization. The boundary system also defines the relationships between and among the occupants of different positions in the organization, as well as the relationship between and among its organizational units (departments, schools, district offices, and so on).

- *Evaluation system.* Systems that define the way measures of merit and worth are assigned, status determined, and honor bestowed, as well as when and how negative sanctions are applied.

- *Power and authority systems.* Systems by which the use of sanctions is made legitimate, the proper exercise of power is defined, and status relationships are determined.[11]

[11]My understanding of these systems has been enhanced and inspired by the early work of Ronald Corwin, with whom I had the privilege of studying when I was a young man.

WHY REFORM IS SO DIFFICULT

As long as any innovations that are introduced can be absorbed by the existing operating systems without violating the limits of the social systems in which they are embedded, change in schools is more a matter of good management than one of leadership. Such changes can, in fact, be introduced through programs and projects and managed quite well by technically competent people who are familiar with the new routines required by the innovations and skilled in communicating to others what they know.

In these cases, while it is sometimes difficult to break old habits, usually after a brief period of resistance, old certainties are abandoned and new certainties embraced. For example, teachers now routinely use PowerPoint slide shows where once they used overhead projectors and slate boards. The reason this transition was relatively easy to accomplish is that it did not change the role of the teacher. Indeed, PowerPoint makes it easier for teachers to do what they have always done, just as a DVD player is easier to use than a 16 millimeter projector. Moreover, the technical skills required to use a PowerPoint slide show are easily learned and communicated, making the process of diffusion relatively simple.

But when innovations threaten the nature and sources of knowledge to be used or the way power and authority are currently used and distributed—in other words, when they require changes in social systems as well as operating systems—innovation becomes more difficult. This is so because such changes are disruptive in inflexible social systems.

The reason change in schools is so hard is that the innovations that are most likely to have an impact on learning are those that are most intimately connected to the directional system, the knowledge development system, and the recruitment and induction system; whereas the social systems that determine the flexibility and adaptability of the school organization are the power and authority systems, the evaluation systems, and the boundary systems. When an innovation threatens existing patterns in the operating systems most directly affected by the way power and authority are arranged, the way value is assigned, and the way boundaries are defined, if these three systems are not arranged in a flexible way, the odds of the innovation working are limited indeed. An extended case study from an earlier era of school reform will illustrate this point.

A Lesson from the Past: The Curriculum Reforms of the 1960s

Following the launching of *Sputnik I* in 1957, there was a great demand for school reform. As is the case today, many politicians, pundits, journalists, and academic leaders surveyed the world of the public schools and found them lacking. Too many children could not read or were geographically, scientifically, or mathematically illiterate, and too many of their teachers were not much better, or so it was argued. Given the crisis mentality that prevailed, the American public and the Congress that represented them were willing to engage in actions that would not previously have been accepted, up to and including federal intervention into the life of local schools. (As will be shown later, this was a defining moment with regard to the role of the federal government in the life of schools.)

One of the most significant of these interventions was the involvement of the prestigious National Science Foundation in sponsoring and supporting a variety of curriculum development projects that centered on improving instruction in such fields as biology, physics, chemistry, and, later, in geography, sociology, and other social sciences. Although these curriculum projects varied in format and design, most involved collaboration between persons who were recognized scholars in the academic disciplines and leaders in the design of curriculum materials and instructional processes. Most of these projects were also based on assumptions that students learned better through discovery processes and inquiries similar to those engaged in by scholars in the disciplines than by didactic approaches and heavy reliance on lectures. Indeed, many of the arguments that surround issues of school reform today are the same ones made in the 1950s and 1960s.

For the most part, these reforms failed to have the impact it was then assumed they would have. I have spent much time thinking about why this occurred and have come to believe that those who led these reform efforts proceeded from one of two faulty assumptions:

- They assumed that the innovations they wanted to install would not call for fundamental changes in the social systems that defined the schools. They thought the only changes needed were in the operating systems and the skills of the operators. Simply making the materials available and offering proper training and leadership development for teachers would be enough.

- Or they assumed that the directional system and the knowledge development and transmission system would serve as the leading systems in the organization and that the other systems would adapt to the conditions required by changes in direction or changes in knowledge development and transmission. Put differently, they assumed that the logic underlying their innovations would provide opportunities for a fair and sustained trial of their products and that the results would be sufficiently impressive to ensure that needed systemic changes in the power and authority system, the evaluation system, and the boundary system would be forthcoming.

Those who worked to implement these new curriculum materials, myself included, vastly underestimated the disruptive nature of the innovations they were providing the schools. It turns out that the proper incorporation of an inquiry-oriented curriculum not only requires better-trained and more highly qualified teachers, but also changes in the power arrangements that typify the traditional relationship between teachers and students. Student inquiry, rather than teacher-dominated instruction, had to define the direction to be taken in the classroom. Student learning, rather than teacher control, had to be the guiding concern.

The prevailing notions of boundaries were threatened as well. Some of the science materials, for example, required students to engage in experiments that required more time than the class periods in the typical high school's standardized schedule. Some of the social science materials called on students to conduct surveys and do action research that some faculty members found too invasive of the boundaries of their own classrooms or that encouraged students to inquire into areas of school life that some felt were best left unexamined. For example, the Sociological Resources for the Social Studies project (SRSS) has a unit on leadership that took black leaders as examples in their case studies. This encouraged students in local school districts to want to interview black leaders in the local community at a time when the impact of *Brown* v. *Board of Education* was just beginning to be felt in some schools. Many school administrators were, to say the least, a bit anxious about what such inquires might unleash in their schools and their communities. I personally know of two superintendents who simply would not permit these materials to be used in their schools and I heard anecdotal reports of many others.

Installation of these materials also required changes in evaluation and evaluation systems. With regard to the evaluation of students, few of the standardized tests then available made any real effort to assess problem-solving skills or creativity. They were designed to assess broad and shallow understanding of lightly held information, not the presence or absence of profound understanding.

Similarly, existing evaluations of teachers proceeded from the assumption that teachers were by and large performers, and that the most important determinant of what students learned was the performance of the teacher. The new curriculum materials, however, were more focused on the activity of students than on the actions of the teacher. Many who designed the new materials assumed that the teacher was a leader, facilitator, and intellectual guide rather than simply a performer.

Moreover, existing evaluations did little or nothing to encourage teachers to pursue the profound goals implicit in the new curriculum materials. Indeed, goals and results had little to do with the evaluation process. (This reference to results is not an implied endorsement of the idea of evaluating teachers by the examination of test scores. I do not endorse this idea, as will become clear as my arguments unfold.) Teacher as leader was an idea that was—and still is—absent from most teacher appraisal processes. Yet the National Science Foundation materials assumed, implicitly at least, that the most important aspects of the teacher's role required leadership skills.

In addition, many of these materials required changes in the way textbooks were produced and purchased, and they challenged the authority of some of the groups and agencies that had controlled these matters. In states where state-wide textbook adoption was the norm, textbook committees found it difficult to endorse some of these materials, especially when the format made some elements expendable, requiring regular replacement.

Finally, the successful implementation of the new curriculum material required collaborative efforts that were uncommon among teachers and generally uncharacteristic of schools. They required devising schedules to allow teachers to meet together to review materials and intensive professional development—two resource allocations that few schools were prepared to accommodate. Those who found the innovation threatening to their own interests were thus provided ample support in their demands for abandonment of the program.

Collateral Lessons

There is a great deal more we can learn about systemic reform from the experiences of the 1960s. For example, one of the major barriers to systemic reform is what some sociologists refer to as *bureaucratic practicality*. Bureaucracies encourage a preference for external controls, rationality in decision making, and objectivity. Therefore, bureaucracy encourages a preference for data that can be collected in an efficient and easily standardized way and managed from afar.

While it is true that most things can be measured, not all things can be easily and efficiently measured, especially from afar. "Learning how to learn," for example, may be an admirable aim, but it is hard to measure progress toward such a goal in terms that will satisfy the bureaucratic bent toward standardized measures that can be administered efficiently. Creativity, insight, and the ability to frame problems, as well as to solve them, are difficult to measure in standardized fashion. Another collateral lesson is that the political and literal messiness caused by implementing some types of changes often causes discomfort among some who occupy power positions. Given an issue around which to organize, those who are distressed by the change will seize any opportunity to abandon the effort. This is especially the case when the change threatens existing power arrangements or when students are encouraged to explore ways of thinking that are at odds with prevailing local customs.

The Process of Abandonment

Programmatic efforts to improve schools are seldom overtly abandoned. Rather, the programs disappear, and the old systems are reestablished without acknowledgment or fanfare. The abandonment of the curricular reforms of the 1960s is no exception. There were moments of noise and drama, but more often these efforts were abandoned quietly—so quietly that few new teachers today know they ever happened, and even experienced teachers have forgotten about them.

The unfortunate fact is that the success or failure of the inquiry-oriented curriculum materials of the 1960s was dependent in large part on undisciplined volunteerism, with little encouragement or support from higher levels in the bureaucratic structure. Indeed, the textbook adoption practices of school systems, existing patterns of staff development, and insistence on bureaucratic uniformity all worked to discourage teachers from adopting these new materials. And when they did try to use them, the structure and culture of the school discouraged them from continuing.[12]

Failed Efforts to Increase Flexibility: Another Example

There are many useful and necessary innovations that do not work in the context of schooling but nonetheless address important issues. In these cases, we

[12]I spent nearly a decade working with these materials and working in a variety of efforts to install them in schools. My conclusions are based on this experience, but it is an experience that has been shared by many others and is well documented.

should ask, "How might we change the context so that these needed innovations can work?" Clearly one of the problems that must be confronted is the lack of flexibility inherent in the bureaucratic structure of schools. Efforts to tinker with this structure have not been particularly successful in the past and are unlikely to be any more successful in the future unless they are approached from a system perspective rather than programmatically. Consider flexible scheduling, open classrooms, and student-centered decision making.

Reformers have complained for years that the biggest barriers to school improvement are the inflexible use of time and space and the standardized placement of people. Many novel notions about ways to address these matters have been advanced, but efforts to act on these ideas almost always run into major difficulties. Indeed, more often than not, after a trial period, traditional calendars and schedules are reestablished, open classrooms are closed, and "batch processing" of students is reestablished.

One of the largest and most comprehensive efforts to make the use of time and space in schools more flexible and to more clearly focus instruction on the individual student was the so-called Trump plan. Named for J. Lloyd Trump, associate secretary of the National Association of Secondary School Principals (NASSP), the plan was admittedly complex. Nevertheless, it contained many of the components that would be necessary for schools to serve as platforms for learning as opposed to platforms for instruction. For example, the school day was broken into small time modules, and all students had a schedule based on an assessment of their instructional needs. Sometimes a period would be twenty minutes, sometimes two hours. Classrooms and learning spaces were of various sizes, and space was arranged in a flexible manner.

With support from the Ford Foundation, the Trump plan became something of a movement throughout the United States. Indeed, many new high schools that were being built during the 1960s and 1970s reflected the thinking of Trump. Schools that adopted the Trump strategy met with varying levels of success, but for the most part, after a few years of effort, traditional schedules began to reappear, open classrooms were walled off, seminar rooms became offices or storage rooms, and students were once again assigned lockers rather than work spaces. Today the Trump plan and its derivatives are parts of the lore that older high school teachers, older school board members, and many school administrators refer to when mounting arguments against this or that effort to manage time, space, or people in innovative ways. "We already tried that and it did not work," they say. "Students do not have enough self-discipline to pursue studies independently," some argue.

Today we see some derivatives of the Trump plan (for example, block scheduling), but even these more limited innovations confront difficulties that are embedded in the system itself. For example, the Carnegie unit, an accounting mechanism introduced in the early twentieth century to ensure uniform quality through standardized seat time, continues to make it difficult to organize student work in any way other than that suggested by traditional class arrangements. Although two reports by NASSP have called for the abandonment of the Carnegie unit, there seems to be little will to take this small step toward freeing up schools to install innovations that violate the way knowledge is organized in schools.

Similarly, much of the standards movement assumes that the graded school is a part of the natural landscape of school life. Otherwise, why would one have grade-level testing? However, as long as the idea of grade level dominates the ethos of schools, the idea of the nongraded school is nothing but a fiction to be bypassed. What reformers view as a nongraded classroom becomes a classroom where teachers feel harried to teach a mixed class of first-, second-, and third-grade students so that each can pass the appropriate test at the appropriate time.

In spite of these realities, in the face of the changes in learning technologies available to students outside school and the threats and possibilities that digital learning opportunities present to and for students, it is difficult to see how schools can survive unless educators are prepared to accept many of the ideas that Trump advanced years ago. However, before such changes can be successfully implemented, it will be essential to create a more collegial work environment than is typical of most schools—and there are many other problems that will need to be confronted as well.

Most important is the matter of discipline and control. In schools as they are now organized, any change that erodes the traditional base of teacher authority erodes the entire control structure of the schools. It was this erosion, probably more than any other factor, that led to the abandonment of the Trump plan.

If flexibility is to be introduced and student needs and interests, rather than teacher preferences, are to be the basis on which decisions are made, new systems of social control must be instituted. It is likely that these systems will need to be invented school by school and designed in ways that have meaning to students and provide teachers and parents with the assurances they need. This means that the way the power and authority systems are structured will need to be changed, as will the boundary systems and the evaluation systems. That is why real change in schools is so hard.

COMMON LANGUAGE, POWER, AND SEPARATION

Toward the end of *Disrupting Class*, Christensen, Horn, and Johnson suggest three strategies for making schools more adept at using disruptive innovations: development of a common language, power, and separation. This book has a strong bias for the first of these strategies. The reason is that I am as much concerned about the school as a community-building institution as I am about the school as the deliverer of an educational "product." Without a common language that expresses common values and common concerns, democratically oriented education is not possible. Education is not a commodity or a privately held good. Education, especially in a democracy, is a common good, and the safest repository for such a precious commodity is the citizenry of the democracy itself.

In my view, the power strategy and the separation strategy are both, potentially at least, antidemocratic in their conception. The power strategy, which involves such things as turning schools over to strong mayors or the state, removes from local publics the right to make meaningful decisions regarding the direction of their schools. The separation strategy, essentially a form of a charter school strategy, argues for the balkanization of schools—developing schools in such a way that they serve, relatively exclusively, students from specific backgrounds whose circumstances are pretty much alike, thereby ensuring the social-cultural homogeneity required to run an effective school.

The common language strategy would require school leaders, including school boards, to redefine their roles and become as concerned with community building and creating a public for public education as with trying to respond to the disparate claims of a factionalized and increasing balkanized constituency. Such leadership is in short supply, but it is for such leaders that this book is written.

Bureaucracies Versus Learning Organizations

I f we are serious about having great schools for every child, we begin by trying to understand the schools we have and the reasons they function as they do. Next, we try to imagine what schools would look like if they were to function as they would need to for all children to learn at high levels. This chapter provides a framework for assisting leaders with both of these tasks.

This framework posits two modes of organization that can frame our thinking about how schools should be organized and how they should function. The first of these is the *bureaucracy*, an organizational type initially described in detail by Max Weber (1864–1920), a German sociologist who was particularly interested in understanding the nature of large-scale organizations based on rational principles, clearly differentiated roles, and hierarchically arranged systems of authority. To assist him in this understanding, he employed the idea of bureaucracy as an ideal type. Since Weber's initial formulation, literally thousands of books and articles have been written on the subject of bureaucracy.

Weber did not, however, invent bureaucracy or the idea of bureaucracy. The term *bureaucracy* was first used in France in reference to the operation of the French government prior to the revolution of 1789. Weber transformed this term into a tool for technical analysis by describing bureaucracy as an ideal type.

The second mode of organization is the *learning organization*, a relatively new concept. Much of the original thinking underlying the notion of the learning organization was developed by Peter Drucker as he struggled to understand and explain how changes in the mode of work that typified American industry were creating a new type of worker—what he called the *knowledge worker*—and a new type of organization—what he called the *knowledge work organization*. Peter Senge built on this set of ideas and is probably the originator of the term *learning organization*.[1] Since the seminal work of Drucker and Senge, many others have contributed to our understanding—and misunderstanding—of these ideas.

What I have to say in this chapter is therefore a compilation of the thinking of many social theorists (there may even be an idea or two here that I can blame on no one but myself).

IDEAL TYPES: A TOOL FOR ANALYSIS

The effort to describe and explain the similarities and differences in organizations has occupied social scientists for many years. One of the most powerful of the tools developed to support this work is the *ideal type*: efforts to present in an idealized manner a model "expressing in a pure—and therefore unreal—form, the core characteristics of a pattern of conduct." Above all, ideal types are efforts to state the patterned regularities that "sustain an enduring system of relationships."[2]

Ideal types are intended to bring attention to factors that are worthy of notice and should be considered when trying to understand a phenomenon; they are not statements regarding the actual condition of the phenomenon. For example, Max Weber used the *rational bureaucracy* as an ideal type to describe and explain behavior in organizations with which he was concerned. As conceived by Weber, rational bureaucracy is a means of organizing human activity so that the impact of human emotion and sentiment is minimized, thereby ensuring rationality in all decision-making processes. Few organizations attain this idealized state, but it is important to consider the role that a preference for rationality plays in the decision making of an organization and the creation of the systems that lead to and reinforce decisions.

[1]See, for example, Peter Drucker, *The Essential Drucker: The Best of Sixty Years of Peter Drucker's Essential Writings on Management* (New York: HarperCollins, 2001). Peter Senge, *The Fifth Discipline: The Art and Practice of the Learning Organization* (New York: Doubleday, 1990).
[2]Everett Wilson, *Sociology: Rules, Roles, and Relationships* (Homewood, Ill.: Dorsey Press, 1971), p. 644.

Another function of the ideal type is to provide a basis for considering the extent to which an organization fits or deviates from any given model or type, the difference such patterns make in the lives of people in the organization, and the effects the organization has on the outside world. Organizations based on bureaucratic assumptions, for example, always have trouble dealing with and taking advantage of persons whose primary tasks call on them to create or uniquely apply technical knowledge and who function generally as what these days are called *knowledge workers,* a term that appears to have been coined by Peter Drucker. The productivity of *knowledge worker* has to do with employing ideas, theories, and mental processes, in contrast to the activity of the manual worker, which has more to do with the exercise of muscle and sinew. Bureaucracies operate best when work is routine and the means of doing the job are relatively well known and certain. They are not highly adaptive organizations and do not encourage creativity. If adaptive behavior and creativity are required, a learning organization is required.

In this book I use the notion of the school as a bureaucracy to show how a preference for compliance and control has driven educators to model schools after factories, aimed at the mass production of products like automobiles, and governmental agencies and other types of organizations that give preference to operating systems that reflect compliance and control as core values.

The contrasting idea of the learning organization provides a way to describe a more flexible and creative mode of organization, one where working on and working with knowledge and putting knowledge to work are primary modes of operation. Peter Senge defines learning organizations as "organizations where people continually expand their capacity to create the results they truly desire, where new and expansive patterns of thinking are nurtured, where collective aspiration is set free, and where people are continually learning to see the whole together."[3] Table 3.1 lists side by side the defining characteristics of these two ideal types.

Are Schools Learning Organizations?

Are schools learning organizations? When asked this question, Peter Senge said, "Definitely not.... Most teachers feel oppressed trying to conform to all kinds of rules, goals and objectives, many of which they don't believe in. Teachers don't

[3]Senge, *The Fifth Discipline,* p. 3.

Table 3.1
Characteristics of Schools Operating in a Bureaucratic Versus a Learning Organization Context

Bureaucratic Schools	Learning Organizations
The primary purpose of the school is identified in a way that defines the student in a passive or submissive role—for example, the student as product, raw material, client, or conscript.	Students are viewed as volunteers rather than conscripts, and it is assumed that for them to learn what the community wants them to learn, they must be provided with work that has qualities and characteristics that respond to the students' own motives.
The willingness and ability of students to comply with uniform performance standards set by various "end users"—such as the business community or colleges and universities—are usually of central concern.	A well-articulated set of norms places task engagement and profound learning at the center of the school's system of values and clearly defines the core business of school as the creation of engaging work for students.[a]
Student docility and compliance are defined as virtues.	
Teachers are customarily viewed as employees and as lower-level members of the adult hierarchy.	Teachers are viewed as leaders, designers of work for students, and guides to instruction.
There is considerable separation between employee groups and management groups.	
The principal is usually viewed as a first-line supervisor, in the lower echelon of management.	The principal is expected to be a leader of leaders within the school, as well as a member of the superintendent's administrative team at the central office level.
Routine, standardization, and predictability of response are desired end states.	The idea of continuous innovation aimed at continuous improvement is embraced as a core value, and behavior is guided by clear moral and aesthetic norms combined with a fluid set of technical norms.[b]

(Continued)

Table 3.1
(*Continued*)

Bureaucratic Schools	Learning Organizations
Rules, procedures, and policies are elaborate and rigidly enforced.	Local conventions place emphasis on fairness, equity, excellence, loyalty, courage, persistence, constancy of purpose, and duty as values that define "the way we do business around here."
Communication flows from the top down with little attention to bottom-up communication or horizontal communication. Management by memorandum is typical. Coordination of effort is a management function.	Conversation and dialogue about the core business of the school and its success in doing that business are the primary tools for building and maintaining the school culture and ensuring the disciplined pursuit of a shared vision of the future.
Carefully crafted job descriptions are used to delegate and assign responsibility and authority. Boundary disputes are common, especially between school faculties and central office personnel or among middle-level operators and semiautonomous operating units such as departments within schools.	The central office staff is expected to work to develop the capacity of both the school district and the community to support and sustain innovations that promise to increase the quality of schoolwork provided to students.
The superintendent is typically viewed as a manager rather than as a leader and is expected to carry out the directives of bureaucratic superiors (school boards, state officials) without significant input into the way such directives are framed.	The superintendent is expected to serve as a moral and intellectual leader for the district, to continually focus all participants on the direction in which the schools are heading, and to reinforce the cultural and moral basis for the direction that has been set.

(*Continued*)

Table 3.1
(Continued)

Bureaucratic Schools	Learning Organizations
The role of the board of education is typically defined as representative of various stakeholders, particularly the special interest groups, factions, and parties that elect or appoint them.	The school board is expected to establish a clear sense of community for itself and to market the identity it develops to constituencies as a means of building a community of interest around the schools and the students served by the schools.

[a]By *core business* I mean the goals and activities that define what the school is about. A core business is identified by answering the question, "What do people do around here, and what meaning do they attach to what they do?"

[b]Moral norms have to do with judgments about good and bad, corrupt and honorable, purpose and value. Aesthetic norms have to do with taste, standards of beauty, and so on. Technical norms have to do with the way tasks are to be done, usually based on research and disciplined knowledge. Conventions have to do with "the way things are done around here" and are justified by tradition. These ideas were first suggested to me in Robin M. Williams's now-classic book, *American Society: A Sociological Interpretation*, 3rd ed. (New York: Knopf, 1972).

work together; there's very little sense of collective learning going on in most schools." With regard to students, Senge continued:

> We say school is about learning, but by and large schooling has traditionally been about people memorizing a lot of stuff that they really don't care too much about and the whole approach is quite fragmented. Really deep learning is a process that is inevitably driven by the learner, not someone else. And it always moves back and forth between a domain of thinking and a domain of action. So having a student sit passively taking in information is hardly a very good model for learning; it's just what we're used to.[4]

Generally I agree with Senge when he asserts that schools are not learning organizations. I do have some difficulty with his assertion that schools are not

[4]John O'Neil, "On Schools as Learning Organizations: A Conversation with Peter Senge," *Educational Leadership*, Apr. 1995, p. 28.

learning focused. They are learning focused, but they are typically focused on the wrong type of learning.

Senge is, however, concerned only with what he calls *deep learning*. (I usually refer to this type of learning as *profound learning*, meaning learning that calls on the student to think and reason as well as to remember.) The kind of learning that most schools now promote tends to focus on a type of learning that can be produced by forms of compliance not associated with engagement.[5] This type of learning is superficial but it does have the advantage of being easy to measure on standardized tests.

Profound learning requires that students remember what they learned over a long period of time rather than just to pass a test. It thus provides them with a level of mastery of what they have learned that is sufficient to ensure that the knowledge they gain or develop is of use in contexts beyond that in which it was learned.

Critical thinking is essential to the acquisition of profound knowledge, as are reflection, re-creation, and reconfiguration. Such learning seldom occurs when the tasks that are intended to produce the learning have no inherent meaning or value to the learner. For profound learning to occur, meaning, personal value, and the engagement that result from these are essential ingredients.

One of the reasons that bureaucracy is so commonplace in American schools is that the type of learning valued in schools can be most efficiently produced by inducing compliance through the use of extrinsic rewards and the threat of punishment. The pedagogical procedures needed to produce this type of compliance are generally more certain and better understood and codified than is the case when the concern is to produce engaging work for students. Therefore, the procedures needed to produce superficial learning are relatively easy to rationalize and standardize and submit to bureaucratic control.

Profound learning is more likely to result from compliance that comes about as a result of students' finding meaning, personal significance, and value in the tasks they are asked to complete and their work products. The pedagogy that produces this type of engaging work is less certain, more difficult to codify, and less predictable than is the pedagogy that produces more superficial forms of learning.

Bureaucracies are designed to organize and manage certainty and ensure predictability. Learning organizations are designed to create the type of leadership

[5]This is not an indictment of individual teachers. Many teachers, indeed most teachers, work hard to ensure that students learn at profound levels in a system that often does not value profound learning. The problem is that the bureaucracies in which they work neither expect nor support these efforts, and thus the task of great teachers is made needlessly difficult.

structures needed to deal with uncertainty in disciplined, productive, and creative ways—to transform problems into possibilities and perplexities into insight. The result is that bureaucratically organized schools tend to show a strong preference for programs and activities that are designed to reliably produce superficial learning. Schools that are organized as learning organizations are much more likely to be supportive of the kinds of pedagogical styles that will result in greater creativity, problem-solving ability, and other so-called twenty-first-century skills.

Which Systems Are Emphasized?

One of the most important differences between learning organizations and bureaucracies has to do with which of the critical systems described in Chapter Two receive the majority of leaders' attention. This prioritization is illustrated in Figure 3.1. Leaders in bureaucracies are primarily concerned with strengthening formal controls that support the enforcement of operational standards and minimize disruption to routines. Leaders in learning organizations are primarily concerned with establishing direction, creating and transmitting knowledge, and developing people who are capable of self-direction and self-control. This attention results in collateral differences with regard to the systems that are most likely to be well developed and carefully defined.

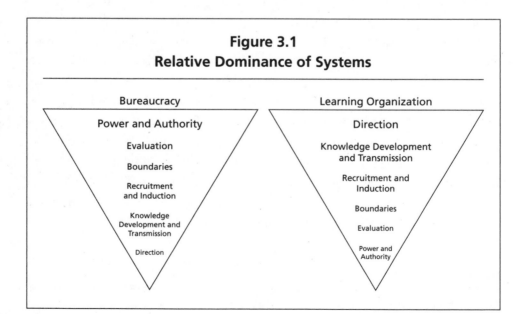

**Figure 3.1
Relative Dominance of Systems**

Bureaucracy

Power and Authority

Evaluation

Boundaries

Recruitment
and Induction

Knowledge
Development and
Transmission

Direction

Learning Organization

Direction

Knowledge Development
and Transmission

Recruitment and
Induction

Boundaries

Evaluation

Power and
Authority

Power, authority, evaluation, and boundaries are all more closely associated with formal control than are the directional, knowledge development and transmission, and recruitment and induction systems. Bureaucratic leaders are concerned with such questions as these:

- Who is in charge?
- What are they in charge of?
- Who decides, and how are things decided?
- What are the standards for performance?
- Who judges this performance?
- What are the metrics to be used in rendering these judgments?

Leaders in learning organizations are concerned with questions such as these:

- What kind of organization are we, and what do we want to become?
- What accomplishments will make us most proud?
- What will it take to satisfy those we intend to serve?
- What are the core values and beliefs we want to ensure that new members will embrace and uphold?
- How do we identify, import, and develop the knowledge we need to engage in the kinds of continuous innovation required to survive and thrive in a constantly changing environment?
- How will we know when we succeed, and how will we measure success?

Unlike leaders in learning organizations, bureaucrats are seldom visionaries; they are more often functionaries. Typically they have little concern about vision or direction, for the direction of bureaucracies is generally determined by agencies external to the bureaucracy itself, for example, by a state legislature. Leaders in learning organizations spend much of their time communicating clear visions to others and inspiring others to join them in the pursuit of those visions. (In schools organized as learning organizations, teachers as well as administrators are looked on as leaders. See Chapter Four and Chapter Five.)

In fact, bureaucrats usually have little patience with discussions of direction and matters related to direction, whereas issues of direction are of central concern to leaders in learning organizations. In bureaucratically oriented schools, strategic planning usually involves nothing more than a ritualistic bow to the need to "have a vision statement," followed by detailed attention to the development of clear and measurable goals that may themselves be directionless or may lead in many directions simultaneously.

Indeed, the closest some bureaucratically oriented school leaders come to discussing issues of direction is when they endeavor to establish indicators of progress toward goals that have been established, often paying little or no attention to the direction these goals may imply. It is therefore not uncommon for bureaucratic goals to compete with each other, one goal leading in one direction and the other in another direction. And one of the unfortunate consequences of this lack of attention to direction is that often the direction taken leads only to more bureaucracy.

In learning organizations, discussions of direction always take precedence over those of goals. Goal setting is often the responsibility of the individuals who will become responsible for them, with the caveat that the goals selected make an important contribution to the pursuit of a direction that has been collectively agreed on.

Because control is so important in bureaucracies, bureaucratic leaders tend to define many problems as boundary problems. If the new knowledge imported into the system is not congruent with the existing power and authority arrangements, then the system that is of most value to them—the power and authority system—may be threatened or disrupted. Therefore, the new knowledge and those who are trying to import it are seen as boundary threats. Indeed, changes in the knowledge development and transmission system will be tolerated only if these changes do not let unsettling knowledge cross the boundaries, or if the means of generating the knowledge does not threaten the existing internal power arrangements. (The examples of the National Science Foundation projects and the Trump plan presented in Chapter Two illustrate this point.)

In learning organizations, leaders take an entirely different view of matters. The power and authority system is almost always subordinate to the directional system. In learning organizations, when power arrangements become barriers to the introduction of a promising innovation, leaders are more likely to change the power arrangement than they are to domesticate the innovation so that it fits the system of power and authority. In a learning organization, power and authority are viewed as shared resources for maintaining direction. They are not a means of exercising control in a system that may be without direction yet dominated by attention to often competing operational and strategic goals, each of which may be leading in a different direction.

Leaders in learning organizations also recognize that energy and resources spent on recruitment and induction decrease the need for supervision, formal evaluations, and inspection. When self-control is present, the need for formal control is decreased. When all employees share and embrace performance standards, the informal controls exercised by peers who are committed to these standards will be a more powerful means of ensuring needed compliance than can ever be gained by compliance-focused evaluation systems.

In bureaucracies, the formal understandings on which the organization proceeds are usually made available through policy manuals, memoranda, corporate briefings, management-dominated conferences, committee meetings, and announcements. In learning organizations, the understandings on which the organization proceeds are likely to be enshrined in myths, lore, stories, and semisacred traditions and transmitted through fully developed induction processes. (This is not to say that learning organizations do not have policies and policy manuals, for they do, but such materials do not have the prominence that they have in bureaucracies.)

To function well and efficiently, bureaucracies depend on the application of negative sanctions and differential access to status and the rewards associated with it. The systems that facilitate this formal control—power and authority, evaluation, and boundary systems—thus receive the most attention. In the absence of shared beliefs and values to provide direction, uniformity is most likely to be maintained through the use of power.

Furthermore, in a bureaucracy, the way the power and authority, evaluation, and boundary systems are structured will determine the way the induction, knowledge development and transmission, and directional systems are and will continue to be structured and how they function. Induction, for example, will likely be dominated by attention to the way formal evaluations are conducted and direction by those who have formal authority. Control of knowledge and information will be carefully regulated so that departmental boundaries are honored and the status of prominent individuals is reinforced, or at least not threatened.

In brief, the structure and culture of bureaucracies are defined by the way power and authority are distributed, the way evaluations are conducted, and the way internal and external boundaries are determined—and the other systems are shaped to respond to these dominant structures. Official status is power; title and position, rather than knowledge, determine who is empowered to act. People can act only if they occupy positions that formally entitle them to act, regardless of what they know and what others know they know.

In a learning organization, authority follows knowledge. Knowledge indeed is power. Those who are most knowledgeable are empowered to act on what they know, regardless of their position or title. Because those who know what needs to be done are empowered to act, learning organizations are nimble in the face of novelty. Bureaucracies, in contrast, are often slow and cumbersome because novel situations do not have rules, and action without rules is frowned on. Furthermore, those who are authorized to make or legitimize rules are usually far removed from the point of action.

Appendix A provides detailed matrices that contrast the bureaucratic and learning organization types. These tables are organized around the six systems presented in Chapter Two. These more detailed descriptions are useful tools for those who are interested in more fully understanding the way their own school or school district operates. It has also been useful in helping school leaders assess where their organizations now stand with regard to their organizational form.

HOW IS SOCIAL CONTROL ESTABLISHED?

The effectiveness of any formal organization depends on the ability of leaders to maintain direction, mobilize efforts in pursuit of common goals, and coordinate those efforts in an effective and efficient manner. This means establishing *social control:* the means by which groups and organizations induce their members to engage in tasks, fulfill roles, and support norms that are important to the survival of the group or the achievement of organizational goals.

Sociologists commonly distinguish three types of social control:

1. *Formal control,* where official sanctions, rewards, and punishments are in play.

2. *Informal control,* where peer groups and informal networks enforce agreed-on rules and norms through the use of such devices as humor, embarrassment, corrective feedback, and personal confrontation. In these situations, group members have internalized the norms to the point that they take responsibility for enforcing them, up to and including bringing members who deviate from the norms into line.

3. *Self-control,* where individuals have internalized the norms that regulate behavior in the group to the extent that they feel personally obligated to do what they are expected to and regulate their behavior accordingly.

Bureaucracies are heavily dependent on formal control; learning organizations rely more on informal control and self-control.

Social control usually involves the exercise of power and authority and may also involve the exercise of personal influence. As should be clear from the preceding discussion, how power and authority are distributed and exercised, and the way influence is viewed and dealt with, define many of the differences between bureaucracies and learning organizations. It is therefore useful to be clear about the way the concepts of power, authority, and influence are used in this book:

- *Power* has to do with the ability to gain acceptance of directives and support for norms that are held as important in the life of the organization. Power in organizations is based on access to organizational resources, for example, financial resources, personnel resources, and the symbolic rewards the organization has to offer.

- *Authority* has to do with the right to exercise power. To say that one has authority is to say that one has the officially condoned and legitimized right to impose sanctions and distribute rewards. In other words, it refers to the recognized right to exercise the power made available through the physical, fiscal, and symbolic resources the organization controls.

- *Influence* has to do with personalities and personal relationships. Unlike power and authority, it is not embedded in the formal structure of the organization. People have influence due to who they are and what they do with and for others rather than because of the authority assigned to the positions they occupy.

Types of Power and Sanctions

Amitai Etzioni, a highly regarded sociologist, has described three types of power: normative, remunerative, and coercive power.[6] On this typology, he suggests three types of sanctions that might be used to establish and maintain social control:

- *Normative sanctions,* which are based on the assumption that participants have internalized the values of the organization so deeply that symbolic acts

---

[6]In his early career, Etzioni wrote a book in which he used power and compliance as critical elements in the classification of differences between and among organizations. I drew on his ideas in the first book I wrote in 1976, and I see no reason to abandon these ideas now. See Amitai Etzioni, *A Comparative Analysis of Complex Organizations: On Power, Involvement and Their Correlates* (New York: Free Press, 1961).

that support norms (for example, praise and support from colleagues) are sufficient to maintain direction. In such situations, self-control, informal controls, and peer influence are the primary sources of control.

- *Remunerative sanctions,* which are based on such considerations as receiving or being denied bonuses, promotions, and other material benefits. Usually these sanctions are formally administered and carefully defined within the authority structure. Generally, remunerative sanctions are related to the idea of extrinsic rewards, whereas normative sanctions are associated with what are sometimes referred to as intrinsic rewards.

- *Coercive sanctions,* which are based on the ability to inflict physical or psychological pain, deny mobility, or preclude access. Dismissal for poor performance (denial of access), furloughs, and detention are all forms of coercion, as are public humiliation and official ridicule.

Clearly there is a great deal of variability between and among organizations with regard to the extent to which these sanctions are available and are likely to be used. Bureaucracies usually rely little on normative sanctions, whereas learning organizations are heavily dependent on normative sanctions to maintain control. The reason this is so is that normative power depends on the ability of the organization to develop affective ties between and among participants, as well as emotional attachments to the beliefs and values on which the organization is based. Sociologists often distinguish between expressive functions and instrumental functions, by which they mean, and I mean here, functions that are value loaded and not easily observed or rationalized (expressive) and functions that have to do with ends that are more or less concrete, observable, usable, and subject to rationalization (instrumental). Normative power requires careful attention to the expressive functions of the organization.

Bureaucracies are designed to suppress the effects of personal sentiments. Moreover, they emphasize instrumental relationships more than personal ones. Bureaucracies are based on the assumption that emotion, personal attachments, and affect lead to lack of objectivity and interfere with the kind of rational decision making that bureaucracies are designed to foster.

Learning organizations, in contrast, are dependent on the capacity to develop and maintain shared commitments to common beliefs and shared meanings regarding the good, bad, beautiful, and ugly. They require a common attachment to shared symbols and the creation of a common identity. They proceed on the assumption that all members have a shared understanding of duties and obligations that membership imposes on them, as well as a shared understanding of the rights and privileges that membership ensures. Consequently, it is incumbent on leaders of learning organizations to give a great deal of attention to recruitment, retention, and symbolic acts that signify continuing support for established members.

Leaders in bureaucracies are less likely to attend to systematic approaches to induction or continuing support for staff other than executives and officers.[7] They are more likely to orient new staff and explain the rules to them than purposefully induct them into the culture of the organization. Bureaucratic managers are more likely to teach by exception—that is, when a rule is violated, to punish the violator—than to teach by example.

Bureaucratic managers are concerned with developing systems for rationalizing the way remunerative rewards are distributed, promotions are gained, and punitive measures can be applied than with developing the sentiments of staff toward the moral order of the organization. This is so because bureaucracies are designed to control for the messiness that human emotion introduces into the life of organizations. Learning organizations, to the contrary, are designed to capitalize on the creativity that human sentiments, controlled by disciplined discourse and reason, can produce. They are as dependent on commitment to the moral order that characterizes the organization as they are to the exercise of technical skills, for it is through shared commitments to this order that social control is exercised.

Principles of Authority

Max Weber identified three types of authority: scientific-rational, traditional, and charismatic.[8] *Scientific-rational authority* is based on rules, procedures, and processes that have been rationalized and codified into job descriptions, policy manuals, and specified technical procedures. It is the authority on which bureaucracies proceed. *Traditional authority* has to do with deeply embedded and often

---

[7]Clearly this generalization has many exceptions. The military, for example, is in many ways quite bureaucratic, and induction, especially among the officer corps, is a major concern. Indeed, as the fighting of war has required more knowledge work, many areas of military life are being transformed into organizational forms more like that of a learning organization.

[8]Max Weber, *Theory of Social and Economic Organization,* ed. Guenther Ross and Claus Wittich (Los Angeles: University of California Press, 1978).

tacitly understood ways of doing things. The basis for such authority is often shrouded in mystery and myth and is sometimes provided legitimacy through religious sanctions and long-standing habit. Families and small communities are illustrative of systems that typically proceed on the basis of traditional authority.

Charismatic authority has to do with authority that derives from some perceived special attribute of the person who is assigned whatever authority there is to assign. Historically and in primitive cultures, such an attribute was (is) thought to have to do with a special relationship with a divine spirit or a god. Over the years, the word *charisma* has come to stand for any type of authority that flows from the perception that a person is specially and uniquely endowed or blessed as a leader. Social movements are sometimes organized around individual leaders who are believed to have special qualities that entitle them to authority. Adolf Hitler was certainly charismatic, but so were many people of more noble character, such as Dr. Martin Luther King Jr. In education, it is common to attribute the success of effective principals to charisma. If charisma is essential to principal success, this does not bode well for schools. Charisma cannot be taught or learned; it just *is*.

Weber's distinction among rational, traditional, and charismatic authority is not, of course, the only means of framing the issue of authority. Indeed, political scientists spend much time and energy in discussions on the nature of authority derived from democratic principles, that is, authority based on the will of the people. They contrast this type of authority with the kind of authority one finds in autocratic regimes, that is, authority based on the will of a dictator or ruling party.

John French and Bertram Raven, for example, have described five types of power: coercive, reward, referent, legitimate, and expert.[9] (Later they added two additional types.) Their discussion is useful and provocative, but their framework, as well as several other variations of that framework I might have chosen to use, confuse power and authority in ways that are not useful for my purposes. In my view, authority is best thought of as the legitimized right to exercise power.

Power has to do with resources, symbolic and material. Authority involves the right to use these resources and distribute them to others. Coercive power, for example, can be legitimate or illegitimate. The principal who assigns a student to detention is exercising legitimate coercive power in that he or she is exercising

[9]See, for example, John French and Bertram Raven, "The Bases of Social Power," in D. Cartwright, *Studies in Social Power* (Ann Arbor, Michigan: Institute for Social Research, 1959).

the right to limit the mobility of the student. The student may be assigned detention because he too employed coercive power when he engaged in a fight on the playground, but his exercise of coercive power was not legitimate.

The type of authority one has is determined by what is used to legitimize the granting of authority. In a bureaucracy, for example, authority is usually granted based on rationalized principles. Those principles often include the assumption of expertise as the basis of gaining access to a power position. In contrast, charismatic authority is granted based on the assumption that the person who is granted the right to exercise power is entitled to it by virtue of his or her own unique characteristics or unique relationship with mystical forces and sources. Charismatic authority therefore is extraorganizational in nature, and the person who exercises it does not base his or her claim to power on the authority assigned to the position he or she occupies in the system. Traditional authority is based on honorific positions that entitle one to claim deference from others, for example, the authority of the parent over the child, elders in tribal communities, and religious leaders in sacred societies. (It is not without significance that the effort of teachers to base their authority on professional expertise has become more prominent as the tradition-based authority of the teacher as sacred community figure and surrogate parent has been eroded by the same forces that have eroded the sense of community that defines many schools.)

Consensual Authority

It is my view that participation in the life of a learning organization requires embracing an authority principle that may be compatible with many of the existing models of power and authority but is a sufficiently different phenomenon to deserve a different label. I refer to this type of authority as *consensual authority*.

Consensual authority has some elements in common with rational authority and some in common with democratic authority. It involves some aspects of what French and Raven refer to as *connectional power*, meaning authority that derives from the trust built through networks and relationships. It also has some of the dimensions that French and Raven refer to as *expert authority*. Groups may learn to turn to persons for direction where previous experience with the person indicates he or she has superior understanding in the area of concern.

Consensual authority gives high priority to the idea that the basis of decisions needs to be transparent and submitted to public inspection and verification.

Hidden agendas are taboo in learning organizations. Open discussion, conversation, and dialogue are the primary means of making decisions. Persuasive argumentation, where facts are mustered, values are expressed, and meanings are explored is the lifeblood of a learning organization.

In bureaucracies, facts and data are weapons for exercising control and inducing compliance. In learning organizations, facts are viewed as tools with which ideas are disciplined rather than as weapons with which adversaries are dispatched.

In learning organizations, personal values and biases are assumed to be among the facts one must consider when determining the merit and worth of an argument. Unlike the scientific-rational frame, however, consensual authority does not try to discount unique insights that come from inspiration rather than research. It simply insists that these ideas and their likely consequences be submitted to the discipline of public discourse. Ideas and values drive learning organizations.

The categorization, manipulation, and codification of facts and data are the driving passion of bureaucracies and bureaucrats. Facts and data are important in a learning organization, but ideas are prized above facts, and advances are made on the basis of ideas disciplined by facts. This is why disciplined conversations are so critical in learning organizations and why issues of personal character and integrity are so important. It is also why bureaucracies tend to bleed the life out of facts and the excitement and imagination out of research.

Unlike organizations based on rational authority, organizations based on consensual authority honor values and traditions and openly embrace the notion that culture, as well as structure, is important to the life of the organization. Moral and aesthetic norms are as important to those who proceed on the basis of consensual authority as are technical norms. In organizations where consensual authority reigns supreme, people and their value are at the center of decisions as much as or more than are processes and their value.

Passion and empathy are given space and honor, as are logic and objectivity. Although the participants in the life of learning organizations are adept at testing hypotheses and developing theories, they are equally adept at making the case and telling the story. They are as interested in the journalistic values of fairness, accuracy, completeness, and balance as they are in the scientific values of validity, reliability, and objectivity.

In organizations based on consensual authority, individual men and women have authority not because it is assigned to them by bureaucratic superiors, granted through traditional entitlement, or bestowed by some mystical or unique attribute. Rather, they have earned the right to act on behalf of others through their proven judgment, commitment, and fidelity to the values of the organization and to the welfare of those who are dependent on it. They are entitled because others have learned to respect them rather than because a title was bestowed by superordinates.

Consensual authority emerges out of conversation, dialogue, and arguments aimed at seeking a common course of action and empowering people to act. Men and women with special talents are more likely to be empowered to act than are those without needed talents, but the traditions of a learning organization will bestow honor on all who participate in the life of the organization and contribute to that life. The talents of all are valued, no matter how meager these talents may seem to be.

Learning organizations celebrate the human spirit and strive to inspire the creativity that men and women possess. They nurture strong personal bonds and community sentiments, which are essential to the authority from which learning organizations proceed. This is why the systematic induction of students and staff is so critical in schools that function as learning organizations. It is also the reason that induction is usually only an afterthought in many bureaucratically organized schools. It is the reason that storytelling, myths, and legends are important in learning organizations, for much of the genius of the organization is stored in these symbols.

The Importance of Influence

Consensual authority derives from a synthesis of rational, traditional, charismatic, and democratic authority. Furthermore, as with any other true synthesis, the whole is greater than the sum of its parts. Consensual authority is authority by consent, but it is not authority by consensus or even by vote. Consensual authority involves power, that is, the control of resources, but it is also based on personal influence.

In a learning organization, people have power because they have influence. When they cease to have influence and must resort to the use of power to gain support from others, they will lose the right to exercise power. In a bureaucracy, those who have power are likely to try to barter their power for influence, for it is through personal influence developed through the strategic use of power that bureaucrats become entrenched.

For this reason, bureaucracies often treat personal influence as a problem, because such influence is difficult to control by formal means. In bureaucratic systems, in fact, informal networks sometimes develop that are bent on subverting the formal authority system. For example, strategies intended to increase productivity through piecework incentives are often subverted by groups of workers who reach informal agreements that set the upper limit of permissible performance well below that which a competent individual could produce, and they then use informal means of influence (humor, embarrassment, and shunning, for example) to sanction "rate busters." Another favorite ploy of disaffected workers in bureaucracies is to work to the rule, which means doing exactly what the rules require regardless of the contradictions and inefficiencies introduced. Militant union action sometimes uses such strategies in lieu of strikes.

Sometimes these informal agreements and understandings, while technically in violation of rules, make it possible to solve problems the bureaucracy has otherwise been unable to solve. In fact, if it were not for the willingness of members of informal networks to support deviations from the official rules, changes in the external environment would almost certainly overwhelm bureaucracies. For example, in one school district in which I was conducting research, the board of education, in the effort to encourage teachers to engage in professional development activities, had made it possible for teachers to gain salary increments through participating in training activities approved by the principal. This was called in-service credit. In this same school district, it had also been a common practice for principals to assume they had the authority to assign teachers, without additional remuneration, to do extra-duty activities such as monitoring athletic events and chaperoning dances.

When a new union contract required such duties to be paid and principals discovered that the money budgeted to pay teachers was nowhere near the amount required to pay for the level of work customarily assigned on a non-voluntary basis they began to offer "in-service credit" to teachers who "volunteered." This made it possible to comply with the union contract and at the same time get the necessary work done.

This practice was not exactly illegal or in violation of policy, but it was certainly not consistent with the intent of providing in-service credit. This practice became part of the lore that experienced principals passed along to new principals as they brought these neophytes into their informal networks.

Because the subtleties of such deviations are complex and the rules do not appear in the operational manuals of the system, much of the induction of new members in a bureaucracy has to do with established members and informal networks helping new members understand "what we really do around here," especially when the rules make no sense in the real life of the organization. Sometimes these informal socializing networks become much more powerful in communicating the culture of the organization than are official orientation efforts. Such practices can also be used to subvert the intentions of official leaders as well as to make an otherwise unworkable system work passably.

Unlike bureaucracies, learning organizations encourage the development of informal networks among influential individuals. Indeed, such networks serve as one of the primary means by which social control is established and maintained. Given that self-control, rather than formal control, is valued in learning organizations, this is not surprising. It is also not surprising that learning organizations are much more attentive to providing systematic induction of new employees, for it is through such induction that organizational norms become internalized and informal networks supportive of the beliefs and values of the organization are established and maintained.

In a learning organization, for example, persons who are recognized by their colleagues as exemplars of practice are most likely to be those designated to be mentors and trainers for new recruits. They will also be likely to serve as continuing leaders of learning communities as well as exemplars and status leaders in the organization more generally. That is, they are given consensual authority.

In bureaucracies, mentors and trainers are more likely to be those who have job seniority and occupy official positions in the bureaucratic hierarchy that manages human resources, training, or staff development. The de facto mentors, however, will likely be powerful members of the informal groups that define "how we really do business around here." Thus, in learning organizations, informal status and reputation are affirmed by job assignments, whereas in bureaucracies, job assignments are determined by the position one occupies in the hierarchy.

Influence, like power, has to do with the ability to gain acceptance of directives and support for norms, but influence is based on personal attributes and personal relationships. Personal reputation and informal status among colleagues and peers determine influence. People who have authority may use it to generate influence; for example, sometimes people in authority overlook minor infractions of rules which may generate a certain amount of social exchange influence with subordinates. (Social exchange theory refers to the idea that human interactions can be viewed as exchanges, much like economic interactions can be viewed as exchanges.) Similarly, those who develop a great deal of influence are likely to be assigned responsibilities that bring with them considerable authority. Thus, power, authority, and influence interact in ways that are sometimes subtle and sometimes blatantly obvious.

Commitment and Involvement

Many years ago, following ideas developed by Amitai Etzioni, I suggested that there were three ways that school employees and students might relate to the culture of the schools with which they are involved: moral involvement, calculative involvement, or alienation.[10]

Morally involved individuals find meaning and significance in the life of the school. They have a feeling of belonging and a sense of obligation and duty toward the school, and they embrace its symbols and its activities. They respond positively to the symbolic rewards associated with affiliation and membership in the life of the school and are not particularly concerned with the utilitarian value of these rewards outside the context of the school and its culture.

Calculatively involved individuals are involved in a way that reflects an emphasis on social exchange values. They are likely to participate in school activities because their participation promises to produce some extrinsic benefit they value. For example, student athletes often comply with the expectations of their teachers for no reason other than that they want to remain eligible for varsity athletics. Good students frequently do tasks they find meaningless for no reason other than the desire to please their parents or gain entry into college. Teachers frequently attend seminars for no other reason than to accumulate certificate renewal credits.

Alienation can produce at least two types of responses, one passive and the other active. The passive response is generally congenial, accompanied by an "if-you-don't- bother-me-I-won't-bother-you" attitude. A more active response might be overt refusal to comply with expectations, open rebellion, or the substitution of a course of activity more to the liking of the alienated individual. For example, in some middle schools, there are many alienated students who go through the day unnoticed because the take a passive posture—they just "hang out and chill." Others become aggressive and are treated as discipline problems.

---

[10]See Phillip C. Schlechty, *Teaching and Social Behavior: Toward an Organizational Theory of Instruction* (Needham Heights, Mass.: Allyn and Bacon, 1976).

Bureaucracies depend on calculative involvement to ensure compliance, and in the face of extreme alienation, they are likely to apply some form of coercion. Learning organizations seek moral involvement, and leaders spend much time and attention on the management of symbols and the design of engaging activities that tend to bind participants to the moral order of the school. That is why induction of students as well as of faculty is so important in schools that are being transformed into learning organizations. It is through such induction that moral norms are internalized and the value of the symbolic rewards available in culture is enhanced.

WHAT IS THE SCHOOL'S FUNCTION?

Like other formal organizations, schools are purposefully established to serve valued functions or attain certain ends. Sometimes these functions are announced and officially proclaimed, and sometimes they are only tacitly understood, if recognized at all. Among the most frequently articulated of these are the following:

- Providing students with experiences that promote intellectual and moral development and support the transmission of culture

- Ensuring that nearly all students meet the performance standards set for them by those who make and enforce policy related to schools and schooling

- Supporting and assisting in the distribution of talent (meaning such things as labeling, grading, and recommending students) as that talent is represented in the graduates of the school

- Satisfying custodial needs by providing students a place to be and a time to be there under safe conditions

- Ensuring discipline and order

Discussions regarding issues related to cultural transmission, performance standards, and the distribution of talent occupy much of the attention of those concerned with school reform today. Such discussions are often cast in terms of what students should know and be able to do. Sometimes they are framed around economic needs, such as the need for the schools to produce a "world-class workforce." Sometimes they fasten on real or perceived problems such as grade inflation, or the fact that too few students are enrolling in math and science courses. Such discussions are increasingly shaped by the notion that schools need to ensure that all children are prepared to meet college entrance requirements. The failure of schools to meet this standard is viewed by some with great alarm.

As increasing numbers of children come from families where both parents work outside the home, the custodial function of schools is becoming ever more apparent. In fact, it is not uncommon for schools to develop before-school and after-school programs as well as summer school programs that are ostensibly to serve academic ends, but are in fact intended primarily to meet the child care needs of parents working outside the home. Indeed, *latchkey child* and *extended care* are now common terms that educators have created to help categorize children in need of this custodial care.

For parents and others concerned about the day-to-day operation of schools, discipline and order are clearly understood to be matters of great importance. Indeed, the absence of discipline and order in schools is viewed as a critical matter, both within schools and among the public generally. Nothing so harms public confidence in the schools as does the perception that schools, especially inner-city high schools, are places of violence and disorder.

Keys to Direction

In schools, as in other purposeful organizations, goals are important. They serve to orient action, provide standards for assessing progress, and help to coordinate effort. Goals do differ, however, and the way they differ sometimes has more to do with the functions they serve than with the actions they inspire. Some goals are conditioned by moral and aesthetic choices and are stated in ways that clearly express the values that are intended to guide all that is done in the school. R. T. Pascale and A. G. Athos, well-regarded management consultants, refer to these direction-setting goals as *superordinate goals,* by which they mean the goal or goal set that provides "the significant meanings or guiding concepts that . . . [the school] imbues in its members."[11]

Other goals are more utilitarian and are conditioned more by assessments of opportunities and problems. These goals serve to define the short-term and long-term action agendas of the organization. Such goals commonly carry such labels as *strategic goals, operational goals,* and *action goals.*

[11]R. T. Pascale and A. G. Athos, *The Art of Japanese Management: Applications for American Executives* (New York: Warner Books, 1982), p. 125.

Superordinate Goals   The way leaders prioritize the critical functions to be served by the schools they lead goes far toward determining what they will view as the superordinate goal of the school, which will determine how the core business of the organization comes to be defined. Because learning organizations are inherently value expressive, leaders who are striving to transform their schools into learning organizations are likely to be especially attentive to superordinate goals. It is, after all, these goals that give order and coherence to all the other elements of the system of direction.

Leaders in bureaucratic schools tend to be uninterested in issues of direction. Consequently, they often become impatient with discussions of superordinate goals, considering such discussions too philosophical and not sufficiently practical and preferring to concern themselves with matters that have more to do with power and authority, boundaries, and evaluation.

Indeed, because bureaucratically organized schools are rarely intentional in determining superordinate goals, such goals often go unrecognized, even by leaders. These goals are, however, just as powerful as if they were consciously chosen. The old saw that says, "If you don't know where you are going, you will probably wind up where you are headed—and you probably won't like it when you get there," is illustrative of this commonplace problem in bureaucracies.

Defining the Core Business   The core business of an organization has to do with the essential activities it engages in as superordinate goals are being pursued. The answer to the question, "What is your core business?" sets out the most important things you are trying to accomplish or produce and what you do to accomplish those things.

Whether schools are organized on the principles of learning organizations or on the principles of bureaucracies depends in large measure on the way leaders define the means by which they intend to go about defining and prioritizing the functions the school or schools are intended to serve. These definitions in turn identify the core business of the organization and provide answers to such questions as, "What are the most important things we do around here?" The answers define whether the school is likely to function as a learning organization or a bureaucracy; they also define the way the principles underlying each of these organizational types will be applied. Table 3.2 illustrates the way functions, superordinate goals, and the core business of schools are related.

Table 3.2
Relationship Among School's Perceived Function, Superordinate Goal, and Core Business

Function	Superordinate Goal	Core Business
Promoting intellectual, aesthetic, and moral development and the transmission of culture.	Provide students with engaging tasks that result in their learning those things of most value to themselves, their parents, and the larger society.	Designing engaging work for students that calls on them to complete intellectually demanding tasks and leading students in the successful completion of these tasks so that students learn those things it is intended that they learn.
Ensuring conformance with performance expectations.	Ensure that the needs of individual students, as determined by externally defined standards, are the primary determinants of actions taken.	Diagnosis, prescription, intervention, and treatment.
Distributing talent and developing a productive workforce.	Support and assist in the distribution of talent as that talent is represented in the graduates of the school and provide operating processes that ensure uniformity and the enforcement of product standards set by external customers.	Shaping, molding, testing, placement, and reporting.
Providing custodial care.	Provide students a place to be and a time to be there and ensure safety for those who are being "stored away."	Labeling, categorizing, containing, and entertaining.
Ensuring discipline and control.	Ensure tight supervision and the maintenance of decorum and order.	Containment, monitoring, corrective action, and punishment.

In a school organized as a learning organization, leaders assume that the core business of the school is designing engaging work for students—work that calls on students to complete intellectually demanding tasks—and leading students in the successful completion of those tasks. In a school organized as a bureaucracy, where compliance rather than engagement is the major concern, the core business is more likely to be seen quite differently.

Clearly, the decision regarding the priority order of the various functions of the school will determine the superordinate goal of the school, and this in turn will determine the way resources are allocated and energy is invested. It will also shape the way decisions are made and the meaning that is given to those decisions. For example, in schools where discipline and control are the superordinate goals, efforts to increase student or staff commitment and engagement will be evaluated in terms of their potential impact on existing patterns of discipline and control.

Of course schools that emphasize engagement nonetheless need to attend to discipline and control. After all, the idea of order and discipline is inherent in the life of all organizations, regardless of their type or mission. Without order and some degree of predictability in relationships, there is no organization. In a school where student engagement is given high priority, however, actions taken to ensure discipline will always be evaluated in terms of their impact on student and staff engagement and commitment.

Goal Conflict and Goal Displacement

Goal conflict occurs when the pursuit of one goal requires the commitment of resources (time, people, space, information, technology) already considered essential to the pursuit of another goal that has, or is perceived to have, equivalent legitimacy in the school. For example, some states have set goals for smaller class size, resulting in requirements that a class be reconstituted (broken into two classes) when it reaches a threshold number. But it is also generally accepted that students, because of the attachments they develop to their teacher and classmates in the first few weeks of school, need the assurance of a stable environment and that this assurance is an important determinant of later success. Thus, many schools have also implicitly or explicitly adopted a goal of ensuring stability in classroom assignments.

Students do not, however, enroll in school in convenient batches of fifteen, twenty, twenty-five, or even thirty students. Moreover, they do not always enroll when school starts and initial class rolls are developed. A class that is under threshold at the beginning of the school year may go over threshold three to six weeks into the school year. In such a case, the principal and teachers are confronted with a conflict embedded in the goal system. On the one hand, there are bureaucratic compliance goals, and on the other hand, there are goals having to do with the welfare of students. If the class is reconstituted, the need of children for stability will be dishonored, but if the class is not reconstituted, state laws will be violated. This is goal conflict.

Goal displacement occurs when a goal that has official sanction within the directional system is replaced by goals and actions that have greater real or perceived support from those who have official authority in the system. It also occurs when those who are assigned responsibility for a goal become inattentive to the goal and the actions needed to support it.

Because leaders are sometimes unclear about direction and priorities, they may overlook or look past some goals and give preference to other goals. It also happens occasionally that goals that have been officially endorsed as legitimate within the organization are replaced by unofficial goals that may not be sanctioned by the official directional system but have great support within the power and authority system. It is commonplace, for example, for superintendents to complain that the demands of individual school board members on the time of the superintendent and his or her immediate staff become so burdensome that there is little time left to do those things it was assumed the superintendent was hired to do. This is goal displacement.

An equally important illustration of goal displacement is the tendency of the maintenance needs of school organizations to overwhelm developmental needs, leading to the tendency of school district officials to co-opt resources officially assigned to support developmental activity and the installation of innovations for the purposes of supporting and sustaining ongoing operating systems. For example, it is not uncommon for grant money intended to be used to provide staff support to train teachers in new teaching techniques and administrative processes to be diverted over time to providing staff support for existing programs. I first observed and reported on practices such as these when conducting a large-scale study of the management of staff development programs in a large urban school district.[12] Others have made similar observations. Indeed, this type

---

[12]See, for example, Phillip Schlechty and Betty Lou Whitford, "The Organizational Context of School Systems and the Functions of Staff Development," in G. Griffin (ed.), *Staff Development: Eighty-Second Yearbook of the National Society for the Study of Education,* Part II (Chicago: University of Chicago Press, 1983).

of practice is so common that some philanthropic foundations now directly provide technical assistance to schools with which they become involved rather than give the schools flexible dollars to employ consultants or supplemental staff.

In schools where the superordinate goal has to do with ensuring standards are met, it is likely that teachers will see most of their work as having to do with testing, diagnosis, and remediation. In schools where the priority goal is distribution of talent, testing will also be present, but the purpose of the testing will be more for student placement than for diagnosis and treatment. In schools where discipline and order are the superordinate goals, attention is likely to be given to behavior modification strategies and the systematic application of sanctions to signs of misbehavior.

When leaders are unclear regarding which functions should be given priority, confusion regarding superordinate goals, and the core business as well, will be likely. One of the most frequently heard laments from classroom teachers today is that the shift of the attention of schools from learning to testing has caused educators to be less concerned with whether students have learned what it is intended they learn and more concerned that all students can meet minimal performance standards on state-mandated tests.

It is not, in fact, uncommon for school leaders who are under pressure to ensure that a predetermined percentage of students meet standards on a state-wide test to engage in practices that are at best dubious if the goal is to ensure optimal educational experiences for all children. The goal of substantive learning becomes displaced by the goal of performance on tests.

Some schools have taken up a practice that critics refer to as "educational triage," categorizing students into three categories: those who will undoubtedly meet the standard, those who will undoubtedly not meet the standard even with strenuous intervention, and those who are "on the bubble" and may get over the threshold with considerable coaching and individual support.[13] The preferred strategy becomes concentration of efforts on the third group, because that is where the payoff is for the teacher and for the school.

Such practices illustrate why many educators are concerned about the direction of school reform in America today. The rhetoric leads to the belief that the intent is to improve the capacity of schools to develop the intellectual, moral,

[13]Jennifer Booher-Jennings, "Below the Bubble: Educational Triage and the Texas Accountability System," *American Educational Research Journal*, 2005, *42*, 231–268.

and cultural abilities of the young. But the activities that are sometimes encouraged make it clear that the core business assumed by some reformers is far removed from what it would need to be if the superordinate goal were creating engaging work for students.

IMAGES OF SCHOOL

The next two chapters continue this discussion of the differences between the bureaucratic and learning organization types by examining metaphors that are often used to describe schools. The intent of this discussion is to illustrate the need for transformation. As will become clear as the remainder of this book unfolds, I am persuaded that metaphors and their systematic use are one of the most powerful tools available to leaders seeking to transform schools.

It is not my intent to provide a definitive description of school types. Rather, I suggest metaphors that can be used to reveal some of the more salient features of different types of schools. Certainly the metaphors I use are not the only possibilities. However, taken as a set, they illuminate many of the important features of school life and help to make even clearer why bureaucracy is not now and never has been an appropriate form for schooling and why the idea of the school as a learning organization points the way to a brighter future for democratic education.

Bureaucratic Images of Schools

I f schools are to be transformed, those leading the transformation must have a clear image of what is going on in the schools they are trying to change. This chapter shows the power of metaphorical reasoning in developing such a picture. I use five metaphors in this effort: the school as a *factory,* the school as a *service delivery organization,* the school as a *warehouse,* the school as a *prison,* and the school as a *learning organization.* In each case I discuss the system of rules, roles, and relationships these metaphors suggest. I pay special attention to the roles of students, parents, teachers, principals, central office staff, superintendents, and school board members.

There are, of course, many other roles and role groups that could have been included in this analysis—for example, clerical staff, custodians, teachers' unions, parent advocacy groups, and so on. The intent of this discussion, however, is to demonstrate how various mental models based on different kinds of organizational assumptions affect life in schools, and that is best done by hewing closely to the main point.

Discussion here is limited to metaphors that can illuminate mental models based on assumptions consistent with the bureaucratic ideal type described in Chapter Three. And in Chapter Five, I discuss images associated with the school organized as a learning organization.

ABOUT THE METAPHORS

Peter Senge wrote that mental models consist of "deeply ingrained assumptions, generalizations, or even pictures and images that influence how we understand the world and how we take action."[1] Mental models are not the same as metaphors, but the two concepts are closely associated. The mental models people use to frame their social reality are sometimes revealed by the metaphors they use to discuss those parts of the world with which they are concerned. Moreover, the metaphors used to express mental models sometimes take on a life of their own and become the de facto mental models that are used to frame action.[2]

I chose the metaphors used here in part because the words that educators, students, parents, and others who comment on schools use suggest that these images have some meaning in the real world of schooling. For example, educators frequently speak of diagnosis and prescription and sometimes quite literally refer to students as clients, thereby suggesting that someplace in their minds lurks a mental model reminiscent of a service delivery organization such as a hospital. Similarly, the language of the factory—for example, the idea of the student as product—is so deeply embedded in the language of schooling that the use of this metaphor needs no further justification.

The idea of the school as a warehouse is not so obvious in the language of educators. The tendency of some schools to simply store some students away is so frequently commented on by critics of schools that it is clear that warehousing is not an unfamiliar aspect of life in some schools. Warehousing, when it exists, is a condition that needs to be identified and confronted. The warehouse metaphor can help to reveal the extent to which warehousing is going on in a school.

The idea of the school as a prison and teachers as guards is not a happy notion. Nevertheless, there are troubled schools in which teachers complain that they are compelled to perform more as prison guards than as educators and where principals complain that they feel like wardens. Students—sometimes in jest, sometimes in earnest—may refer to the school as a prison or jail. The idea of the school as a prison helps to illuminate the sometimes coercive nature of relationships between students and schools. It also may shed light on other

---

[1]See Peter Senge, *The Fifth Discipline: The Art and Practice of the Learning Organization* (New York: Doubleday, 1990), p. 8.
[2]See George Lakoff and Mark Johnson, *Metaphors We Live By,* 2nd ed. (Chicago: University of Chicago Press, 2003).

aspects of relationships in schools that might not at first be obvious. For example, the tendency to treat parents as outsiders is sometimes encouraged in part by the view that parents, like visitors in a prison, are not to be trusted.

A BASIC FRAMEWORK

Table 4.1 presents a framework for the discussion in this chapter. It lists the five organizing metaphors used in this discussion; a summary of the five possible ways the core business of a school or school district might be defined; and descriptive labels for each of seven roles of concern in this discussion: students, parents, teachers, principal, central office staff, superintendent, and school board. Clearly, in real life, there is much more differentiation among roles than I have used here. Central office roles vary greatly, and important differences exist between teacher roles at various grade levels, for example.

These are important distinctions, but for the discussion at hand, I use these metaphors to demonstrate how the assumptions made about the way schools should be organized affects what goes on in schools and in classrooms.

It should also be clear from a careful examination of Table 4.1 that I assume a strong correspondence among the views leaders have about superordinate goals, the core business of the schooling enterprise, and the way schools come to be organized. For example, schools that are organized on the assumption that the top priority is discipline and control are more likely to reflect the style of a prison than that of a learning organization or even a factory. In such schools, students are likely to define their own roles as that of inmates, and, like inmates, many of them are alienated from the norms and values of the organization in which they are "imprisoned." Consequently, the control strategies that are most likely to be employed lean toward coercion, as there is little of a positive nature that the system has to provide to students who are alienated from its values.

Where the core business is defined as diagnosis, prescription, intervention, and treatment, it is likely that the students will be defined as clients. It is especially likely when teachers choose to define themselves as service delivery professionals, for example, as diagnosticians and clinicians along the lines of medicine. In this case, it is also likely that teachers will expect the principal to function in ways that protect them from the demands of the larger bureaucracy in which the school is embedded.

Table 4.2 illustrates the relationships among guiding metaphors, superordinate goals, and the core business. In combination with Table 4.1, it provides a

Table 4.1
Five Metaphors for Schools and Their Related Core Businesses and Associated Roles

Guiding Metaphor	Core Business	Students' Role	Parents' Role	Teachers' Role	Principal's Role	Central Office Staff's Role	Superintendent's Role	School Board's Role
Factory	Testing, remediation, and reporting	Raw material and product	Supply source and determinant of product quality	Skilled worker	Shop foreman	Inspectors and supervisors	Plant manager	Owners and advocates
Professional service delivery organization	Diagnosis, prescription, and treatment	Client	Guarantor and questionable ally	Professional performers and presenters or clinicians and diagnosticians	Chief of staff	Technicians and support staff	Chief executive officer	Board of directors
Warehouse	Labeling, categorizing, placement, and recording	Excess inventory	Primary shipper and receiver	Clerk and keeper of records	Midlevel: Bureaucrat and keeper of the keys	Directors of maintenance, shipping, and personnel	Property manager	Safety inspectors and fire marshals
Prison	Containment, monitoring, corrective action, and punishment	Inmate	Distrusted visitor	Guard	Warden	Department directors, hearing officers, and parole officers	Bureau chief	Officers and parole board
Learning organization	Designing engaging academic work for students and leading them to success in that work	Volunteer and knowledge worker	Partner and member of the school community	Leader, designer, and guide to instruction	Leader of leaders	Capacity builders	Moral and intellectual leader	Community builders and advocates for schools

Table 4.2
Relationship Among School's Guiding Metaphor, Superordinate Goal, and Core Business

Guiding Metaphor	Superordinate Goal	Core Business
The school as factory	Support and assist in the distribution of talent as that talent is represented in the graduates of the school and provide operating processes that ensure uniformity and the enforcement of product standards set by external customers.	Shaping, molding, testing, placement, and reporting
The school as professional service delivery organization	Ensure that the needs of individual students, as determined by externally defined standards, are the primary determinant of actions taken.	Diagnosis, prescription, intervention, and treatment
The school as warehouse	Provide students a place to be and a time to be there, and ensure safety for those who are being "stored away."	Labeling, categorizing, containing, and entertaining
The school as prison	Ensure tight supervision and the maintenance of decorum and order.	Containment, monitoring, corrective action, and punishment
The school as learning organization	Provide students with engaging tasks that result in their learning those things of most value to themselves, their parents, and the larger society.	Designing engaging work for students that calls on them to complete intellectually demanding tasks and leading students in the successful completion of these tasks so that they learn those things it is intended that they learn

clearer understanding of some of the sources of confusion, conflict, and ambiguity that often exist in schools. For example, the emphasis that No Child Left Behind places on ensuring that students meet standards that will satisfy external customers (such as universities and potential employers) almost forces teachers to view students as products. This image of students requires teachers to view themselves as skilled workers subordinated to a principal who is required to operate very much like a shop foreman, even though their teacher education programs may have encouraged them to view themselves as service delivery professionals and principals to view themselves as instructional leaders.

Understandably, many teachers and principals chafe against this image of themselves. Such tensions are structural in nature and have their origin in public policy, though they may be experienced as private troubles. Moreover, these tensions will eventually be resolved in some fashion: the policy will be changed, or the noncompliant employees will be brought into line, voluntarily leave, engage in sabotage, or be dismissed.

THE SCHOOL AS FACTORY

As Raymond Callahan demonstrated many years ago, ideas that guided the development of the American system of manufacturing, especially the ideas of Frederick W. Taylor and others who were committed to "scientific management," have had a deep and lasting impact on the organization of America's system of schooling.[3] Indeed, with the possible exception of the metaphors of the family and the small community (which I touch on in the next chapter), the metaphor of the school as factory has probably had more impact on the thinking that has guided the design of schools than any other sets of ideas. The reason this is so has to do with both historical accidents and the special interests of educators. These developments are discussed in detail in Chapter Six, but it seems well to foreshadow some of this later discussion here.

Until the twentieth century, public schooling in America for the most part constituted only what is now called elementary school. Moreover, schools were viewed as community institutions and extensions of the family, so it is not surprising that the formative image of the elementary school was that of the family and community center.

[3]Raymond Callahan, *Education and the Cult of Efficiency* (Chicago: University of Chicago Press, 1962).

The creation of the American high school in the context of urbanization and industrialization encouraged educators to seek new models for their schools, and the most obvious models were those that were demonstrating so much success in the business sector, especially in the automobile industry. In fact, the factory metaphor emerged as a guiding notion primarily because the social organization of the modern American high school occurred at the same time that the assembly line system of manufacturing and ideas about scientific management were becoming dominant in the world of business.

In addition, the self-interest and status concerns of school administrators intent on establishing a professional identity were well served by making school administration a part of the management class and embracing scientific management as a set of guiding principles. Positioning school administration in this way was thought by some to imbue educational management with the aura of science and scientific rationalism. At the same time, this view was thought to be a way to boost the status of administrators, especially urban superintendents, in the political and social worlds in which some found it necessary or desirable to move.[4]

The principles of scientific management are also compatible with the principles of behaviorist psychology, a branch of psychology that has long had a strong influence on members of the testing community. Furthermore, the assumptions of bureaucracy generally, and the factory in particular, are quite compatible with the assumptions that underlie behaviorism. Such views are therefore most compatible with the views of those who champion science and research as the primary means of directing educational programs and actions.[5]

Finally, with its emphasis on selecting, sorting, inspecting, and processing—and with the assumption that the quality of outputs is determined by the characteristics of inputs and the ability to standardize processes—the factory metaphor is clearly congruent with the idea that the superordinate goal of schools is, or should be, facilitating the distribution of talent to various end users. This goal promotes the notion that students are products and that the customers of the schools are the business community and higher education. This idea is so deeply

[4]I am not alone in this view. Similar observations have been made by many others. See, for example, Callahan, *Education and the Cult of Efficiency,* or David Tyack and Larry Cuban, *Tinkering Toward Utopia: A Century of Public School Reform* (Cambridge, Mass.: Harvard University Press, 1995).
[5]See Lauren Resnik and Megan Williams Hall, "Learning Organizations for Sustainable Education Reform," *Daedalus,* 1998, *127*(4), 89–118.

embedded in our culture that many advocates of school reform continue to affirm this image at the same time that their rhetoric condemns the impersonal nature of schools and the resultant lack of creativity in students.

Student as Raw Material and Product

Most educators would disclaim any allegiance to the idea that students are, or should be, treated as products and raw material. Yet the everyday language and conversations of teachers, principals, and many other educators betray their disclaimers. It is not uncommon, for example, to hear teachers explain academic excellence among some students as being due to the fact that some students are "just better academic material" than are others.

There is no doubt that academic ability, like other abilities, is not equally distributed among students. The factory model, with its emphasis on the production of a single uniform product, amplifies this fact. Indeed, one of the problems that has plagued educators for many years is the fact that as schools are now organized, many students, perhaps most of them, seem ill equipped, unable, or unwilling to pursue an academic curriculum that requires employing higher-order thinking skills and pursuing topics that require rigorous thought and analysis.

As America's secondary schools were being formed, many educators dealt with this problem through tracking and offering a differentiated curriculum— ideas that are certainly congruent with an image of school as factory and student as product. Today, for both ethical reasons and practical ones, such a model is subject to considerable challenge. Moreover, even within groups of students who are placed in tracks, there remains a great deal of variability in talent and motivation. Learning to live and benefit from this variability rather than insisting on uniformity as a condition of life is part of the genius of democratic life.

Separating the most talented students from the masses does nothing to solve the problem of democratic education so long as the masses are submitted to batch-processed schooling while their more fortunate peers in the academically gifted group receive an education customized for them. In a democracy, a customized educational experience should be the birthright of every child.

The problem is that conventional approaches to teaching and learning—those approaches most subject to standardization and control—depend on standardized inputs in order to produce standardized outputs. Universities have long acknowledged this fact through the use of selective admission standards. A rational system works only if policymakers are willing to limit inputs to those who fit the mold the factory requires. Systems based on the principles of rational bureaucracy do not work when diversity of inputs and talent are valued and creativity is an intended result.

In the face of these problems, some educators argue that academic studies are for the most part irrelevant to most students and that the academic curriculum therefore should be abandoned in favor of a curriculum more in tune with students' interests and the needs of the workplace. This is the rationale that gave rise to vocational education. Some reformers today see vocational education as a new avenue to academic studies, potentially more inviting to many students. Others see vocational education simply as a more efficient means of providing industry with a better supply of trained crafts workers, assuming that academic studies are best reserved for the intellectual elite.

In schools organized on principles reminiscent of the factory, the problem of variability in "product quality" is often handled through labeling, for example, "honors students" as contrasted with "C students." Sometimes different types of diplomas are viewed as a means of ensuring "truth in labeling." And sometimes the problem is not attended to at all, resulting in wide variability of output or, perhaps equally disturbing, a homogenization of output in which regression toward the mean is accepted as the dominant reality in a system of mass education.

The school organized as factory does take customer needs into account, but the student is not the customer of concern. The customers of concern are the groups and organizations that are, to use an unlovely phrase, *end users*: business and industry, colleges and universities, and so on. The performance standards that are of concern are those that will satisfy the needs of such external groups and agencies.

It is critical to recognize that in the school organized as a factory, standards are not standards *for* students. Rather, they are standards that others apply *to* students in making judgments about the students' merit and worth. (I have more to say about the difference between standards for students and standards that are applied to students in Chapters Seven and Eleven.) Satisfying the needs and values of students, if considered at all, is important only as an instrumental matter. In the factory, teachers are expected to work *on* students—to mold them and shape them if they are malleable, and to sort them and label them if they are not—so that the end users will have a basis of determining their value.

Schools as factories tend to depersonalize teaching and compartmentalize learning. Students are expected to learn on a predetermined time schedule and in a predetermined way. Those who cannot or do not learn in this way acquire an inferior label, or they are sent to the scrap heap or pulled out for recycling and repair. Schools are therefore, designed to push information and prepackaged knowledge at students rather than help students pull knowledge from the many sources available to them and then help them to construct conceptual packages (ideas and frameworks) that suit their own needs and interests.

Like variations in raw material, variations among students are often treated as a nuisance to be transformed into a categorical response. If, for example, a student does not meet grade-level standards, the student is often retained, or "recycled." When large clusters of students fail to meet standards, they are likely to be subject to batch-process remediation at the end of the ordinary "manufacturing cycle." For example, it has become increasingly common to assign underperforming students to special after-school and summer school programs, where it is assumed that they can be and will be given some type of remedial treatment.

Parents as Supply Source and Determinant of Product Quality

As Diane Ravitch and many others have shown, the assumption that the social class origins of students should affect what students should be expected to learn has long guided the design of America's schools.[6] Not only is such thinking ethically problematic in the context of a democracy, it is potentially at odds with the condition of the modern economy. Unlike the time when only a few people were required to be well educated, today both civic and economic life require that all citizens have a profound grasp of the academic disciplines as well as the intellectual processes implicit in these disciplines. Moreover, if American workers are to compete in the world economy, it will be necessary that they be creative as well as disciplined and skilled.

Schools organized as factories encourage the assumption that "an apple does not fall very far from the tree." Who the parent is, what the parent does for a living, and the type of social and cultural milieu provided by the family are assumed to be primary determinants of the performances one can expect from children. However, it is not politically correct to explain poor performance by reference to race, ethnicity, or social class. Such distinctions are made nonetheless, but the euphemisms used sometimes conceal the intent. Educators speak and write of *at-risk children, the academically challenged, special youngsters,* and

[6]For an excellent discussion of these matters, see Diane Ravitch, *Left Back: A Century of Failed School Reforms* (New York: Simon & Schuster, 2000).

children with learning disabilities, where once they spoke of lower-class children, discipline problems, the nonacademic, the problem child, the slow and retarded, and so on.

Certainly in a school organized as a professional service delivery organization, clinical categories like those commonly used by special educators may serve as useful ways of categorizing client needs. It is, for example, clearly the case that dyslexic students, autistic students, and blind and hearing-impaired students need to be identified and treated in ways that are responsive to their special circumstances. Labels that help to ensure that special treatment is available and provided are certainly justified as a means of personalizing instruction. In the factory setting, however, student labels often tend to serve to manage performance expectations and to communicate to others the performance capabilities of the "product" more than to increase the ability of the school to respond to the needs of its students.

The faculties in many factory-like schools often assume that middle-class and upper-middle-class youngsters are more inclined to find academic work engaging than are children of the poor. Therefore, children from poor families are perceived to require a less-challenging curriculum than are children from more affluent families. It is also common to assume that the aspirations of middle-class parents for their children's occupational future require a different form of curriculum than is required for children from blue-collar families—a vocational curriculum for the working classes and an academic curriculum for the children of managers. In large urban school districts, these tendencies are often built into the arrangements of buildings themselves, with schools that serve the poor being organized more along the lines of factories, warehouses, and prisons, and schools that serve the affluent being organized more like professional service delivery organizations.

The result is that children from less affluent families are more likely than their more affluent peers to be confronted with highly scripted programs and with teachers and schools that provide much less freedom of action. Indeed, some of the negative sanctions that government agencies tend to impose on low-performing schools include provisions that ensure that the faculties of these schools are submitted to more restrictions and denied fewer opportunities to introduce variability into their classroom procedures. It is also likely that supervision will be tighter and students are afforded less opportunity to participate in the arts, music, or even the pleasure and freedom that recess might provide.

One of the consequences of this policy may be that schools that serve predominantly middle-class children but fail to develop strategies that improve the performance of a small minority of children will be compelled to abandon the service delivery model they are employing and embrace a model of education that is increasingly factory-like in implementation. Although I am not convinced that the service delivery model is the best option available, within the context of models consistent with bureaucratic assumptions, it has much to recommend it as contrasted with the factory. It is a more humane and decent view of the world of schooling than is suggested by the model of the school as an efficient factory spewing forth children who fit predetermined molds serving narrowly defined and short-term economic interests. Nevertheless, current policy seems bent on making schools more like factories and less like the client-centered organizations envisioned by many of those committed to the professionalization of teaching.

Finding ways to provide all students, regardless of social class or ethnicity, meaningful access to a sound grounding in academic studies is a challenge to which school leaders have yet to find a way to respond. I believe that they are unlikely to find a way to deal with this matter until they embrace the idea that continuous innovation and student engagement must be central in schools.

Schools organized as factories, or any other bureaucratic form, lack the capacity to respond to the variability a multicultural society requires if the intent is to provide an elite education for nearly every child. More than that, bureaucracies tend to stifle creativity rather than nurture it, and it is creativity, a playful mind, and the ability to think and reason in disciplined ways that are the attributes most needed in the modern world.

Teachers as Skilled Workers

The idea that teachers should be treated like workers in factories is certainly not new. Neither is the idea of "teacher-proof curriculum materials." In the first quarter of the twentieth century, when the basic structure of our bureaucratic school system was being formed, school administrators were quite open about their views on teaching and teachers and about their assumptions regarding the need to treat teachers like workers on an assembly line.[7]

---

[7]See, for example, Linda Darling-Hammond, *The Right to Learn: A Blueprint for Creating Schools That Work* (San Francisco: Jossey-Bass, 1997).

Few reformers today are willing to openly advocate such a view, but a review of some of the more scripted programs that are now popular in schools, especially those that have to do with reading and arithmetic, reveals that the idea of teacher-proof materials is not dead. Nor is the idea that teachers should be treated as workers, though it is not clear whether this view includes the idea of skilled workers. Although the No Child Left Behind legislation calls for "highly qualified teachers," the programs that are touted as exemplifying best practice often assume that the main qualifications of a highly qualified teacher are docility, compliance, and willingness to submit to authority, even when the teacher believes that what authorities want done may be harmful to children.[8]

It is indeed something of a paradox that at the same time that policymakers are mandating activities that relegate teachers to a role that makes them little more than low-level bureaucratic employees with little real authority with regard to the conditions of their work, these same policymakers are arguing that the key to improved schooling is the presence of highly qualified teachers in every classroom. Seldom do these policymakers stop to ask, "Why would highly qualified teachers want to teach in an environment in which their qualifications provide so little respect and their creativity is so little valued?" The fact is that schools that are most likely to reflect a factory-like image or, worse, the image of a warehouse or a prison, are also the ones that are having the most difficulty recruiting and retaining highly qualified teachers—that is, schools that serve mostly poor children.

Early in my career, I conducted a number of studies, in collaboration with Victor Vance who was one of my graduate assistants, dealing with the characteristics of those who entered the teaching profession and those who were most likely to leave it.[9] What we found is that teaching has some difficulty in attracting students from the top half of their graduating class, and once these people are attracted, they are among the most likely to leave teaching within five years.

I have kept up with related research since then, and I see no evidence that things have changed much. The only difference I see now is the possibility that more people enter teaching after trying their hand at other things than was the case when these initial studies were conducted and that it is even more difficult to attracted highly qualified minority teachers than was the case thirty years ago.

[8]See, for example, Sharon L. Nichols and David C. Berliner, *Collateral Damage: How High Stakes Testing Corrupts America's Schools* (Boston: Harvard Education Press, 2007).
[9]Phillip C. Schlechty and Victor Vance, "Recruitment, Selection and Retention: The Shape of the Teaching Force," *Elementary School Journal*, 1983, *83*, 469–487.

If policymakers were really serious about attracting highly qualified teachers, their first question would be, "How do we organize schools to take advantage of the talent we have so that we can ensure that there will be even more talent available in the future?" As the experiences of some large urban schools are showing, payment of bounties and even coercion may not be enough to encourage teachers to teach in schools where they are treated as low-level employees in a factory-like setting. The following excerpt from a recent article in the *Charlotte Observer* (North Carolina) illustrates this problem:

> Gorman [the superintendent of the Charlotte-Mecklenburg Schools] said Wednesday that some efforts to boost teacher quality at high-poverty schools have fallen short or even backfired. For instance, many veteran teachers left four low-scoring high schools last year, when Gorman said he'd fire any faculty who couldn't boost scores. But the offer of $15,000 signing bonuses and a 15-percent pay bump didn't lure enough experienced teachers to replace them, he said.
>
> "It is very clear to me that trying to pull people in with incentives will not completely close the gap," he said. "We will have to push some people to move to certain sites against their will."
>
> Such a move risks a backlash from parents and teachers.
>
> "They're pushing—they're also pushing teachers out of the school district," said Judy Kidd, head of the Charlotte-based Classroom Teachers Association. "There are people taking pay cuts every day to get out of Charlotte-Mecklenburg Schools."[10]

Principal as Shop Foreman

Until recently, much of the research that was used to inform thought about the role of building principals was derived from studies of first-line supervisors in industrial settings. Notions like span of control (the number of persons who may be supervised and evaluated by an individual supervisor) and the need for tight supervision of observed teacher performances are clearly notions that have their origins in the research conducted on the shop floor. Many of the classroom behavior checklists that principals use to evaluate teachers are reminiscent of the checklists used in time-and-motion studies in the factory. This is especially true

[10]Ann Doss Helms, "CMS May Go Beyond Moving Teachers," *Charlotte Observer,* Jan. 25, 2008.

of checklists that have grown out of applications of the time-on-task research and studies of teachers' behavior.

As first-line supervisors, principals are usually viewed as occupying the lowest rung on the management chart. Assistant principals and others who hold lesser administrative or quasi-administrative positions in schools are treated as job setters, tool-and-die makers, and timekeepers are treated in the factory—necessary functionaries, but not a part of the line system through which authority is exercised and decisions flow.

Operating as a supervisor requires that both the principal and the teachers assume that the principal is relatively expert in the job the teacher is doing, else the ability of the principal to evaluate the performance of teachers, a common requirement, is compromised. (In some bureaucratically organized school systems, central office subject matter specialists are also used in evaluating teachers, thereby offsetting with specialization what cannot be accomplished with delegation.) More frequently, schools deal with the principal's supervision dilemma by avoiding altogether the issue of content. Principals are expected to evaluate teachers strictly on the basis of the instructional processes employed—with the consequence that a teacher could be judged to teach very well, even though the content presented to the students might be suspect and shallow.

Central Office as Supervisors and Inspectors

When school districts are organized on principles similar to those that govern factories, the authority and prestige of central office personnel are substantial. As supervisors and program managers, central office personnel usually have a great deal of discretionary control over budgets, and they can also exercise their supervisory responsibilities in such a way that they can build up a relatively sizable staff that reports to them.

These staff members, usually technicians and subject matter specialists, are also a part of the central office, and they have an interest in maintaining bureaucratic structures, for it is in these structures that their authority and security reside. This provides central office personnel with powerful incentives for resisting fundamental changes in the culture and structure of the organization, for the principles of scientific management contribute to the authority of central office managers more than any other bureaucratic form that might be devised.

It is assumed that the occupants of central office positions hold these jobs because of their expertise, usually signified by supervisory certificates. Once they are in these supervisory positions, however, the authority of the position rather than the authority of expertise provides the basis of credibility for their actions.

In schools organized as factories, the right to evaluate programs and the work of others, combined with control of discretionary resources, is critical to defining the authority of central office employees. Moreover, to the extent that special knowledge is the basis of authority, the kind of knowledge that is most valued is knowledge of the sometimes arcane rules through which state and federal programs are administered and controlled—administrative knowledge rather than knowledge of matters dealing with teaching and learning.

As a result, persons in central office positions that control large, federally mandated budgets often enjoy unusual influence with those above them as well as those below. The reason is that they control the knowledge necessary to ensure that the funds allocated can be expended in ways that are within the regulations. These regulations are often so complex that central office supervisors are required to spend days in workshops designed to teach them the arcane rules they are expected to promulgate and enforce.

In a factory system, the central office tends to be organized in separate units—silos, in contemporary parlance—each operating relatively independent of the others. Theoretically, activity in these silos is coordinated through the superintendent's office and by those who report directly to the superintendent. In practice, however, the persons who head such departments or units often operate with considerable autonomy that has been delegated or assigned to them through policy, procedures, and job descriptions. This autonomy and lack of centralization at the top is responsible for the mixed messages that principals and school faculties often receive. And it is one of the reasons that many teachers and principals speak disparagingly of the "central office bureaucracy."

Superintendent as Plant Manager

In the early days of the American manufacturing system and before the creation of the elaborate management systems that now exist in large corporations, owners played a direct role in the way the business was run and operated. Henry Ford, for example, hired plant managers, but when Mr. Ford was on the floor, there was little doubt about who was in charge. The job of the plant manager was to carry out the directives of the boss.

The relationship between superintendents and boards of education is sometimes similar to that between the plant manager and Mr. Ford in the early days of the Ford Motor Company. Given the way some boards operate, however, the superintendent is likely to feel that he or she is accountable to five (or as many as twelve) "Mr. Fords," each with an agenda to push and a program to advance.

In many school districts, each board member feels empowered to act as a boss. The authority of the superintendent, as a plant manager working for these "owners" or "owners' representatives," is almost always clouded and subject to usurpation by individual board members. Moreover, in many school districts, it is often the individual board member (rather than the board as a collective body) who controls the power.

The idea that schools and school districts should reflect a sense of community and common commitments is hard to maintain in such a circumstance. It is equally hard for the superintendent to maintain a clear direction, for there are too many directors to whom he or she must attend. All the superintendent can do in this case is manage. There is no context in which to lead.

One of the consequences of this condition is that in school systems where the board of education defines the role of superintendent as plant manager, as many large urban district boards do, there is likely to be high turnover in the superintendent's office. Quite often this turnover serves to strengthen the power and authority of those who occupy midlevel and second-order positions in the district—those found in the central office. The reason is that turnover at the middle level is rarer than at the top. Superintendents come and go, but midlevel operatives continue on, as do the systems they value.[11]

School Board as Owners and Advocates

Within the context of a factory model, it is commonplace for school board members to assume that their job is to act as owners of the schools or representatives of those who own the school. So long as a white middle-class majority was able to exclude from ownership those who brought different values and different needs to the table, the factory model worked relatively well—at least for the owners. Thus, schools were expected to prepare a few youngsters for high-level positions, a larger group for vocational and technical jobs, and the vast majority for a minimally trained, blue-collar world.

---

[11]For a discussion of how bureaucratic cultures are maintained in the face of high turnover at the top of the organization, see Michael Crozier, *The Bureaucratic Phenomenon* (Chicago: University of Chicago Press, 1964).

The civil rights movement increased consciousness of the meaning and value of cultural diversity. It is now accepted that the cultural diversity embedded in the local community must somehow be represented in the governance of the schools. It is also coming to be understood that in the face of changes in the larger society and the economy, the parochial needs of local communities must somehow incorporate the more universal needs of a society where international standards must be taken into account on every turn.

In order to respond to the demands of previously excluded groups and in an effort to ensure diversity on school boards, it has become increasingly common to elect school board members to represent subunits (for example, regions) within a school district rather than being elected at large. Unfortunately, when boards elected in this manner continue to function as owners and advocates, the operation of the board often becomes fragmented, contentious, and directionless. In these circumstances, board members are likely to vote in ways that reflect greater concern for the welfare of the special interest groups that elect them than for the general welfare of students and the larger community.

A recognition of the inefficiency and ineffectiveness of such arrangements and the parochialism these disputes engender has led to increasing pressure to do away with local school boards and turn instead to the state and federal government as sources of guidance and direction for America's schools. Recently, for example, Lou Gerstner, the former CEO of IBM and a long-time activist in the area of school reform, made a recommendation to the incoming Obama administration via the *Wall Street Journal,* in which he advocated the abolition of local school boards as a necessary step to the improvement of the schools.[12] Apparently it is assumed that since local managers are incompetent to do what is required, authority should be further centralized so that those at the top (state elites and federal bureaucrats) will be in a better position to control the action in local schools. For those who would avoid this result, the first step is to seek ways to reorient boards of education so that they cease to behave as corporate owners and begin to behave as community leaders. (See Chapter Five for a further discussion of this matter.)

[12]See Louis V. Gerstner Jr. "Lessons from 40 Years of Education 'Reform': Let's Abolish Local School Districts and Finally Adopt National Standards." *Wall Street Journal,* December 1, 2008.

THE SCHOOL AS PROFESSIONAL SERVICE DELIVERY ORGANIZATION

When educators discuss the professional status of teaching, it is not long before someone suggests a comparison between the role of teachers and the role of such professionals as physicians and lawyers. There are, however, significant differences in the perceived status of the medical profession, which seems a preferred model among some educators, and the status of the teaching occupations.

Because physicians developed professional standing—much of which has been enshrined into law and custom—prior to their involvement in bureaucratized hospital systems, they have retained considerable moral authority in the context of the hospital, even though most hospitals have become bureaucracies. Because physicians base their authority on membership in a relatively autonomous profession, they are, in fact, capable of resisting many efforts at bureaucratic intrusion into the way they conduct their practice.

Teachers, however, had no collective identity as an occupational group prior to becoming members of the formal education bureaucracy. Teaching started as a craft, a calling, and a semisacred vocation. The idea of teacher as solitary employee was well established long before teachers felt the need to develop a collective identity as a professional group. Indeed, much of the collective identity of teachers arose from adversarial relationships that emerged between teachers (as employees, or "labor") and "management" as the "profession" became bureaucratized. Indeed, the management of schools was professionalized well in advance of efforts to professionalize teaching.[13]

Furthermore, as the struggles of physicians with health maintenance organizations, insurance companies, and for-profit hospitals show, even occupational groups as powerful as physicians have difficulty maintaining professional authority when the resources they need to do their work are under the control of bureaucratic managers. Indeed, the antagonism between professionals and bureaucracies is so well understood that the study of these problems has occupied sociologists for many years.

Students as Clients

From the perspective of teachers and many students, schools organized on the principles suggested by the service delivery metaphor certainly have advantages

[13]See, for example, David Tyack and Larry Cuban, *Tinkering Toward Utopia: A Century of Public School Reform* (Cambridge, Mass.: Harvard University Press, 1995).

over schools organized on the basis of principles reflected in factories, warehouses, or prisons. The status of teachers is surely enhanced. The idea that students are clients is certainly more attuned to serving the interests of students than is the idea of students as products, inventory, or inmates.

There is, however, a downside. The client-provider relationship always requires trusting submission on the part of the client. The client voluntarily accepts the directives of the professional on the assumption that the professional knows better than the client what is required. It also assumes that the professional has the long-term interests of the client at the center of his or her attention and is bound by a professional code of ethics to enforce this view. Students can be served as clients only if they are able and willing to submit to the will of the teacher and if their parents are willing to support whatever directives the teacher prescribes.

Students who voluntarily submit to such a relationship because they find academic work inherently engaging will do quite well in schools organized as professional service delivery organizations. Indeed, these students are likely to do well in most schools, regardless of the way the school is organized. Even students who are willing to comply for more calculative reasons (like good grades as a ticket for admission to the college of their choice) may find their school experience sufficiently rewarding to produce high levels of satisfaction with the services provided.[14] Those most likely to create problems for the teacher who defines students as clients are those who are, for whatever reason, unwilling to comply with directives solely because the teacher gives them.

In fact, in the school organized on a service delivery model, students who do not do what is required, or who initially will not or cannot, are more likely to be viewed as problems than as potential recruits. Indeed, in such schools (especially high-performing schools) such students are likely to be excluded from the school or placed in programs and areas of the school that more closely resemble the model of the school as a factory or a warehouse. (Special education is generally an exception to this argument because special educators take on clients that other parts of the system cannot seem to serve well.)

---

[14]*School of Dreams,* a book that tells the story of a high-performing high school, provides numerous examples of students who are willing to work hard at academic tasks that they find to be intrinsically without meaning or value because they believe the pursuit of these tasks will result in the grades they need to enroll in the college of their choice or may help them develop the test-taking skills needed to excel on college entrance exams. See Edward Humes, *School of Dreams: Making the Grade at a Top American High School* (Orlando, Fla.: Harcourt, 2003).

Sometimes, of course, teachers acting as professionals try to modify student behavior so that the students do comply with the standards set by the bureaucracy. This is especially likely to occur in schools that serve large numbers of poor children and in special education settings. Perhaps this is one of the reasons that behavior modification techniques have so much appeal in many schools serving large numbers of poor children and special education students. Such an approach permits teachers to cling to the view that they are skilled professionals in control of a specialized body of knowledge rather than simply skilled workers in a factory setting, warehouse clerks, or prison guards.

Parents as Guarantors and Questionable Allies

The assumption that teachers are service delivery professionals presents peculiar problems with regard to relationships with parents. In the traditional view, the authority of the teacher flowed from the same source as the authority of the parent. In schools organized on the principles illustrated by a professional service delivery organization, the authority of the teacher flows from the claim of special expertise.

Parents therefore are expected to guarantee that students will do what the teachers and the school expects them to do. It is also likely to be expected that parents will do what the school requires without questioning or equivocation.

Having an abundance of such parents is viewed in such schools as evidence of "strong parental support." In this context, to say that the parent is a partner is equivalent to the claim that doctors sometimes make when they insist that patients are partners. In both cases, to be identified as a *partner* means that one is willing to do what the expert suggests should be done. The "partner," however, is not involved in prescribing what *should* be done.

Those parents most likely to resist the unqualified acceptance of the guarantor role may have one or more of the following characteristics:

- They lack the economic, social, or educational resources to adequately perform the role of guarantor. For example, parents who work two jobs to provide food and shelter might find the expectation that they supervise their child's homework to be more than they can do.

- Their life experiences have taught them to be distrustful of bureaucratic officials in general.

- They have the resources and the skills to provide the needed support but believe that it is up to the schools and teachers to do this job.

- Whether affluent or poor, well or poorly educated, they believe that they are in a better position to define the needs and interests of their children than are school officials. Therefore they expect their views to be taken into account when decisions are made regarding the education and destiny of their children.

The internal dynamics of schools that prefer to define parents as guarantors are frequently shaped by responses made to parents who refuse to play the role they are expected to play. Sometimes such parents are treated as boundary invaders and outsiders, making it difficult for them to communicate their concerns except through official channels. In such cases, the principal is usually expected to protect teachers from interference by uncooperative parents.

Sometimes such parents are managed by co-optation, for example, by encouraging involvement in school-sponsored parent groups where the concerns of dissident parents can sometimes be channeled, dissipated, or domesticated. Sometimes dissident parents are managed by exclusion or by highly formalized interactions such as a conference with a team of teachers rather than an individual teacher or principal acting alone.

This is not to say that parent involvement is devalued in the school organized on a professional service delivery model. Rather, in the professional service delivery organization, just as in the prison, parents are often perceived as possible threats to the security of the ongoing operation and a potential source of unwanted interference. This perception is reinforced by the fact that even though teachers in a service delivery organization are afforded professional status, the ethos of a bureaucracy still undergirds the organization of the school. One of the functions of bureaucracies is to protect boundaries and keep outsiders out and insiders in.

Moreover, teachers who adopt a service delivery perspective are likely to assume that their professional expertise makes their judgments superior to those of parents. This further encourages teachers in schools organized as professional service delivery organizations to view parents with some suspicion.

In schools organized on a service delivery model, uninformed parents are likely to be distrusted because they are thought to know too little. The well informed are likely to be distrusted because they are perceived to think they know too much. Such a view does not generate the type of mutual respect from which real partnerships evolve. This attitude can also serve to reinforce the notion, especially among poor parents, that locally run public schools are not responsive to students and to parents.

One of the results is that in the effort to make the local bureaucracy more responsive, parents sometimes turn to state and federal agencies for support. Indeed, one of the strategies that some government officials have used to ensure that the policies they promulgate are implemented in local schools is the creation of special training programs for the parents of special education students. These programs are led by persons (sometimes called child advocates) whose loyalties are to the interests of students as defined by state and federal bureaucracies rather than as defined by the locally dominated bureaucracy.

Schools in small towns and rural areas are likely to have more success in enticing parents to become guarantors than might be the case in inner-city schools. It is probably the case, however, that the authority of the teacher in small towns and rural schools rests more on traditional respect for authority than on the assumption of professional expertise. Indeed, some small town and rural schools have retained their position as centers of communities. Unfortunately, recent reform efforts promulgated at the state and national levels may be threatening even these more relatively idyllic schools and communities.

It is also probably the case that parents in more affluent urban and suburban areas may be willing to play the role of guarantor if they can be assured that their children will in fact benefit in the long run from doing what the school requires—even if doing these things causes both them and their children considerable distress and discomfort. Indeed, I would argue that in schools that operate as professional service delivery organizations, the motive force behind parent involvement in the school is as likely to be calculative in nature as it is to be reflective of the parent's moral commitment to the purposes of the school.[15]

Teachers as Performers, Presenters, Clinicians, or Diagnosticians

The image of the teacher as a professional performer or as a clinician and diagnostician certainly enhances the status of the teacher beyond that of a skilled worker, clerk and record keeper, or prison guard. As performers, teachers are sometimes viewed, as the saying goes, as "the sage on the stage." Here, it is the work the teacher does that is important. The work students do is secondary. Like trial lawyers, such teachers know that most of what they do is behind-the-scenes preparation. Also like trial lawyers, it is their performance in the public forum that is attended to and evaluated.

[15]See, for example, Edward Humes, *School of Dreams: Making the Grade at a Top American High School* (Orlando, Fla.: Harcourt, 2003).

When teachers see themselves as performers, they plan lessons that emphasize what the teacher is going to do and what the students are expected to learn from what the teacher does. What teachers expect students to do is at best an afterthought and consists primarily of the expectation that the student will listen to the teacher and do the tasks and chores assigned.

The assumption is that what the teacher does is the primary determinant of student learning. This enhances the importance of the teacher, but it does little to honor the well-established notion that what students do accounts for most of the variance in learning outcomes. If all students are expected to do is to admire the performance of the teacher, it is unlikely they will learn much from it; at least they will not learn much at a profound level. Imitation does teach, but learning through imitative means is limited and seldom encourages creativity.

The teacher as diagnostician and clinician has gained considerable support among some educators, particularly among special educators and some members of the educational research community. The mental model that leads to this notion assumes that, as in medicine, the individual student is the center of the attention of the professional. Something seems almost warm and personal about this view, but closer inspection reveals a number of problems inherent in the assumptions on which it is based:

- Most of the research on which such clinical notions are based derives from behavioral psychology, which emphasizes conditioning more than educating. This view often encourages a highly manipulative and unimaginative form of teaching, inadequate to the task of educating and liberating minds. It is, however, a form of research that is compatible with the assumptions on which bureaucracies are based and from which scientific management has been derived.

- In medicine, the proper focus of action is almost always the individual. In teaching, while the intent is to affect individuals, the focal point of action is almost always groups and collectives, even sometimes mobs. Little that teachers do is accomplished one-on-one. Individuals learn, but in the bureaucratically organized school, batch processing is the norm, and teachers teach *classes*.

- It is true that teachers need to diagnose, and even prescribe, but they need to do so more in the sense that leaders diagnose and prescribe. They need to diagnose the situations in which they find themselves and the motives students and others bring to those situations. They need to think long and hard about the ends they want their students to pursue and then set about determining courses of action that they and their students might take in order to attain those ends. Behavioral psychology is not a good source of guidance in such endeavors. As one wag once observed, "B. F. Skinner did not put thirty rats in a maze at the same time."

- The idea of teacher as performer makes the teacher, rather than the student, the center of attention in the class. The quality of the learning experience afforded students is sometimes as much associated with the teacher's theatrical abilities as with anything over which the student has control.

Principal as Chief of Staff

I have chosen the label *chief of staff* for the role of principal in a professional service delivery organization only because the hospital metaphor is such a convenient means of expressing the principles I wish to express. I could instead have used the term *managing partner* or *first among equals*. The point is that in a school organized as a professional service delivery organization, the principal is likely to come from the ranks of teachers and be perceived by both self and others as a colleague rather than as a bureaucratic superior.

Within the context of a school organized as a service delivery organization, it is likely that teachers will perceive the principal as a teacher with a special administrative assignment—in other words, as "one of us." Others, especially central office personnel and other representatives of what is often referred to in local schools as "the board," are seen as bureaucratic outsiders and potential boundary threats. Indeed, in many schools where a service delivery ideology prevails, one of the primary tasks of the principal is to protect his or her teacher colleagues from interference from "downtown."

The fact that most school districts are organized on bureaucratic principles makes it possible for some individual schools to function as professional service delivery organizations, while others function as factories, warehouses, and prisons—or some combination of these. It is, in fact, one of the peculiarities of the service delivery model that schools reflecting such a structure and culture depend for their existence on a highly decentralized bureaucracy that ensures that local building units have considerable autonomy from the larger system.

This is perhaps one of the reasons that charter schools are growing in popularity among more independent-minded principals and teachers. One of the ways to protect professionals from bureaucrats is to remove them from the bureaucracy. Used in this way, charter schools do not change the fact of bureaucratic dominance, they just make it easier to conceal this dominance. (In the next chapter, I argue that a better way would be to transform the bureaucracy into a learning organization.)

As a colleague and first among equals, the principal is less a supervisor and more a facilitator and advocate for the local faculty. Indeed, in the service delivery model, the principal is likely to spend most of his or her time dealing with cross-boundary issues—issues related to parents, the bureaucratic requirements of the local district or the state, and so on. To the extent that the principal gets directly involved in instruction, he or she probably takes great care not to interfere with the autonomy of teachers and will do what he or she can do to ensure that that autonomy is respected by others as well.

The role of the principal in a service delivery–oriented school imbues the principal with professional status within the school. Bureaucratic superiors may, however, expect the principal to be a loyal member of the administrative team, which of course leads to considerable role conflict and tension for the principal. As a professional colleague, the faculty expect him or her to uphold the norms of the profession as these norms are defined by the local professionals. As a member of the bureaucratic hierarchy, the principal is expected to enforce bureaucratic mandates that are passed down, even when these mandates conflict with the judgment of the faculty and the interests of clients.

Central Office as Technicians and Support Staff

In the factory model much of the power of the bureaucracy will likely have been delegated to central office staff, and the occupants of these offices will enjoy considerable prestige as a result of exercising this power. (See the previous discussion of the school as factory.) Organizing the central office in a way that would be congruent with a service delivery model requires a fundamental shift of power and authority away from the central office and down to the school level. It requires central office staff to see themselves more as technicians and support staff, persons with limited power and authority, whose primary worth to the system is found in the work they do for teachers, principals, or the superintendent.

Such reduced status produces considerable ambivalence on the part of central office staff and often leads to much resistance to building-level decentralization and increasing the decision-making autonomy of school faculties. This resistance is one of the primary reasons that the service delivery model seldom can be observed beyond the building level—and even the school is likely to exhibit conflict and boundary struggles born of role ambiguity and allegiance to the idea of bureaucratic hierarchy.

When the superintendent and the school board are inclined to support the forms of decentralization needed to make the service delivery model work, central office staff often find ways to sabotage the effort. After all, the model makes them losers in the power and status games that factory-like bureaucracies encourage, and the last recourse for losers is sabotage.

Superintendent as Chief Executive Officer

In the 1980s and though the 1990s, there was considerable fascination with viewing the role of superintendent in a way that reflected a romanticized image of the corporate CEO. Recent events such as the Enron scandal, the Wall Street scandals and the decline of the big three automobile manufacturing companies have done much to cool this enthusiasm, though many continue to embrace the image of the superintendent as CEO as a viable and valuable one. It certainly continues to have considerable appeal to some policymakers and some school boards.

Among the consequences of the view of the superintendent as CEO is the increasing tendency of school boards to seek "nontraditional candidates" to occupy the office of superintendent—for example, retired military officers or corporate executives. The assumption is that "management is management" and there is such a thing as a professional manager. Just as the CEO of a large hospital need not be a physician, the CEO of a school district need not be a professional educator. The skills needed to manage and lead the corporate bureaucracy of schools are precisely those needed to manage large military units and corporations—or so it is argued.

Key to the idea of the superintendent as CEO is the idea that the superintendent should be free from micromanagement by his or her board, as are CEOs in well-run companies. In this view, the job of the board is to establish policy, provide oversight—especially oversight of the budget and financial matters—and ensure the continuation of strong executive leadership. It is also expected that, as in great corporations, the CEO will be the primary source of strategic direction and will work with the board to establish and maintain that direction. Finally, it is expected that as CEO, the superintendent will know how to delegate authority to others and be especially attentive to the development of new leaders.

As will be shown in Chapter Five, there are many similarities between the role of superintendent as CEO and the role of superintendent as moral and intellectual leader. In organizations in which learning is an end as well as a means to an end, however, the superintendent's primary job is moral and intellectual leadership. In an organization in which knowledge and learning are only a means to an end (for example, a bureaucratically organized hospital), moral and intellectual leadership are secondary, and management is the primary concern. Skill as a manager and planner is much more important than skill as a designer of systems or a leader of disruptive change.

Superintendents who fasten on the idea that they are, or should be, CEOs often work very hard to redefine the way power and authority are distributed in the system. In delegating considerable authority to building principals they simultaneously strengthen, rationalize, and centralize the evaluation system so that both the power of the superintendent's office and the operating authority of principals is enhanced.

Principals often find such an increase in authority exhilarating. Then they discover that although it is much easier to resist the invasion of boundaries by central office bureaucrats, it is more difficult to resist those that occur when evaluation systems are rationalized, shaped, and directly controlled from the top of the organization.

When superintendents operate as CEOs, they tend to take authority away from central office functionaries concerned with instructional matters and assign this authority to building principals. In the process, they often create a new category of bureaucratic offices, such as those having to do with testing, measurement, compliance issues, and public relations. Whether this is good or bad for children is a matter that deserves considerable study and debate.

School Board as Board of Directors

The idea that school boards should function more like boards of directors and less like legislative bodies is not new but it is a concept that is difficult to implement. Boards of directors are concerned primarily with the internal operation of the organizations they direct. If they are directors of nonprofit corporations, they are more likely to be appointed than elected. The expectation is that they will exercise their best judgment regarding how the organization can best accomplish those things it was chartered to accomplish. Typically they do not represent factions and constituencies. (Struggles by shareholder groups to wrest control from existing management and the presence of consumer advocates and employee representatives does sometimes make this assertion suspect.) Their goal is to establish and maintain clear direction for the organization—direction that will best serve the interests the organization was chartered to serve, or so it is sometimes argued.

School boards are usually elected, and those who elect them often expect them to represent their particular interests, even when such interests are inconsistent with the more general interests of the community. As a consequence, many board members see themselves as responsible for negotiating the direction of the school district in whatever way is necessary to provide advantage to the interests they represent, rather than to serve the common good the public schools in a democracy are intended to serve.

If it functions well, a board of directors does not interfere with the day-to-day operations of the organization it heads. These matters are left up to management, although with oversight from the board or committees of the board. Generally corporate boards are more concerned with long-term strategy, financial strategy, decisions about new construction or closing of existing facilities, and similar large issues.

Spending authorization tends to be in very broad categories, with much executive discretion. In the case of school boards, however, state laws regarding the frequency of meetings, narrow categories of funding, and stringent limits on executive discretion—combined with open meeting laws that encourage political posturing on the part of board members—have served to make it difficult for school boards to function as boards of directors, even when individual members are inclined to do so.

The Dilemma of Professionals in Bureaucracies

Peter Drucker,[16] whom many view as the father of the field of management studies, coined the phrase *knowledge workers* to describe a class of persons who make their contributions to organizational life through the manipulation of symbols, the application of ideas and theories, and the use of words rather than through the exercise of muscle and sinew. Drucker recognized, as others have come to, that a different set of demands is placed on leaders who manage others who work with

---

[16]See, for example, Peter F. Drucker, *Management: Tasks, Practices, Responsibilities* (New York: HarperCollins, 1974).

ideas than are placed on those who are primarily concerned with the application of physical skills and the production of things. This is particularly true of those who have come to be called professional knowledge workers, such as physicians, lawyers, accountants, and, in the service delivery model, teachers as well.

Service delivery professionals are knowledge workers in that they are members of an occupational group that puts knowledge to work on behalf of others. In a service delivery organization, there are other professionals as well, chief among these being management professionals. Management professionals, in fact, dominate bureaucracies because they are in charge of the systems of most concern to the maintenance of bureaucratic forms: the power and authority systems, the evaluation systems, and the boundary systems.

The problems that arise when service delivery professionals are compelled to work within the context of bureaucratically arranged organizations are relatively well documented in the literature on occupations. This literature primarily reveals a fundamental antagonism between service delivery professionals and the bureaucratic organizations in which they operate. Try as they might, bureaucrat managers have difficulty accommodating service delivery professionals, precisely because these professionals are part of an external authority system as well as an internal one.

Sometimes schools attempt to reconcile such long-established conflicts by a system of shared governance, incorporating the interests of the professionals into the bureaucratic hierarchy through such mechanisms as union-negotiated arrangements ensuring that professionals are represented in the decision-making process. These arrangements do provide some relief, but tensions persist.

So long as the bureaucracy is left in place, tensions between bureaucratic authority and professional authority will exist, and the impersonal ethos of the bureaucracy will be likely to prevail. Moreover, when these matters are dealt with through union contracts, the contracts often become as constraining to professionals as the bureaucratic rules that guide the system more generally. Union contracts often become a part *of* the bureaucracy rather than an alternative to it.

The fundamental problem has its root in the fact that members of professions are expected to submit to the norms of their professional group as well as to the norms of the bureaucracy in which they are employed. The norms of bureaucracy center on efficiency and standardization, while the norms of service delivery professions center on meeting the needs of clients. Bureaucracy requires commitment to rules and the uniform application of rules to categories of cases. Management professionals manage by the rules and with the rules.

Professionalism, as service delivery professionals define the term, requires commitment to understanding the unique circumstances of clients and the application of tested principles as opposed to rules. These are differences that make a difference, and these differences almost always produce conflict.

Nonetheless, many educators find much to admire in the professional service delivery model, especially the medical model. For example, the National Board for Professional Teaching Standards is clearly based on ideas similar to board certification in medicine. The idea of "best practice" and the idea that practice should be based on research are reminiscent of a medical model. So is the idea that the special knowledge teachers have should entitle them to authority over children, even when that authority may be in conflict with the authority of the parent.

Teaching is, or should be, a profession, but it is not a service delivery profession. It is a leadership profession and like other members of the leadership professions, the goal should be to empower others to act rather than simply provide them services they cannot provide themselves because they lack the knowledge and skill.

Certainly leadership professionals provide services to others, but service is not their aim. Their aim is to enable others to do things they might not otherwise do and pursue goals they might not otherwise think were attainable. Such a role is not likely to be available to a teacher in bureaucratic structures because teachers must be empowered to be leaders.

Empowerment, unlike delegation, is based on the assumption that those who are empowered are entitled to act because of who they are and what they are judged by their peers to be able to contribute to the pursuit of shared goals. They have authority because they need it to do what they are expected to do rather than because they occupy a position to which authority has been assigned. It is the processes through which such entitlement is gained, that is, induction processes, that should be of concern to those who would have teachers be members of a leadership profession.

THE SCHOOL AS WAREHOUSE OR PRISON

The factory-like qualities of some schools have been widely commented on. Similarly, the notion that schools and students might be well served if the teaching occupation had more of the qualities of the medical professions, and if schools were organized more like hospitals, has also had some positive support among educators. Thus, the ideas of the school as factory or hospital are sometimes much more than metaphors—they are almost blueprints for the design of schools.

The metaphors of the warehouse and the prison are not blueprints. Rather, they conjure images that are sometimes used to criticize schools in which the factory-like attributes become too pronounced, or they are used to explain the way schools and subunits are organized to cope with students who are unable or unwilling to yield to the demands that the factory-based system makes on them. Thus, in schools in which some students are so alienated that they are unwilling to comply with the rules of the factory, such students may be labeled and "shipped" to special programs where they are stored for safekeeping rather than educated—or, in the extreme, treated as prisoners might be treated in a prison. The image of Joe Clark, principal in a troubled inner-city high school who became much admired for his get-tough, punitive approach to alienated students, patrolling the corridors of his school with a bullhorn and a baseball bat comes to mind here.

It is not, however, common to organize school districts or even a single schoolhouse on principles reflective of those illustrated by either the warehouse or the prison. Though some politicians have held Clark up as a model for all principals, few educators would agree with this judgment.

In the real world of public schools, what usually happens is that some subunit within the school takes on the characteristics of the warehouse or the prison and the students in it are those who cannot be made to fit into the factory system. The fact is that even in the most bureaucratic schools, guard-like and warden-like behavior are only admired when situations are pathological in nature. For example, large urban school districts have begun to develop alternative schools especially for students who misbehave in "regular schools." Sometimes such schools function like hospitals and try to provide remediation, counseling, and help. Sometimes, however, these alternatives serve as nothing more than warehouses where students who present behavioral problems are stored away until they can be shipped out, or as prisons where students are incarcerated until their sentence has been served.

Students as Inventory or Inmates

The warehouse and the prison metaphors and the images they suggest are useful in shedding light on the way schools often respond to students who cannot or will not comply with the demands of the system. When student noncompliance is perceived to result from some condition beyond the student's control, it is likely that the student will be categorized as a special education student. In the school characterized by a manufacturing ethos, the student "product" is likely to be placed on a special track where behavior modification techniques may be applied. In a service delivery organization, such students will be sent to instructional units for service by specialists trained to work with students with the "presenting problems." In some schools, however, special education students, especially those who have been identified as behaviorally disordered, are likely to be stored away in the hope that some magical change might come about that will allow them to be returned to the mainstream population.

There are several types of inventory in a warehouse. Some is stored only temporarily. Other forms may be stored for prolonged periods—so long in some cases that even the shipper forgets about it. (This, of course, stirs up sadder images than even a cynical observer might be reluctant to explore.) Some inventory is highly valued, and both the shipper and receiver are concerned with its care while it is being stored away. Other forms of inventory are of indeterminate value: of enough potential use in the future that they are not discarded, but sufficiently without value that they are placed in the warehouse so as not to clutter up the factory floor.

Students who are treated as inventory may be high-performing students or students who do not perform at all. Sometimes scheduling problems cause schools to warehouse subsets of students. Such warehouses are usually given a euphemistic label such as *study hall* or *homeroom*. (I am not suggesting that all study halls and all homerooms are warehouses, but many certainly are. Furthermore, as one sign of improvement in high schools, there are many fewer study halls than there used to be.) Some critics would go so far as to argue that the senior year in high school is little more than a warehouse experience for most students.[17]

Historically, vocational education served a warehousing function for many students for whom it was assumed academic studies were "beyond" but were "good compliant youngsters who could work with their hands if not their minds." With the increasing demands of modern manufacturing processes and the uses of technology in businesses, such a view of vocational education is on the wane. Nevertheless, the mental model that many Americans hold of vocational education is one that represents it as a holding pen for students who would not or could not fare well in more elite academic programs.

[17]See, for example, Leon Botstein, *Jefferson's Children* (New York: Doubleday, 1997).

It is also the case that some self-contained special education classes with poorly trained teachers become little more than warehouses for the unfortunate. The fact that special education is an area of major short supply of teachers makes this more likely to occur, especially in schools organized around the notion that students should be considered products or clients.

When faculties view student noncompliance with the rules as overt rejection of the norms and values of the organization—that is, the faculty believes that such students are terminally alienated—the only response available to the bureaucratically organized school is to treat the students as patients in a mental hospital might be treated or to treat them as prisoners. The school that is generally organized on a service delivery model is likely to take the former approach and invest heavily in special programs that make extensive use of behavior modification techniques. Schools that are generally organized more like factories are likely to set up special units that are designed to treat such students as inmates—or they may simply refuse to serve them, by means of extended suspension or expulsion.

Schools that treat children as inmates are not as numerous as the popular press and talk show hosts would have the public believe, but they do exist. Many other schools, especially those that clearly reflect a warehouse mentality, are often on the brink of a crisis that could evolve into a prison-like mentality. This may be one of the reasons that faculties of high schools organized on the factory model are often eager to have district leaders create alternative schools. Such alternative schools can then be organized on assumptions that can accommodate alienated and noncompliant youngsters without their being forced to fit in a factory-based system.

Ironically, sometimes alternative schools are granted considerable autonomy within large bureaucratic structures. In part, this autonomy is granted precisely because such alternatives relieve the bureaucracy of a problem created by the bureaucracy itself.

Some alternative schools produce wonderful results with students who might otherwise have been failures in the system. Indeed, if an alternative school has the right principal and a few of the right faculty members, it may evolve into one of the few authentic learning organizations in a system that otherwise operates factories or hospitals. This is, of course, one of the arguments for charter schools.

Absent the protection of bureaucratic controls, however, and absent a clear set of beliefs and values to guide decisions in the district (as would be the case in a learning organization), such alternative schools are just as likely to become places to store or punish children as they are to become nurturing environments. Charter schools might work, but only if the larger organization in which they are embedded is in fact a learning organization operating with a clear set of beliefs that defines the core business of all schools in the district as that of designing engaging work for students and leading students to success in doing that work.

Parents as Outsiders

Although the preachments of schooling suggest that parents should be viewed as partners, friends, or at least guarantors, the practices of schooling often result in parents having a very different experience than such warm definitions might suggest. As Willard Waller put the matter many years ago,

> A marked lack of clear thought and plain speaking exists in the literature touching the relation of parents and teachers. From the ideal point of view, parents and teachers have much in common, in that both, supposedly, wish things to occur for the best interests of the child; but, in fact, parents and teachers usually live in a condition of mutual distrust and enmity. Both wish the child well, but it is such a different kind of well that conflict must inevitably arise over it. The fact seems to be that parents and teachers are natural enemies, predestined each for the discomfiture of the other. The chasm is frequently covered over, for neither parents nor teachers wish to admit to themselves the uncomfortable implications of their animosity, but on occasion it can make itself clear enough.[18]

Many high schools are organized on the assumption of infrequent and highly stylized and controlled interactions with parents. The primary role of the parent in this case is that of a shipper and a receiver, making sure that the student gets to school and has a place to return to when school is out.

Schools and faculties that are indifferent to the home life of students and the values and expectations of parents place parents in the position of outsiders. Parents who are indifferent to the school lives of their children—so long as their children are safe and are returned undamaged—implicitly accept this role definition.

---

[18]Willard Waller, *The Sociology of Teaching* (Hoboken, N.J.: Wiley, 1967). (Originally published in 1932).

Distrust and increased social distance between teachers and parents is most likely to become apparent when students exhibit disruptive behaviors and pose a threat to other children, leading them to be labeled behavior problems. This divide can be compounded by the fact that children from racial and ethic minority groups and children of the poor are more likely to be defined as persistent behavioral problems than are children from affluent homes.

Even in the best of circumstances, parents are never fully integrated into the bureaucratic system. It is expected that they will provide support, but when they do not, the school is generally powerless to compel them to do so. In addition, even when parents do voluntarily comply with the directives of school personnel, such compliance is always looked on with some skepticism: the parent is a questionable ally, not to be consistently counted upon. Few parents are totally trusted and treated as insiders or partners.

In the extreme, parents (especially parents of limited economic means) may be treated much like visitors to prisons. They are viewed with suspicion, treated more as strangers than as friends, and compelled to follow specific rules, limit their interactions, and not go to places where they are not invited. Indeed, some critics of public schools argue that this is a widespread phenomenon and use this as an argument to justify abolishing public schools altogether. Joel Turtle, an outspoken critic of public schools, writes, for example:

> Most parents don't realize that school authorities don't want their opinion. Too often, school authorities ignore parents' suggestions or complaints because they truly believe they are the experts and parents are just annoying amateurs. As a result, some teachers, principals, or administrators feel insulted when parents make suggestions or complaints. Many school officials believe parents should not have any real input in their children's education. That is one reason why school authorities hold their committee meetings in secret.[19]

It has been my observation that affluent and better educated parents are likely to complain about the nature of the curriculum, teaching strategies, and so on. Less well-educated parents complain too, but more often their complaints have to do with feeling that their child has somehow been personally mistreated

---

[19]Joel Turtle, "Parents' Complaints—Arrogant Public Schools Turn a Deaf Ear." 2005. http://www.mykidsdeservebetter.com.

or treated with too little respect. In either case, there are parents who feel that school officials often treat them as distrusted visitors and interlopers. The fact that persons with influence in the public media share this sentiment does not bode well for the future of public education.

Teachers as Technicians, Clerks, or Guards

One of the laments of many teachers, and especially of special education teachers and teachers who work in federally funded programs, is that they are increasingly overburdened with paperwork—so much that they have less and less time to think about students and instruction. The extent to which this is empirically verifiable may be subject to debate (my observation is that the complaining teachers have it about right), but the fact that many—if not most—teachers perceive it to be so is beyond doubt. Teachers in fact often refer to themselves as clerks and record keepers.

This condition is especially prevalent in schools that are under scrutiny because they are ranked as "underperforming" and are therefore increasingly subject to bureaucratic mandates and new forms of inspection. Such forms of inspection almost invariably require more paperwork for teachers and for principals. Indeed, producing evidence of compliance with bureaucratic mandates, including producing test scores and practicing to produce test scores, often takes up much of the time of teachers, even of teachers who are working in situations where they are trying to treat students as clients, or perhaps even as volunteers.

Another lament of teachers is that persistent discipline problems are so distracting that they find themselves spending more time on discipline issues than on matters of instruction. This perception is sometimes so widespread that teachers report feeling "like a prison guard" rather than a professional educator.

It is common for teachers to lump many of the problems they have with individual students under the general category of "discipline problems." The effort to integrate into the regular classroom students who once were in self-contained special education classes (mainstreaming), efforts to reduce tracking and ability grouping, and a perceived breakdown in discipline in the home are all pointed to as sources of discipline problems, as is the perceived change in the attitudes of youngsters toward adult authority more generally.

In one poll, for example, 78 percent of teachers reported that students who are persistent discipline problems and who should therefore be removed from the classroom have not been removed. In the same poll, 52 percent of the teachers reported an armed police officer on their school grounds. A third of the teachers surveyed in this poll reported that they had considered quitting teaching or knew a colleague who had quit because of the pressures of discipline problems. In focus groups some teachers reported that they are in the "business of crowd control, not education."[20]

Being in charge of crowd control may not make one a guard, but it is not far from it. It would seem, then, that while in most schools, teachers are not guards and do not want to be guards, at least some teachers in some schools feel under considerable pressure to act as if they *were* guards—and some find this expectation unbearable.

Concerns about discipline are not new in American education. The difference seems to be that in an age in which test scores count for more and more, student noncompliance has more of a negative effect than it did in the past, and schools in which students are most likely to be noncompliant are also those most likely to have lower test scores: urban middle schools and urban high schools. [21]

Principal as Minor Bureaucrat

One of the most common images of the principal in the media, especially the high school principal, is the martinet and bureaucrat. Although this is an unfair characterization of most principals, there is much in the way schools are currently organized that encourages principals to behave more like bureaucratic managers than like the leaders most want to be.

If the ethos of the factory prevails, principals are likely to be evaluated more on the way they manage their staff than the way they lead their staff. Indeed, the way teachers are evaluated is likely to be of more import than is the way new teachers are inducted into the system. The way forms are completed and the way meetings are attended is likely to be of more importance than is the quality of the teacher development programs that are provided in the school. Moreover, when teachers see themselves as nothing more than skilled workers, they often want someone who will be forceful in telling them what to do. In this way, there can be no ambiguity about where they stand relative to a set of rules with which they have little personal involvement other than the requirement to comply.

[20]See *Teaching Interrupted: Do Discipline Policies in Today's Public Schools Foster the Common Good?* (Washington, D.C.: Public Agenda, May 2004).
[21]Ibid.

In such circumstances, there are also clear indications that many teachers feel that their condition could be considerably improved if their principals were empowered to act more like wardens.[22] Forty-six percent of teachers, for example, felt things could be improved if principals were given much more authority than they now have to handle discipline problems as they see fit. Moreover, 57 percent of teachers were in favor of establishing alternative schools for "chronic offenders" (of discipline codes), and 70 percent of teachers wanted a "zero-tolerance" policy to put students on notice that they could be kicked out of school for serious offenses. In this study, teachers, and to a lesser extent parents, felt that discipline in schools had been negatively affected by the threat of lawsuits and by the fear administrators have of aggressive parents. Principals who do not stand up to such pressures are certain to lose status, just as surely as would a warden who turned the prison over to the inmates.

Central Office as Directors or Hearing Officers

In the effort to decentralize a school district, central office positions are often downgraded from supervisory to support positions. Although the titles people are given vary, the idea is that they direct only programs and resources; they do not direct people or the ideas that drive people. They become, in the truest sense of the word, managers. They are never leaders and are not expected to lead. Their role is to ensure that programs are implemented with fidelity and to report to line superiors (assistant superintendents, deputy superintendents, and so on) when this is not so.

Sometimes, however, program directors are able to exchange what they have in the way of authority over things for some degree of influence over people.[23] This in turn leads to considerable dysfunction and conflict between and among central office departments, as well as between the central office and principals in local schools. Such struggles often create conditions that reveal the most inefficient sides of bureaucracies.

In school districts where a warehouse ethos is predominant, instructional matters are likely to be of little concern, especially among central office personnel. The most prestigious positions are likely to be those that have to do with finance and personnel (without human resource development) and perhaps communications and public relations.

[22]Ibid.
[23]See Phillip C. Schlechty, *Creating Great Schools: Six Critical Systems at the Heart of Educational Reform* (San Francisco: Jossey-Bass, 2005) for a more detailed discussion of this phenomenon.

Curriculum and instruction do not play prominent roles, because the concerns of the central office and the superintendent have more to do with managing things than with leading people and developing ideas.

One of the major growth areas in the operation of central office bureaucracies, especially in large urban schools, is in those areas that have the potential for legal action and government sanctions. Some of these have to do with programs, but increasingly they have to do with student personnel matters, especially special education students and discipline referrals. It is not uncommon for school districts to have relatively large departments that do nothing but deal with such matters. Department staff prepare materials for board hearings or hearings by panels required by state and federal laws, conduct interviews and investigations, and maintain contacts with the courts and with law enforcement officials. The growth of these roles and the special education enterprise in general has added much to the public perception that the public schools are overly burdened with central office personnel—sometimes referred to in the press as "downtown bureaucrats."

Superintendent as Property Manager or Head of a Bureau

The image of the superintendent as property manager or chief of the bureau of prisons, as suggested by the metaphor of the school as a warehouse or a prison, is much more common in the real world of public schools than the limited applicability of the two metaphors might suggest. In school districts undergoing rapid growth, it is not at all uncommon for school boards to hire superintendents with an eye toward their demonstrated skills in negotiating contracts, supervising construction, managing efficient budgets, and so on, giving little attention to the candidates' views on instructional matters. Even in more stable environments, there are some superintendents who are more concerned with the material side of the operation of schools—school facilities, budgets, maintenance, and so on—who have little interest in the direction the district is headed and find discussions of such matters distractions from their "real" work.

School boards in districts that are undergoing dramatic growth or dramatic reductions in size often put pressure on the superintendent to emphasize the role of property manager and attend less diligently to the human side of the organization. This is sometimes reflected in the formal and informal evaluations board members provide the superintendent, but more frequently, it is a matter left to implication rather than a specific mandate. The role of the superintendent as property manager is especially salient when building new schools or closing old ones, for it is in these conditions that the vested interests of school board members operating as owners are likely to come to the fore.

Other environmental factors discourage superintendents from attending to those systems most critical to transforming schools into learning organizations. For example, the fact that many school districts are embroiled in so many legal actions encourages superintendents to behave more like prison bureau chiefs than intellectual leaders. Indeed, the fact is that superintendents often become involved in matters of law that would boggle the mind of the most accomplished bureau chief.

Some school districts outsource legal services, and some set up entire departments that provide ongoing legal support. In either case, when major lawsuits confront the district, the superintendent is likely to become so distracted by the demands of lawyers, accountants, and other technical staff that it is difficult, if not impossible, for him or her to provide the kind of intellectual and moral leadership required to ensure constant direction to the system. Simply to survive seems quite enough.

School Board as Safety Inspectors or Parole Board

Referring to school board members as safety inspectors or fire marshals is a shorthand way of pointing out that sometimes school boards give inordinate attention to details of school life at the expense of attention to the big picture. This is not to say that school safety is a minor matter, for it is not. Yet there is little that school board members can or should do about these matters other than to ensure that the school district has policies and procedures in place that ensure they are attended to—and then to monitor to ensure these policies are enforced.

Some school board members take it on themselves to respond personally and directly to parent complaints about such matters as textbooks not being available, bus schedules being inconvenient, bleachers producing splinters, and so on. Rather than referring these matters to the office of the superintendent or using these calls as a signal that there may be a need for a different policy mix, some board members step into a supervisory role and demand corrective action.

Micromanagement of this kind is especially likely to happen when board members see themselves more as politicians and ward heelers than as community builders or members of a board that speaks collectively from a common agenda. Such activity often keeps board members occupied and contributes to feelings of self-importance, but it does little to focus attention on the common needs of children and the future of the community.

Because they are required by law to do so, school boards also sometimes function more as hearing officers and parole boards than as leaders of a major educational enterprise. Indeed, in some instances, an inordinate amount of school board time and energy is given over to holding closed-door hearings dealing with such matters as student expulsions, the dismissal of employees, and various lawsuits with which the district is confronted. Important though these may be, they can distract the board from thinking about broad matters of policy and contemplating the future direction of the school system. Even more unfortunate, perhaps, is the fact that for school board members whose mental model of the board is that of a quasi-legislative body, being on the board can be seen as a stepping-stone to higher office. This not only demeans the status of the school board but it encourages board members to be more attentive to the special interests that elect them than to the common good which they should be obliged to serve.

GETTING THE PROBLEM RIGHT

Recognizing that too many public schools, especially schools serving poor children and minority children, operate like warehouses or prisons—and recognizing as well that such arrangements are not good for children or for society—many legislators, including the U.S. Congress, have wittingly or unwittingly set on a course that will result in making all schools even more factory-like.

The result, to date, is that teachers are increasingly coming to view themselves simply as skilled workers, and principals are feeling increasing pressure to behave as shop foremen. Students are increasingly viewed impersonally, more like products than people. They are too often simply programmed, conditioned, and tested rather than inspired, encouraged, and educated.

The following, taken from a recent Public Education Network study, reflects a relatively accurate summary of what I found as I reviewed the literature on the effects of the federal No Child Left Behind (NCLB) initiative: "NCLB's test-based accountability relies on inadequate assessment systems that are narrowing the curriculum, demoralizing teachers and students . . . encouraging school leaders to shed their test-taking enrollments of low-performing students."[24]

[24]*Open to the Public Speaking Out on "No Child Left Behind": A Report from 2004 Public Hearings* (Campaign for Fiscal Equity, New Visions for Public Schools, Good Schools for All, and Public Education Network), 2004. Retrieved December 22, 2008, from http://www.publiceducation.org/portals/nclb/hearings/national/Open_to_the_Public.pdf.

Given the choice between a prison, a warehouse, or a factory, a well-run factory focused on one uniform product certainly does have some appeal. Although the curriculum might be narrow, the teaching unimaginative, and the results generally mediocre, there could be dependable results, and most students would learn something—even if what they learned is pallid compared to what they might learn in a school focused on providing each child with engaging tasks.

Unfortunately, the best the factory model can do, assuming it can be made to work efficiently, is to ensure that most students learn sufficiently well that they will be able to pass paper-and-pencil tests that call for little more than decoding skills and knowledge of basic arithmetic. The processes used to ensure these minimums, however, are almost certain to stifle creativity on the part of teachers and students, and they will discourage students and teachers from pursuing in-depth experiences in any subject.

If one assumes that schools must be based on a bureaucratic model—and I do not make that assumption—then the service delivery model has much to recommend it. This model is not the best that can be done, but given the alternative of a school organized as a factory, a warehouse, or a prison, the service delivery model is quite inviting. At the very least, it honors teachers as professionals and legitimizes their right to struggle against the constraints of the bureaucracies within which they work. It treats students as important human beings—clients—even though it keeps them dependent rather than require them to work toward independence. In contrast to treating teachers as low-level bureaucratic employees and students as products and data points, this seems to me to be the preferable scenario.

The service delivery model is, in fact, the mental model that implicitly and sometimes explicitly guides the thinking of many of the more academically inclined among school reformers, as well as teachers who are, or want to be, considered professionals. It is also the model that implicitly undergirds the organization of many high-performing schools, especially high-performing schools that serve more affluent families. At the very least, the commitment of professionals to their clients affords students some protection from the more intellectually devastating aspects of bureaucratic life and gives some smattering of nobility to the art and science of teaching.

One of the unintended consequences of the NCLB legislation, however, is that many high-performing schools that once functioned more or less as professional service delivery organizations are being forced into a mold that is increasingly factory-like. The likely result will be that many students will become increasingly estranged from schools that they once found rewarding, if not always engaging.

In the bureaucratic accountability systems in which schools often must participate, the leaders of even very good schools sometimes feel compelled to focus on test scores to prove that their autonomy from the bureaucratic structures is deserved. In the effort to produce such scores, and to produce them quickly, the leaders of these supposedly high-performing schools often succumb to the regimentation and standardization they should be seeking to avoid. This increases the likelihood that high-performing students will become increasingly estranged from the public schools and that they and their parents will seek relief in schools that are out from under the bureaucratic constraints now being imposed by state and federal agencies.

It seems clear that reforming bureaucratic structures will no longer suffice. Turning prisons into factories, making existing factories more efficient, or decentralizing operations so that a few schools can function more like professional service delivery organizations will not do the job. This is especially the case if the intent is to ensure that nearly every child is well educated as opposed to ensuring that most children are minimally competent in reading and arithmetic. What is needed are schools that are organized to liberate minds and inspire performance rather than organizations that are designed to ensure compliance with little attention to meaning and value. Such an organization is described in the chapter that follows.

A New Image of Schools

The preceding chapter explored how metaphors can be used to reveal the mental models that might be operating in existing schools. This chapter examines how metaphors might be used to help describe and define an image of schools that has yet to be realized—an image of schooling derived from assumptions based on the notion of the school as a learning organization.

LEARNING ORGANIZATION OR LEARNING COMMUNITY?

In recent years, the concepts of learning communities and learning organizations have gained considerable popularity among educators. As with any other idea that rapidly gains popularity, there is a great deal of confusion regarding the meanings of the terms used.

Richard DuFour, one of the best-known advocates of what he and many others call *professional learning communities,* writes:

> The professional learning community model has now reached a critical juncture, one well-known to those who have witnessed the fate of other well-intentioned school reform efforts. In this all-too-familiar cycle, initial enthusiasm gives way to confusion about the fundamental concepts driving the initiative, followed by inevitable implementation problems, the conclusion that the reform has failed to bring about the desired results, abandonment of the reform, and the launch of a new search for the next promising initiative. Another

113

reform movement has come and gone, reinforcing the conventional education wisdom that promises, "This too shall pass."[1]

I share DuFour's concern and do not wish to add to the confusion. At the same time I want to ensure that the reader understands that when I speak and write of learning organizations, I am not using this phrase as a synonym for *learning community*. Learning organizations do contain learning communities, and many of them, but learning organizations are much more than the learning communities.

Key Definitions

A learning community is a group of people who personally interact, face to face or electronically, and are bound together by the pursuit of common questions, problems, or issues. The members of the group have developed clear norms and procedures to ensure that their interactions go forward in a way that honors the ideas of mutualism, collegiality, trust, loyalty, and friendship, while showing a bias for hard-nosed analysis and concrete action. Learning communities are more likely to be relatively small, though sometimes entire schools may become temporary learning communities. Usually, however, it is best to think of the school as an operating unit within a larger learning organization. As a critical operating unit, the school is a source of connection among a variety of learning communities, some of them focused on matters internal to the school and some may be connected to wider issues in the district or the community at large.

Communities of learners are collections of individuals joined together for the purpose of sharing what they have learned or sharing a common learning experience. Unlike learning communities, communities of learners work together only coincidently on problems, issues, or questions, though they may have strong social bonds, share a common identity, and benefit from the work of other members. Learning communities are distinguished from communities of learners primarily through the presence or absence of a common research and action agenda. Entire school faculties are more likely to be communities of learners than they are to be learning communities. Professional associations sometimes function as communities of learners.

Finally, *learning organizations* are formal social organizations that purposefully create, support, and use learning communities and communities of learners

[1]Richard DuFour, "Schools as Learning Communities," *Educational Leadership,* 2004, *61*(8), 6.

as the primary means of inducting new members; creating, developing, importing, and exporting knowledge; assigning tasks and evaluating performances; and establishing goals and maintaining direction. Learning organizations create and maintain networks of learning communities and use these networks as the primary means by which the work of the organization is accomplished. (This definition is somewhat different from the one I quoted in Chapter Three from Senge. I do not disagree with Senge's definition; however, it focuses attention on the consequences of the learning organization. I am more concerned here with processes and structures.)

The distinctions these definitions suggest are important. They are especially important here because what I am concerned with in this book is understanding schools as complex and formal social organizations and shedding light on how their organizational features might be altered to make the education of young people in America more appropriate to the times in which they live.

Learning Communities in Learning Organizations

Learning communities are the building blocks on which learning organizations stand, but they are not formal organizations. Learning organizations are formal organizations. These formalized systems define, among other things, how and whether learning communities are given legitimacy in the life of the organization, the kind of operating systems that will be employed, and the way the work of the organization will be conducted.

Learning communities can exist in formal organizations based on bureaucratic principles, but their existence is always insecure and usually temporary. Indeed, one of the reasons that the learning community movement is threatened is that many people are trying to install learning communities in schools while leaving essential bureaucratic structures intact. These communities cannot thrive without systems to support them that are far different from those that exist in most schools today.

Among other things, learning communities assume participatory decision making and dialogue between and among leaders and followers in the organization. In bureaucracies, where top-down communication is the norm, such patterns of decision making are always problematic and are likely to be suppressed. This is especially so when the decisions made within a learning community lead to innovations that require changes in rules, roles, and relationships enshrined in current definitions of power and authority.

Consider a small learning community in a bureaucratically organized school that decides to abandon the purchase of new textbooks. It will use the textbooks already on hand, supplemented by materials readily available on the Internet, and then use the money designated for textbook purchases to enrich digital learning opportunities for children. The odds are that this learning community would not be empowered to act without going through many layers of the hierarchy. In bureaucracies, budgets are usually inflexible. Money designated to buy textbooks cannot be used to buy other things. In learning organizations budgets are tools to enable action rather than weapons to control people. In a bureaucracy, accountability means following the funding formula, even if the formula was developed under assumptions that have since changed. In a learning organization, accountability means the ability to explain persuasively why prior commitments should be abandoned and new patterns of expenditure are required. For example, one of the most wasteful periods in many school districts is the month before the financial books are closed for the year and leaders are forced to "spend it or lose it." Many nonpriority items are purchased in such times.

A learning organization would view unspent funds as a resource to be used for development the next year. In addition, the reasons funds were not expended would be studied to understand better what was done right (maybe increased efficiency accounts for the differential) and what was done wrong (maybe the forecasting procedures need some work). In a bureaucracy, unspent funds would be taken as evidence that the department was "overfunded" last year and the department would be penalized in next year's budget.

In learning organizations, learning communities have permanence. Indeed, the creation and networking of learning communities are defining features of these organizations, as is the use of these communities as fundamental features in induction and recruitment systems and in the development and transmission of knowledge. Learning communities are empowered to act on what they learn. Authority is not delegated to them; power is openly available to the learning community acting collectively, and it is up to the community to authorize its use.

This does not mean, however, that learning communities are autonomous and act out of concert with the leadership of the organization. These communities are bound to leadership through a well-developed directional system that encourages the creation of powerful induction programs and intricate networking patterns that link learning communities together throughout the organization. Indeed, it is likely that there will be learning communities whose primary concerns have to do with the creation of ways to ensure coordination of action among various elements in the organization without imposing the arbitrary rules that sometimes typify bureaucracies.

Learning organizations do have a structure and operating procedures, but these are more likely to be based on beliefs, vision, and values than is the case in bureaucracies. In bureaucracies, structure and procedures are based on commitments to rationality and efficiency at the expense of human values and personal growth. In a bureaucracy the key questions are, "What is the rule?" and "Who is in charge?" In a learning organization, the key questions are, "What is the problem?" and "Who is likely to know what to do about it?"

Schools as Learning Organizations: New Mental Models

What mental models would teachers and school leaders embrace if schools were organized on the principles of a learning organization? What beliefs would guide practices in the school? What images would teachers have regarding their own roles and the roles of students? How would parents be viewed, and how might parents perceive themselves? What might one expect to see in a classroom in a school organized as a learning organization, and what results might one expect from such a classroom and from such a school? Here are possible answers:

- Leaders would view the core business of the school district and the schools as designing engaging work that calls on students to complete intellectually demanding tasks and then leading students in the successful completion of these tasks so that they learn the intended things.

- Leaders would persistently and regularly communicate the view they hold to others. They would also discipline all decisions and conversations leading up to decisions by reference to this view of the core business of schools.

- Students would be viewed by teachers and others in the school as knowledge workers, volunteers, and customers for engaging work.

- Teachers would see themselves and be viewed by others as leaders, designers, and guides to instruction.

- Parents would be viewed by all school personnel as partners, and they would also see themselves as partners.

- The principal would be viewed as a leader of leaders.

- The superintendent would be viewed as both a moral and intellectual leader.

- Central office staff would see themselves and be seen by others as capacity builders and what are often referred to as servant leaders.

- The board of education would be seen as community builders and community leaders.

- All who work in and around the school would view their primary task as helping to ensure that each day, each student is provided tasks that are engaging and designed in ways that result in profound learning of those things parents and communities believe are important for students to learn.

One of the more important questions, of course, is what the important things are that schools should teach. In a school system organized as a learning organization, disciplined conversations would need to take place to develop a satisfying answer to this question. These conversations could also become one of the more important community-building activities undertaken by the board of education.

One of the most fundamental problems confronting educators and those who theorize about education in formal organizational settings is the fact that the idea of schoolwork—as distinguished from other forms of work—has never been properly framed. When the workplace metaphor has been applied to schools, it has almost always been applied in the context of the rational systems manufacturing model typical of the factory.

This has led many educators, especially those who embrace a constructivist perspective, to be suspicious of any proposal to change schools based on the idea that students are workers or customers. (The suggestion that students should be viewed as volunteers is not always warmly embraced either, because many traditionally oriented teachers believe that the basic problem in schools is that traditional authority has been eroded and that until traditional teacher authority is reestablished, there is little prospect of improving schools. The idea of viewing the student as a volunteer is viewed by some as tantamount to a compromise with the devil.)

Students as Knowledge Workers

The image of the school as a learning organization requires conceding that the school is a workplace, though a special kind of workplace, and the work that students do is a special kind of work. Peter Drucker called this *knowledge work*.[2]

[2]Peter Drucker, "The Age of Social Transformation," *Atlantic Monthly,* Nov. 1994. http://www.theatlantic .com/politics/ecbig/soctrans.htm.

Up to the past fifty years, only a limited number of people did this kind of work outside the context of schools. Even in schools, only a few students—those few who were most likely to enter the elite knowledge work professions like law, medicine, the ministry, and university teaching and research—were likely to be encouraged to do real knowledge work. Most students in school were expected to put knowledge to work to accomplish routine tasks, much as manual workers in factories put other tools to work to accomplish routine tasks. In school, as well as in the larger society, only the elite were expected to work on knowledge and with knowledge to solve problems and create new products: books, journal articles, sermons, and songs, for example.

Over the past fifty years, however, knowledge work has increasingly become the dominant form of work in America. Today, businesses that are the most productive are those that are most effective at creating an environment that leads and develops knowledge workers. These "learning organizations," described by Peter Senge and others, are structured in a way to support, nurture, and encourage knowledge work.[3]

As a result, the meaning of education has changed dramatically from the past. As Drucker observed in 1995, "Increasingly, an educated person will be somebody who has learned how to learn, and who continues learning, especially by formal education, throughout his or her lifetime." Drucker then went on to caution, however, that

> there are obvious dangers to [the above-mentioned view of the end of education]. For instance, society could easily degenerate into emphasizing formal degrees rather than performance capacity. It could fall prey to sterile Confucian mandarins—a danger to which the American university is singularly susceptible. On the other hand, it could overvalue immediately usable, "practical" knowledge and underrate the importance of fundamentals, and of wisdom altogether.[4]

Ironically, what some business leaders see today as twenty-first-century skills, many educators have long held to be things every citizen needed to know if democracy is to survive. What has changed is not so much what students need to know and be able to do in the twenty-first century (other than those things

[3]See Peter Senge, *The Fifth Discipline: The Art and Practice of the Learning Organization* (New York: Doubleday, 1990).
[4]Drucker, "The Age of Social Transformation."

having to do with information technology), but that the need is now an economic imperative as well as a civic and cultural imperative. The revolution in information technology is heightening awareness that the skills many educators have long argued were needed for the survival of democracy are needed as well for the survival of the economy—such things as the ability to work in groups, to think critically, to discipline ideas with facts (data-based decision making), and to adopt purposeful and disciplined learning as a habit of life.

Critical thinking, which some now call a twenty-first-century skill, is not a new concept in education. Professors in schools and departments of education around the nation have long argued that critical thinking and the ability to work in a group to solve problems are essential to a democratic education. What is new today is that business leaders and editorial writers are now demanding that all students have such skills and intellectual habits whereas in the not-too-distant past, many business leaders and editors saw an emphasis on group work, problem solving, and critical thought as evidence of "soft pedagogy." Some even saw it as downright subversive. Today many business leaders as well as educators agree that the ability to work on and with knowledge is essential to making a living as well as to living well and to functioning effectively as citizens in a society that threatens to overwhelm everyone with information. In this age of easy access to information it is especially important that students understand that knowledge can lead one astray as well as serve as a source of useful guidance and understand as well that not all knowledge is equally valid. Indeed, one of the challenges to those who teach and lead schools is to help students as knowledge workers learn how to discern the differences between facts and opinions and learn how to discipline opinions and propositions with facts. More than that, they need to learn how to verify facts. In summary, schooling must help every citizen develop the skills, attitudes, and habits of mind necessary to make discerning judgments in a world awash with competing claims, all backed by reams of facts and data and each championed by some group or interest.

Getting students to work on and with knowledge is what schools are or should be about. Knowledge work is inherent in the nature of the schooling enterprise. The reason most schools have been successful with the elite and relatively unsuccessful with the vast majority of students is that only a few students were defined as knowledge workers. Most were defined as low-level bureaucratic workers, or what Susan Leddick described as "doers," by which she meant persons who are expected at most to become skilled in the use of a narrow range of intellectual skills and to master some specific content and skills.[5] Real knowledge work, which requires the worker to solve problems, create, think, reason, and critically evaluate, was reserved for the academic elite.

Engaging all students in knowledge work, rather than simply permitting the elite and the especially academically able among the nonelite, to pursue this type of work in school is no longer simply an educational ideal advanced by a few progressive professors and educators. Now, the ability to do knowledge work is an economic imperative as well as the means of achieving a civic ideal and a cultural imperative. Ironically, the economic imperative, properly framed, can be used to transform schools into the kinds of organizations that many educators have always thought they should be: places that prepare the young to thrive in a dynamic democracy where diversity is valued and creativity is expected.

Students as Customers and Volunteers

At the time Drucker developed the idea of the knowledge worker, few American leaders understood how the conditions of modern society were changing the power and authority relationships between workers and managers. Drucker described this new relationship in the following way:

> In the knowledge society the employees—that is, knowledge workers—own the tools of production. Marx's great insight was that the factory worker does not and cannot own the tools of production, and therefore is "alienated." There was no way, Marx pointed out, for the worker to own the steam engine and to be able to take it with him when moving from one job to another. The capitalist had to own the steam engine and to control it. Increasingly, the true investment in the knowledge society is not in machines and tools but in the knowledge of the knowledge worker. Without that knowledge the machines, no matter how advanced and sophisticated, are unproductive.[6]

The fact that knowledge workers, who are becoming the dominant force in American society, are emerging as the "owners" of the means of production confronts traditional management with the same sort of problem that the changing relationship between tradition-oriented teachers and students presents to educators. Knowledge workers in industry are no longer as dependent on their

[5]Susan Leddick "Educating the Knowledge Worker," *School Administrator,* Mar. 2001. http://www.aasa.org/publications/saarticledetail.cfm?ItemNumber=3832.
[6]Drucker, "The Age of Social Transformation."

employers as they were in the old industrial model, just as students are no longer as dependent on their teachers and their schools for their instruction or for their learning opportunities as students once were.

Increasingly, the only control teachers have over what students learn is the control that can be gained by designing tasks that are sufficiently engaging so that students volunteer their attention and commitment. It is only when students are committed to the work they are assigned or encouraged to undertake that they will seek to learn what they need for completing a task or doing work. They are no longer dependent on the school or their teachers as the exclusive providers of their instruction or as the primary determiners of what they will learn. The information society is replete with sources of instruction for whatever it is the school and teachers might inspire them to want to know and be able to do, and it is only through providing engaging work that students will be inspired to learn what they need to.

It is in this sense that students are volunteers: they can choose to invest or withhold their attention and commitment. The decisions they make will alter in fundamental ways the nature of the effort expended on the schoolwork provided. It is in this sense, therefore, that students are also in a customer relationship with the schools and their teachers.

It is up to students to decide how much the work the school is providing them is worth and therefore how much effort they will be willing to invest in it. The nature of the instructional options available to them will go far toward determining how schoolwork will fare in the competition with all of the other learning options students now have.

The image of the student as customer is not intended to be used as a means of defining the relationship between students and schools in commercial terms. Neither is this idea intended to provide the basis for an argument against compulsory education or for school choice. Rather, the intent is to convey the understanding that students are becoming increasingly independent of the traditional authority structures that once bound them to schools and that schools must be organized to take this fact into account.

Students are still compelled to attend school. And while they are in school, most will be sufficiently docile and will comply, however reluctantly, with the directives of adults. After all, adult authority still exists as a reality for most youngsters, and passive acceptance is more common than is rebellion.

However, passive acceptance does not produce profound learning. Although compliance and attendance can be commanded, attention and commitment must be earned. Moreover, student attention and commitment must be earned in the face of growing competition from the world of digital learning, direct marketing to the young, and the growing impact of peer group networking.

Guiding Assumptions

Properly conceived, the image of the student as a knowledge worker would incorporate, at a minimum, the following assumptions about students and learning in schools:

- Learning is an active process, and profound learning requires engaging tasks as well as engaged minds.
- Students learn by doing tasks that call on them to use their minds.

From the day they enter school, students should be viewed as members of the community of learners and will over time become members of learning communities as well. These learning communities will often transcend classroom boundaries and even school and community boundaries. Students will be part of a school community, but they will not be limited by their membership in any one school or any one learning community.

Much that is done with students will be framed in terms of induction problems. Therefore, the social systems of most relevance to defining the position and role of students are the knowledge development and transmission system and the induction system. The constraints of existing boundary systems and the power and authority relationships between students and schools will need to be restructured as well.

Moral involvement and intellectual engagement are at the heart of the relationship of teachers, students, and schools. Therefore, the rules, roles, and relationships that shape behavior in schools should be designed to be supportive of and encourage such a relationship. Key to such relationships are the ideas of volunteerism and moral commitment as contrasted with constraint, compulsion, punishment, and denial of rewards.

TRANSMITTING THE KNOWLEDGE WORK CULTURE

According to Drucker, "The education that is required [for] knowledge work can be acquired only through formal schooling. It cannot be acquired through apprenticeship."[7]

[7]Ibid.

Helping students learn how to learn while at the same time ensuring that they know enough about the fundamentals and the wisdom embedded in the culture is the challenge confronting schools. Mastery is no longer enough. Continuous learning is required not simply to earn a living but also to live a full life and to avoid being overwhelmed by the future.

Drucker has also observed that "the performance of the schools and the basic values of the schools will be of increasing concern to society as a whole, rather than being considered professional matters that can safely be left to 'educators.'"[8]

Schools were initially designed to promote values held by the community, but these values were largely parochial ones and tended to disparage rather than embrace knowledge that is critically held and carefully examined. As Willard Waller, a thoughtful sociologist from a bygone era, suggested in the past, schools served as museums of virtue in which educators took on the task of teaching the young to embrace ideals adults had left behind but were not yet fully ready to abandon.[9] Thus, even before the extreme bureaucratization of schooling, there was a tendency for schools to show a preference for superficial knowledge.

Over the past fifty years, schools have increasingly abandoned teaching any form of values other than the most secular of them. In doing this, they have for the most part abandoned their role in cultural transmission and in the induction of the young into the ways of that culture.

If schools are to be responsive to the needs of the knowledge work society and the demanding intellectual requirements of citizenship in an information-rich environment where facts are plentiful, raw, and unprocessed, and shared values increasingly in short supply, schools are going to need to rediscover their role in the transmission of culture. Today, however, the culture that must be transmitted is the *culture of knowledge work*. Moreover, the work of cultural transmission must be done in the context of a democracy struggling with increasing levels of complex information that is being transformed into knowledge by formal and informal networks of individuals rather than by the traditional institutions that once served these knowledge development and transmission functions.

It is important to understand that knowledge can lead one astray as well as serve as a source of useful guidance. Indeed, one of the challenges to those who teach

[8]Ibid.
[9]Willard Waller, *The Sociology of Teaching* (Hoboken, N.J.: Wiley, 1967), p. 34 (originally published in 1932).

and lead schools is to help students as knowledge workers learn how to discern the differences between facts and opinions and how to discipline opinions and propositions with facts. More than that, they need to learn how to verify facts. In summary, schooling must help every citizen develop the skills, attitudes, and habits of mind to make discerning judgments in a world awash with competing claims.

This means that schools must be much more attentive to inducting students into the norms and values of the knowledge work culture than they have been. They must become the place where all students learn how to learn and learn how to work on and with knowledge. Such learning can no longer be left to chance or reserved for those most likely to be employed in elite knowledge work jobs. In a time in which information technologies are the defining technologies of the epoch, every child must be inducted into the world of knowledge work, and schools are the one place where the need for such learning can be formally recognized and promoted. Without public schools, what most citizens will learn will be determined as much by luck and random chance as by design.

As leaders of learning organizations, educators need to once again assert their tradition-based authority as persons who are charged with the responsibility of inducting the young into the norms and values of the larger society. At the same time, they must help members of the local community understand that the society into which the young are being inducted is a knowledge work society; therefore the most important thing schools can do for the young is to help them on the way to growing continually in their ability to work on and with knowledge and knowledge-related products.

Teachers as Leaders, Designers, and Guides to Instruction

Over seventy years ago Willard Waller advanced the view that teachers are, by virtue of the positions they occupy in schools, leaders. Much has been written about this subject since. One of the unique problems teachers have in this role is that students typically have not yet fully developed their skills as followers. Indeed, helping the young become good followers without destroying their creativity and ability to lead is one of the most difficult tasks teachers confront.

In bureaucracies, it is assumed that good followers are docile and compliant. In learning organizations, it is assumed that leadership and followership are two sides of the same coin.[10]

[10]See, for example, Robert Kelley, "In Praise of Followers," *Harvard Business Review,* 1988, 6, 142–148.

If the mental model teachers have of themselves and others have of them includes the notion that they are leaders as well as designers, the implications for change in the content of teacher education programs and staff development programs might be quite dramatic. Although diagnostic skills, presentation skills, and substantive issues in the academic disciplines will continue to be of concern, these concerns will be subsumed under a more general heading of leadership development. In a school organized as a learning organization, the research and theory related to leadership will be an important part of the content of any staff development effort.

In learning organizations, the attention of teachers moves from planning to designing, a shift with dramatic implications. Rather than seeing themselves as instructors and viewing their primary tasks as planning and delivering instruction, teachers will see themselves as persons who design tasks that are so engaging that students *seek instruction*. Sometimes in their role as leaders, they will provide instruction, but more frequently they will direct the attention of students to other sources of instruction: sources on the Internet, videotaped lectures, books, articles, and so on. They will do this because they understand that there are many useful sources of instruction, some more powerful than the teacher acting alone. Thus, the idea of the teacher as a guide to instruction rather than as the instructor becomes important to a vision of schools based on the assumptions of learning organizations.

The role of the teacher as guide imposes on teachers the expectation that they will be able to make available to students the most effective and efficient means of instruction that can be found. Thus, teachers will need to know a great deal about alternative ways students might learn. They will also know how to assist students in accessing these alternative forms of instruction or be capable of creating or providing these by themselves.

Teachers will lead not only students but also parents and others in the community who might have an impact on students. They might, for example, explore with parents and other significant adults how new information technologies might be exploited to make the linkage among the home, the community, and the school increasingly supportive of the task of designing engaging educational experiences for students. They might take the lead in forming networks of teachers committed to collaborating to develop improved strategies for helping students learn especially difficult concepts.

In addition, teachers might develop networks among parents for mutual support. For example, in one case I observed, a teacher started using e-mail to inform parents about classroom matters, and soon parents beginning to converse among each other. Now parents are using e-mail as a means of checking perceptions, sharing concerns, seeking advice, and generally helping each other as members of a community organized around their children. Some of the issues the parents raise online cause discomfort among school officials, but there is nothing they talk about online that they would not talk about in the grocery store if they ever met there. Building a community among parents may in fact be as important as developing a stronger relationship between schools and parents. Community building among parents is, however, seldom at the forefront of thinking about the relationship between schools and parents.

In school districts where top-level leaders have committed themselves to transforming their schools into learning organizations, those who design and lead professional development are more likely to be teachers than central office staff in charge of staff development. The role of the central office staff becomes one of support to teachers who are taking the lead in professional development.

No single description will define the role of all teachers in any school operating as a learning organization. In fact, my experience with teachers who are trying to work as leaders, designers, and guides persuades me that the learning that occurs in defining these roles is part of the work teachers must do, and this work is continuous. Indeed, the struggles in constantly redefining one's role in schools can do much to enrich the intellectual life of teachers and bring joy back into teaching. One of the most exciting aspects of transforming schools into learning organizations is empowering teachers to learn what it might mean if they were challenged to be leaders and designers rather than skilled workers on an assembly line—or clinicians who are expected to administer prescribed lessons to students.

Parents as Partners

In many schools, the relationship between parents and teachers is undergirded with tension and the potential for conflict. Among other things, the jargon that researchers and federal and state bureaucrats have developed has become so pervasive that teachers often create barriers between themselves and parents by the language they use. *Schoolhouse* (a warm and inviting term) has been replaced by *school facility* (which has the feel of cold porcelain). Teachers are no longer simply teachers; they are *professional employees.* Students are no longer just students; they have become their own labels and categories, for example, *at-risk, free and reduced lunch, EMR, TMR,* and *LD.*

This is not to say that there are not warm and amicable relationships between and among parents and teachers and schools. They exist, however, largely in spite of the systems that have been created rather than because of them. Bureaucracies are designed to protect internal operations from outside influence, and in most schools parents are outsiders.

In a learning organization, parents would be insiders, or at least they would be invited to be insiders. As insiders, however, they must be prepared to participate in experiences designed to induct them into the life and culture of the school and to help them better understand the role of parent as partner in the school. Such involvement would need to go well beyond a PTA open house or even the typical parent education program. For example, some parents might conduct in-home study groups bringing together other parents and a few other citizens to study issues related to the education of their children and associated with transforming schools. Sometimes educators might participate in these groups and sometimes they might not, though they would always provide whatever support the group might need.

Parents would need to be inducted into their roles as partners in the formal education of their children, just as students, teachers, and other insiders would need to be inducted. It is likely that much of the work involved in such experiences would need to be conducted in virtual environments and make heavy use of the Internet and other electronic means of communication. Parents and teachers would need to have regular conversations, not simply attend meetings on such ritual occasions as PTA meetings and open houses. Electronic networking makes such conversations readily available without major inconvenience to the schedules of teachers or parents.

The goal would be to define the role of parent in the school in a way that interactions between parents and teachers would be routine, regular, and informal rather than sporadic and formalized. The intent would be to create a circumstance in which "parents and teachers could meet often enough and intimately enough to develop primary group attitudes toward each other, and if both parents and teachers might have their say unreservedly, such modifications in school practice and parental upbringing might take place and would revolutionize the life of children everywhere."[11]

[11]Waller, *Sociology of Teaching*, p. 69.

To treat parents as partners, educators need to come to understand that in their relationship with parents, their expertise lies more often in the questions they ask than in the advice they give. Their goal should be to understand the motives and talents of each student as well as they can be understood. To do this, they must ask questions of parents that help both themselves and the parent understand what the parent knows about the child. Parents and teachers would be joined together as learners—each learning about the child and in the process learning about each other as well.

Some parents will not be inclined to become so heavily involved in the life of their children or the life of the school, and some children will not have parents who can speak on their behalf. In such cases, the teacher, the school, and other school leaders will need to work to ensure that each child has at least one adult who is significant in their lives and who cares about his or her progress as a student—and who is positioned to make this caring known to the student and communicate it to the school. Sometimes a teacher can take this role, but custodians, cafeteria workers, school secretaries, and community volunteers can, if properly screened and oriented, play such a role as well.

The Principal as Leader of Leaders

There is a large and emerging body of literature on the role of leaders in learning organizations. Principals and those who would be principals are obliged to be aware of this literature and to learn from it. One way to do this is to participate in learning communities and communities of learners (collegial networks, for example) where such literature is reviewed and discussed.

As leaders of leaders, principals must learn how to provide direction as opposed to how to exercise control; they must learn to lead rather than simply manage. They must be clear about their own mental models and able to communicate these images to others in persuasive ways. In a learning organization, the principal would view teachers as leaders and would understand that much that is done by the principal has to do with ensuring that disciplined conversations take place regularly among staff. Especially important are conversations about progress and lack of progress in pursuit of an agreed direction.

The principal who is leading the transformation of a school from a bureaucracy to a learning organization must learn from observing learning organizations. This is not a simple or easy challenge. The following excerpt describing the operation of American-based Toyota plants, as contrasted with their more bureaucratic counterparts at General Motors and Ford, may provide some indication of the dimensions of the problem principals as leaders of leaders may confront:

> "People who join Toyota from other companies, it's a big shift for them," says John Shook, a faculty member at the University of Michigan, a former Toyota manufacturing employee and a widely regarded consultant on how to use Toyota's ideas at other companies. "They kind of don't get it for a while." They do what all American managers do—they keep trying to make their management objectives. "They're moving forward, they're improving, and they're looking for a plateau. As long as you're looking for that plateau, it seems like a constant struggle. It's difficult. If you're looking for a plateau, you're going to be frustrated. There is no 'solution.'"
>
> Even working at Toyota, you need that moment of Zen. "Once you realize that it's the process itself—that you're not seeking a plateau—you can relax. Doing the task and doing the task better become one and the same thing," Shook says. "This is what it means to come to work."[12]

As is the case with leadership at Toyota, in a school organized as a learning organization, the principal is no longer a supervisor in the traditional sense. Rather, the job of the principal is to seek and help others seek ways to more effectively create engaging work for students and ensure that staff members are engaged in their work as well.

It is up to the principal, as the occupant of the most visible moral office in the school, to ensure that the norms of the organization are clearly communicated and that new members of the organization (students, parents, teachers, and other staff) understand the meaning of those norms for the roles they occupy. The principal thus ensures that ongoing and continuous training and development opportunities are provided so that participants have the skills, attitudes, and knowledge needed to fulfill the requirements of those roles. This is no small shift, but without this shift in mental models, the effort to transform schools into learning organizations will go for naught.

[12]Charles Fishman, "No Satisfaction," *Fast Company,* Dec. 2006, p. 82.

Central Office Staff as Capacity Builders

Among the problems confronting those who would transform schools into learning organizations is helping central office staff understand the difference between their roles in service delivery organizations and their roles in learning organizations. Central office staff sometimes resist transformation because they confuse it with reforming factory model schools and turning them into another form of bureaucracy: the service delivery system. As discussed in Chapter Four, in a district designed to support schools organized as service delivery systems, the fate that confronts central office staff is not a happy one. In the learning organization, the central office plays a key role, but it is a role that is not yet well defined.

One of the most fundamental problems of contemporary schools is that most lack the capacity to provide continuing support for the systemic changes that must be sustained if individual schools are to be transformed into vital units in a learning organization. Building those capacities—to focus on the future, maintain direction, and act strategically—should become the primary focus of the central office staff in a learning organization. (See Chapter Ten for a more detailed description of these capacities.)

In a learning organization, it would be assumed that members of the central office staff are more concerned with supporting the action of building-level leaders than with controlling that action. This means that the central office should be subordinate to the staff of schools rather than superordinate. Among the ways such subordination might be symbolized is by using some central office positions as internship positions for persons who aspire to building-level leadership positions—for example, team leaders, assistant principals, and principals. In my view, a properly designed induction experience for principals would include an assignment in the central office. Here the future principal would be afforded the opportunity to see the world from a broader perspective than might be available if he or she were to simply climb the bureaucratic hierarchy within schools.

In the broadest sense of the word, central office staff would be what Ken Blanchard and many others have referred to as "servant leaders."[13] The key point is that servant leaders, regardless of the way the concept is defined, see their role as enabling and supporting others rather than controlling others or managing their works. In a learning organization, central office staff members come to understand that they gain influence by giving away power.

[13]See, for example, Ken Blanchard, *Servant Leader* (Nashville, Tenn.: Countryman, 2003).

The Superintendent as Moral and Intellectual Leader

Many years ago I wrote the following:

> There are two things I know about the office of superintendent. First, whatever moral authority resides in, or is bestowed upon, the school system, that authority resides in the office of the superintendent. Second, the superintendent can delegate to others nearly anything he or she wants to delegate (so long as the board consents) except the moral authority that resides in the office of the superintendent. In the long run, therefore, what the superintendent values, and the style of operation supported by the superintendent, will be manifest throughout the system.[14]

At the time I wrote this, I was not thinking specifically of the role of the superintendent in a learning organization, but today I would argue that that which is true of superintendents in general is even truer of the superintendent committed to transforming a school system into a learning organization. Unlike bureaucracies, learning organizations are held together by commitments to common beliefs, traditions, and values. The office of the superintendent embodies the moral authority represented by these beliefs, traditions, and values, and this authority cannot be delegated. If the superintendent does not exercise this authority, it will remain dormant, or largely so.

Whereas in a bureaucracy the superintendent is often cast as the chief problem solver, in a learning organization he or she is more likely to be expected to be the "chief troublemaker." Rather than mandating solutions to persistent problems, the superintendent in a learning organization must learn to reframe these problems so that they present new opportunities for inventiveness on the part of others and then invite others to design the innovations these opportunities make available.

Designing systems rather than planning programs and courses of action must dominate the thinking of the superintendent. Rather than trying to control events, superintendents must become adept at giving direction to action that is largely outside their own control and that can only be controlled by others.

[14]Phillip C. Schlechty, *Schools for the 21st Century: Leadership Imperatives for Educational Reform* (San Francisco: Jossey-Bass, 1990).

School Boards as Community Leaders

It may be that one of the reasons it is so difficult to transform schools from bureaucracies to learning organizations is that the tenure of superintendents is often too short for the occupant of the position to put his or her stamp on the office. What little legacy a given superintendent leaves behind is likely to be contravened by a new superintendent with a new vision and a different mental model. Indeed, if the board of education and the superintendent are not allied in the most fundamental ways, the disruption caused by transformation is likely to hasten the departure of a superintendent who is serious about transformation.

Therefore, the school board, more than any other element in the school district, is positioned to ensure that direction is maintained even in the face of the turbulence associated with true transformation. This is why it is so important that the role of boards of education be transformed. Indeed, this may well be the key to transforming schools into learning organizations.

Currently, the mental model on which many school boards are based is a quasi-legislative model. It assumes that policymaking is equivalent to law making and that the job of the board's members is to represent the interests of their constituencies in the legislative process. In addition, like legislators at the state and federal levels, they are expected to provide oversight to ensure the executive branch is carrying out the intent of the legislature. The ways in which these assumptions are manifest vary, depending on the larger mental models that shape understandings of the school system more generally. In some instances, school boards may behave like boards of directors of corporations, and at other times, they may behave like owners of the corporation or as appointed overseers and guardians of the public trust.

The role of the board of education in a learning organization would be quite different from that which would be expected of a legislative group. Rather than simply representing the community, they would lead the community. Rather than simply reflecting public sentiment, they would endeavor to inform and shape that sentiment in ways that would fasten attention on the common good as opposed to the needs and interests of special interest groups.

School board members as a collective body would see themselves as the most vital component of the directional system of the school district. Furthermore, they would understand the difference between establishing direction (which involves strategic thinking) and creating goals (which involves strategic planning and action plans). Only the board of education, working in cooperation with the superintendent, is in a position to assert a new direction for the school district and to persuade the community that this direction is needed and desirable. Only the school board is in a position, once the new direction has been established, to ensure that an executive succession plan is in place that ensures that once a vision has been established, those who are employed as superintendent will be willing to embrace that vision rather than substitute another one in its place.

Though much is made of the need for visionary leaders, I am persuaded that there is even a greater need for leaders who have sufficient ego control to lead by visions created by others. All great leaders lead by vision, but only a few leaders are truly visionary. If a vision is established and the district is moving in the direction the community wants it to go, the last thing that is needed is yet another vision or another visionary leader. What is needed is a person who can grasp the vision in place, embrace it, and move the organization forward on the basis of the established direction.

In carrying out their function as community builders, one of the most important tasks of school boards in a learning organization is to find ways to involve the diverse constituencies in the community in continuous conversations and dialogue about the schools and the purposes schools should serve in the community, thereby continuously refining the vision that drives the schools. The most important conversation is the one about what students should know and be able to do as a result of their experiences in school. This conversation is most likely to build a community around the schools while at the same time informing the school board about how the community can best be served.

Such conversations cannot take place if they are treated as hearings or even as advisory sessions. They must be sincere conversations, more in the fashion of focus groups and seminars than in the fashion of advisory groups and committees. Again, the imaginative use of electronic networking could do much to facilitate such community-building efforts, and such networks should surely be built and maintained.

THE SCHOOL AS A SMALL COMMUNITY OR A FAMILY

Recognizing just how unsatisfactory bureaucracy and bureaucratically imposed solutions are in education, some educators have tried to create alternative models based on notions of the school as a small community or the school as a family. There is in fact a long tradition of experimentation with such models, especially among educators who have been influenced by John Dewey.

Such models have considerable appeal, especially to constructivist educators. (Constructivists generally place students rather than teachers at the center of the educative process. They believe that more is to be gained by helping students discover knowledge and construct new understandings than by directly transmitting information from adult to child.) Certainly the image of the school as a family or a community is more appealing than the image of the impersonal bureaucracy. Unfortunately, the conditions of the modern world and the demands of mass education in a democratic society do not fit well with the idea that schools can function as either families or small communities. Consider the following points:

- The smallness and intimacy of the family and the relatively permanent presence of specific adult members are conditions that are difficult, if not impossible, to meet in a world in which the money available to support education is limited and geographical mobility is high.

- Families and communities promulgate particularistic values. The tacit understandings on which families and small communities are based are inherently parochial and specific. To base schools on the model of the family or the small community is to trade the weaknesses of depersonalization for the weaknesses of social and cultural narrowness and the particularistic values that such arrangements rightly encourage and support.

- Democracy depends on the transmission of universal values such as tolerance for political and religious differences. It is the mix of particularistic values in the context of the universal values of democracy that gives a pluralistic democracy its vitality and meaning. Family values and local community are parts of the mix of a democratic education, but they cannot be used to totally define that education. The education of children in a democratic community is not only the concern of parents; it is the concern of the larger society as well.[15]

[15]I do not equate the word *public* with the word *government*. Until the last half of the twentieth century, the idea that the government, especially the central government, had any role in the education of children was alien to the thinking of most Americans. Even state governments were less than aggressive in intervening in the education of children. Since the days of Horace Mann there has been a fear that too much government intervention in schools would transform the schools into state schools rather than locally controlled schools. Americans have historically prided themselves on the fact that their schools were sufficiently independent of government control that they could not be used as a propaganda arm of the state. That the schools of America were never really immune from being used for propaganda purposes cannot be disputed, but neither can it be disputed that Americans value schools that are independent of government influence.

- Leadership in families and small communities is a nuanced matter and not subject to inspection except by those who have intimate and detailed knowledge of the particular situation. Public education, however, necessarily includes the interests of many who have no direct involvement in the life of the school or its participants—nonparent taxpayers, business interests, politicians at the state and national levels, and so on. As formal organizations fulfilling civic functions, the participation of these external groups is a legitimate exercise in democracy.[16]

Bureaucracy and Community: Strange Bedfellows

Those who believe the family and the community—especially the democratic community—are more appropriate models for schooling than are models derived from rational bureaucracies implicitly rest much of their case on the fact that the elements of family and community life are more akin to the purpose of democratic education than are bureaucracies. Bureaucracies, after all, place value on obedience and conformance rather than independent thought. Moreover, in a bureaucracy, creativity is always problematic; therefore it is not encouraged and is sometimes suppressed.

Clearly the impersonal assumptions of bureaucracy are at odds with the personalized assumptions of family and community life. In the family or the small community, for example, the child who falls behind his or her siblings is not "held back." More likely, every member of the family will seek ways to help the lagging child get ahead. In a bureaucracy, where efficiency is a primary goal and ensuring uniformity of response is a central concern, children who fall behind are either segregated from those who are moving ahead or reprocessed in the hope that one more time through the same process will fix them up.

---

[16]It is more than coincidental that parochial schools resist interference from the state and that one of the demands of some parent groups who seek charter status is freedom from monitoring of curriculum matters by the state. Public accountability, which is essential to democratically controlled education, is inherently invasive of the boundaries of family and community life. This is one of the reasons that Americans have traditionally placed so much value on local control of schools and on the rights of families to privacy, even when some family practices seem to others to be abhorrent. Until relatively recently, governmental agencies only infringed on the rights of local communities and of families when it was clear that universal values were being violated—for example, values like equality and fairness, the right of the young to live without fear of abuse, and so on. Furthermore, these invasions were almost always under the supervision and direction of the courts rather than legislative bodies.

So long as schools are organized on bureaucratic principles, any effort to install programs that reflect these more expressive values is almost certain to be expelled or crushed in the long run. For example, the idea of looping, whereby a single teacher stays with a group of students over a long period of time (two to four years) is an effort to incorporate the idea of permanence into the relationship between student and teacher. Looping is almost certain to run into difficulty with bureaucratic rules related to teacher certification, especially in the higher grades. Similarly, abolishing social promotion and installing high-stakes testing, efforts to apply the principles of rational bureaucracy to schools, require teachers to depersonalize their relationships with students in order to ensure "truth in labeling," perhaps at the expense of the moral development of the child.

It remains the case, however, that many policymakers are convinced that the only sure way to improve America's schools is to use the blunt instruments of bureaucracy to make standards clear and then to uphold those standards by punitive measures. Many of these same policymakers see the notion of the school as a small community as an attractive idea. It is perhaps this kind of thinking that leads to the somewhat schizophrenic approach to school reform that mandates simultaneously the further bureaucratization of most public schools combined with the creation of charter schools designed to relieve some public schools from the burdens of bureaucratic regulation.

The Family-Like Qualities of Learning Organizations

Like those who would use the family or the small community as a model for schooling, I believe that bureaucratically organized schools cannot and do not deal adequately with the expressive ends of education. But some type of formal organization is called for if the intention of providing high-quality education to all children is to be realized and the values of democracy are to be preserved. Local communities cannot afford either socially or economically to have a system of schools. They must have a school system for the good of both children and the community at large. (I have more to say about the community-building functions of education in Chapter Thirteen.)

The task that confronts educators is to imagine a formal organization that can meet the conditions necessary to uphold the universal values of democracy. At the same time, this organization must provide a form of education responsive to the needs for personalization, spontaneity, and imagination; it must also be responsive to the moral sentiments of parents and the larger community.

This can be done, but only if educators are willing to embrace a totally new paradigm for thinking about schools: that the school is, or should be, a learning organization.

Because learning organizations are formal organizations, they differ from families in many ways, and thus have other functions. For example, learning organizations are purposeful and are established in part to achieve instrumental ends. Thus, they have within themselves the capacity to embrace universal values and pursue ends that transcend the peculiar interests of local constituencies—local interests that may or may not be congruent with larger societal goals. Unlike bureaucracies, however, and more like families, learning organizations embrace expressive ends, and they embrace expressive functions rather than endeavor to suppress or control them. Discussions of moral intentions and aesthetic values are considered at least as important as are discussions of technical norms and instrumental values. Human variability is prized and nurtured rather than suppressed and thwarted.

In learning organizations, as in families and small communities, conversation, dialogue, modeling, and persuasive discourse are the tools by which rules are conveyed, understandings arrived at, and meanings shared. Likewise, informal group sanctions and self-control are the primary means of social control. Indeed, as centers of community conversation, schools organized as learning organizations might be used to build communities as well as serve them.

Schools organized as learning organizations will never have the intimacy of a family, but this should not be expected of any organization. Still, they can come closer to honoring the dignity and worth of each child and each employee more fully than can a school organized as a bureaucracy—and that, after all, is (or should be) a core value in the education of citizens in a democracy.

CRITICAL STEPS TO TRANSFORMATION

The rules, roles, and relationships that govern behavior in a learning organization differ substantially from those that exist in bureaucracies, regardless of the specific form a bureaucracy might take. Learning organizations are driven by shared beliefs, values, and commitments. Bureaucracies are driven by rules.

Learning organizations are flexible and responsive; bureaucracies are brittle and nonresponsive. In learning organizations, innovation is a continuous and disciplined occurrence. In bureaucracies, innovations, especially major innovations, are disruptive events, more to be managed and domesticated than to be exploited and embraced. Leaders in bureaucracies strive to cope with the future and somehow survive it. Leaders in learning organizations look to the future for opportunities to seize. If schools are to be transformed from bureaucracies into learning organizations, there are three critical initial moves that leaders must make.

First, they must become convinced that the superordinate goal of schooling is to provide students with engaging tasks that result in their learning those things of most value to themselves, their parents, and the larger society. Acting on this conviction will require considerable effort and present some risks. Such a goal will, however, help to ensure that learning has a central place in the directional system of the school and that the attention of every person in the organization will be fastened on those things that make a difference in what students learn and over which teachers and other school leaders can have control.

Second, leaders must ensure that they are clear about the core business of the school and must be willing to use this understanding to shape the direction of all activity in the schools and the school district. The language used to communicate the nature of the core business will likely vary from school district to school district. Nevertheless, the language must fasten attention on the fact that the most important thing schools do is design engaging work for students—work that calls on them to complete intellectually demanding tasks—and lead students in the successful completion of these tasks so that they learn.

Finally, leaders must give, and encourage others to give, a great deal of attention to defining the position and role of students. I have found that for transformation of schools to occur, teachers must fully understand and embrace the idea that they must redefine the role of student. And they must do so in ways that acknowledge both the changes that are occurring in the authority relationship between teachers and students and the changes in the role that traditional institutions play in their lives.

Teachers cannot be leaders until they understand that students are no longer obligated to follow them. Principals cannot be leaders of leaders until they acknowledge and support the fact that teachers are leaders and therefore are empowered to lead. These role changes must occur in the larger context of the operation of the school district in which schools are embedded and the context of the relationship between the school district and the community the schools are intended to serve.

In the end, transformation begins with leaders who are passionately committed to the idea that the core business of schools is to ensure that students are provided engaging, intellectually challenging experiences in school. It also requires teachers who have the imagination and courage to recast the role of students in schools so that all students are encouraged to join a community where they learn to turn information into knowledge and where working on and with knowledge is a central activity of community life.

PART TWO

Getting Our Bearings

The Sociopolitical Landscape

The Bureaucratic Impulse

America's schools are being transformed, but the transformation is not the one for which I have been arguing. Rather, the public schools of America are being transformed from the community institutions they once were into government agencies. If schools are ever to become learning organizations, they must once again be deeply embedded in the communities they serve—so deeply embedded that the boundaries between what is school and what is community are quite blurred.

To make this happen, those who lead the effort to transform schools must understand how and why schools are being transformed into government agencies, for it is only with such understanding that they will be able to design strategies to counter this trend. This chapter addresses some of the issues that are central to such understanding.

HISTORIC ROOTS

The transformation of schools into government agencies started long ago and was for the most part initiated by reform-minded educators who believed that the services of schools needed to be standardized and that the governmental bureaucracy provided the best available means for ensuring standardization.

143

Cuban and Tyack, authors of an award-winning history of school reform in America, put the matter this way:

> Prodded by professional organizations like the NEA [National Education Association], state legislatures increasingly standardized schools across the nation according to the model of a modern school proposed by the policy elite. To carry out their new regulatory roles, state departments of education increased enormously during the twentieth century. In 1890 there was, on average, one staff member in state departments of education for every 100,000 pupils; in 1974 there was one for about every 2,000. Regulations ballooned.[1]

Up through the 1950s, the federal government was generally excluded from direct involvement in the public schools. Indeed, even indirect federal involvement in the public schools was likely to meet strong resistance. Stewart McClure, a long-time proponent of federal aid to public schools and chief clerk of the Senate Committee on Labor, Education, and Public Welfare from 1949 to 1973, noted that many members of Congress would, when confronted with the prospect of federal intervention in local schools,

> get white and scream and wave their hands in the air about the horrible prospects of this vicious, cold hand of federal bureaucracy being laid upon these pristine, splendid local schools that knew better than anyone what needed to be done, and so forth and so forth.
>
> The last thing that could happen in the United States was for the federal hand to be laid on local education, which belongs to the hands of the school boards and local council of education or whatever they're called—which, of course, are all controlled by the Chamber of Commerce.[2]

Defenders of local control of schools, especially political conservatives, were adamant about the fact that the Tenth Amendment to the U.S. Constitution expressly prohibits federal intervention in many local matters, and chief among

[1]David Tyack and Larry Cuban, *Tinkering Toward Utopia: A Century of Public School Reform* (Cambridge, Mass.: Harvard University Press, 1995), p. 19.
[2]Stewart E. McClure, Oral History Interviews, Senate Historical Office, Washington, D.C., Jan. 1983, pp.110–111.

these protected matters was the education of the young. Up through the 1950s, this constitutional defense was largely successful. Then things began to change.

The Erosion of the Tenth Amendment

The use of outside threats to bring about school reform has a long history in American life. Indeed, America's first schools were established to confront an outside threat—what the Puritans referred to as "that old deluder Satan." In the mid-1950s the Soviet Union provided an outside threat that broke, perhaps for all time, America's attachment to the Tenth Amendment as applied to public education.

Through the mid-1950s, most Americans were satisfied that America was a world leader in nearly every area of life. This view was suddenly disrupted when the Soviet Union launched the first earth-orbiting satellite. Fear was palpable throughout America. We were behind the Russians in the space race, and something had to be done about it immediately. Attention turned to the public schools.

Those who had long sought to involve the federal government in the life of public schools found the opportunity provided by *Sputnik* irresistible. Another quotation from Stewart McClure illustrates this point:

> If there was one thing I ever did in my work on the Hill, my work for my whole career, it was to focus Lister Hill's [senator from Alabama] attention on the opportunity which *Sputnik*, this Russian satellite, gave all of us who were struggling, and had been for decades, to establish a federal program of monetary aid to public education, and private, too, in some instances. And I'm really very proud of that.[3]

Furthermore, those who showed reluctance to jump on the bandwagon for federal intervention were subjected to such politically forceful arguments that only a few could resist. McClure said,

> We got the cream of the brains of this country, so that when we went on the floor we could say, "Well, now, does the senator mean that he challenges the distinguished leader of the National Council on Science, Detlev Bronk, who says . . ." We hammered them into the ground. And, of course, if anybody brought up socialism or something like that, the dreadful specter of socialism, we had Edward Teller and the Hydrogen Bomb to clobber them with![4]

[3]Ibid., p. 113.
[4]Ibid., p. 116.

One of the first fruits of this newly found willingness to involve the federal government in public schools was the 1958 National Defense Education Act (NDEA), which did much to legitimize the right of the federal government to provide direct aid to public education. The NDEA became a significant initial thrust for repositioning schools from community institutions concerned primarily with expressive matters (that is, matters of culture, taste, sentiments, civic virtue, and attitudes) to organizations concerned with instrumental matters (that is, skills and competencies that are seen to have implications for the world of work and the utilitarian needs of the government).

Prior to *Sputnik,* debates about curriculum were less likely to be about the need for more math and science than they were to be about dropping Greek from the curriculum and replacing it with modern languages, or whether interdisciplinary social studies should be permitted to replace the study of history. After *Sputnik,* curriculum debates had to do with the nation's need for more engineers and scientists and with the failure of the public schools' curriculum to serve this national interest. The instrumental concerns of the nation began to gain the upper hand over the expressive concerns of communities and the culture more generally. (There were, of course, those who continued to be concerned about matters of culture and values, but their voices were relatively silent compared to the more strident voices concerned about national defense.)

Those who used national defense as a stalking horse for greater federal intervention in schools were not unaware of the danger of what they were doing. McClure, for example, said, "I invented that God-awful title: the National Defense Education Act. If there are any words less compatible, really, intellectually, in terms of what is the purpose of education—it's not to defend the country; it's to defend the mind and develop the human spirit, not to build cannons and battleships. It was a horrible title, but it worked. It worked."[5]

The Advent of Title I

A second landmark in the transformation of America's schools was the Elementary and Secondary Education Act (ESEA) of 1965. Those who authored the NDEA had taken great care to avoid involving the federal government in setting

[5]Ibid., p. 117.

standards for local schools or in any other way interfering with state control of schools. Not so with the ESEA.

In pursuit of the New Deal agenda, Congress had already established that the so-called spending clause of the U.S. Constitution could be used to bypass the prohibitions of the Tenth Amendment. Ann McColl, an expert in school law, notes, "The spending clause is unique in that it allows Congress to enact legislation in areas over which it otherwise has no authority, *if* the legislation is in the form of an offer of a contract—i.e., if federal funds are offered to states to meet certain conditions."[6]

Until 1965, the spending clause had not been systematically applied to education. The feeling that funds provided under NDEA had not always been well spent, concerns about civil rights, and increased concern about special education issues and poverty more generally served to increase congressional willingness to use the spending clause with regard to schools. This is especially evident in Title I of ESEA and the many reauthorizations that have occurred since 1965. The current No Child Left Behind legislation is, in fact, simply a culmination of the series of initiatives that have moved the federal government from a position of noninvolvement to a position where the U.S. Department of Education is viewed as one of the most influential policy agencies in the nation, surpassed only by the U.S. Congress.[7]

The result is that today, few legislators or members of the policy community who advise them seem to fear the prospect of federal control of local schools. Even those who are critical of NCLB tend to center their criticisms on technical requirements of the law and the regulations growing out of the law, for example, the kinds of evaluations the law encourages. Others are concerned about a perceived lack of adequate funding, and some worry about the inability of state agencies to administer some of the more demanding aspects of the law or the lack of realistic time lines set for the standards to be applied. Few, however, challenge the idea that the federal government has any business setting, de facto, standards for schools. Indeed, there are many, including some conservatives, who argue for a national curriculum supported by national assessments.

[6]Ann McColl, "Tough Call: Is No Child Left Behind Constitutional?" *Phi Delta Kappan,* Apr. 2005, p. 605.
[7]See Christopher B. Swanson and Janelle Barlage, *Influence: A Study of the Factors Shaping Education Policy* (Bethesda, Md.: Editorial Projects in Education Research Center, Dec. 2006).

FROM COMMUNITY INSTITUTIONS TO GOVERNMENT AGENCIES

The impulse toward bureaucratizing schools is not a grassroots impulse. It comes from the top down, and from far away. Prior to the 1950s, it came from urban superintendents, state education agencies, and some college deans. Today federal intervention in local affairs is advocated even by the National Chamber of Commerce, which once found the idea of federal aid to education distressing.

Even the general public is coming to accept the fact that the most important decisions to be made about schools and schooling—that is, decisions regarding what children should know and be able to do as a result of their school experiences—are more properly made at the state and federal levels than by local boards of education. For example, each September, the *Phi Delta Kappan,* a publication of a national education fraternity, in cooperation with the Gallup polling organization, publishes the results of a comprehensive survey of public attitudes toward schools. There are always items on the survey regarding attitudes toward local school boards and the role of the state and federal government relative to the governance of schools. One of the most persistent findings of the poll has been the strength of the belief most Americans have that local communities, rather than the state and federal government, should control the schools.

This belief has been eroding over the past few years to the point that the 2007 survey indicated that the majority of respondents felt that either the state or the federal government should be the primary decision makers regarding what students should know and be able to do.[8] This was the first time in the history of the poll that a majority had responded in this way.

There has also been a change in the feelings Americans have regarding whether they have any real attachment to or ability to influence what happens in their schools in any significant way. In many communities, in fact, local school boards are perceived as part of a government apparatus that stands between the public and the schools.[9] Given this fact, citizens find themselves choosing where bureaucratic authority should be located rather than choosing the type of organizational structure that changes the way authority is exercised.

[8]See Lowell C. Rose and Alec M. Gallup, "The 39th Annual Phi Delta Kappa/Gallup Poll of the Public's Attitudes Toward the Public Schools," *Phi Delta Kappan,* Sept. 2007, pp. 33–45.
[9]See, for example, David Mathews, *Reclaiming Public Education by Reclaiming Our Democracy* (Dayton, Ohio: Kettering Foundation Press, 2006).

In the recent debate over the reauthorization of the No Child Left Behind legislation, only a few legislators even suggested that the federal government has no business regulating the operation of local schools. Even the objection of the National Education Association (NEA) to NCLB has more to do with the fact that it perceives the legislation to be underfunded than with the fact that the assumptions on which the legislation is based are flawed.[10] Clearly, federal government control of local schools is acceptable to the NEA so long as that control is exercised in ways that serve the interests of this particular professional group. It is becoming increasingly apparent that many nationally oriented (as contrasted with local community oriented) interest groups, including the NEA, the Chamber of Commerce, and other business-related groups feel they can exercise more control over the schools if control is centralized in Washington, D.C., or state capitals. Thus, the centralization of control of schools serves clear interests, though those interests may or may not have anything in common with the interests of parents, local communities, or the children.

The Mind-Set of American Business Leaders

Despite the increasing importance of knowledge work and knowledge workers in American business, many business leaders continue to operate and think from a bureaucratic, rational systems framework, especially when offering advice to educators on the way schools should be run. When business leaders give policymakers advice regarding school reform issues, the advice likely involves the need to centralize power, especially evaluative power, while delegating operational authority to the lowest level possible.

In addition, business leaders are likely to suggest the need for significant changes in schools' evaluation and reward systems. These suggestions often include the idea that standards should be specified centrally and that evaluation measures should be refined and made more efficient, with the results of the evaluations being more clearly associated with externally enforced outside inspections. The involvement of business leaders in school reform efforts often results in a recommendation for some form of merit pay based on rationalized performance standards that are clearly measurable by some objective means.

[10]See, for example, Joel Packer, "The NEA Supports Substantial Overhaul, Not Repeal of NCLB," *Phi Delta Kappan*, Dec. 2007, pp. 265–269.

Such recommendations are certainly consistent with bureaucratic assumptions—assumptions that include the perception that for the most part, employees are more likely to be motivated by rewards extrinsic to their work than rewards inherent in the work. They are not, however, consistent with growing understandings of what it takes to gain from knowledge workers (and teachers are knowledge workers) the commitments to shared standards of excellence that are required to produce high-quality performance in all aspects of organizational life.[11]

Jim Collins cautions leaders in the public sector to be extremely careful with regard to the business leaders from whom they take advice. Many of them are not doing so well themselves, and many of the problems they have arise from the mental models they hold regarding the way their enterprises should be led. Transformation is not the same as reform, in either business or schools—and what both need today is transformation. Collins has observed:

> We must reject the idea—well-intentioned, but dead wrong—that the primary path to greatness in the social sectors is to become "more like a business." Most businesses—like most everything else in life—fall somewhere between mediocre and good. When you compare good companies with great ones, many widely practiced business norms turn out to correlate with mediocrity, not greatness. So, then, why would we want to import the practices of mediocrity into the social sectors?[12]

The Rise of the Bureaucratic Ethos

In his classic book *The Sociological Imagination*, C. Wright Mills described what he referred to as the "bureaucratic ethos."[13] His essential point was that the social

---

[11]The quality of education provided by schools, regardless of its deficiencies, has produced a new type of worker: one who will not respond to the management styles that once brought about sufficient compliance that men and women became de facto extensions of the machines to which they were attached. Workers today want meaning in their work, even if the tasks in which they are engaged are tedious, small scale, and repetitive. Companies like Toyota that employ many American workers seem to understand this fact, whereas many American manufacturers often seem less attuned to it.

[12]Jim Collins, *Good to Great and the Social Sectors: A Monograph to Accompany Good to Great* (Boulder, Colo.: Jim Collins, 2005).

[13]C. Wright Mills, *The Sociological Imagination* (New York: Oxford University Press, 1959), esp. Chaps. 4 and 5.

sciences are being used increasingly to serve the ends of established bureaucracies: the military, large corporations, and government agencies generally. Mills's concern in the late 1950s was that social scientists were on their way to being co-opted by the bureaucratic forces they sought to serve, thereby limiting the imagination with which they approached their work. There are many parallels between what Mills saw in the social sciences in the 1950s and developments in the field of education since that time.

Partly in response to the feelings of urgency created by the launching of *Sputnik,* partly in response to the rise in the special education industry, partly in response to the pressures desegregation brought to public education, and partly because private bureaucratically managed and organized foundations like the Ford Foundation invested heavily in research and development projects aimed at describing and analyzing schooling in order to improve it, an entirely new class of "academics" developed in American education. Mills called such persons "managers of the mind," "intellectual administrators," and "academic statesmen." Unlike traditional scholars—to whom Mills referred as "intellectual craftsmen"—these new academics develop their reputations not by the research they conduct but by the grants they receive, the committee appointments they are offered, the consultancies they engage in, and the size of the staff they direct and command.

In the 1960s and 1970s, such persons were, by and large, former faculty members at major research universities. Usually they had established reputations as scholars prior to assuming their new roles in the policy world. Sometimes they were former superintendents of large urban schools.

Today, increasing numbers of this growing cadre of intellectual bureaucrats are persons whose only experience in the academy is the experience they had as graduate students studying such subjects as policy analysis. Fewer and fewer have had academic appointments other than as graduate assistants, and those who do get such appointments are more likely to work within the structure center or institute that is only loosely affiliated with the university than they are to work in more traditional academic departments organized around such disciplines as economics, sociology, anthropology, psychology, political science, or history. Moreover, these new types of academic are often appointed to a university position only after their ascendance in the status pecking order of the policy arena. Rather than using their academic expertise to gain access to the right to advise others, they use their acceptance as advisors as a means of gaining access to the status that faculty rank can afford. They are too often generalists who specialize in offering advice about education policy.

Indeed, it seems to be increasingly the case that the career path of this emerging elite leads directly from a graduate assistantship in a research institution to an entry-level position in a foundation, a state education agency, or some other organization where the primary product is advice to policymakers, presented in the form of position papers, commission reports, and so on. Their experience in the real world of academic scholarship or public schools is often very limited, if it exists at all. Moreover, few members of this group have ever had to implement policies of the type they are foisting onto others.

Because of what is expected of them, members of this new policy elite are more likely to nurture professional relationships with private and public power figures well above the level of the local schoolhouse and the office of the local superintendent than they are to spend a great deal of time with those who work in the schools on a daily basis. Over time they seem more comfortable in corporate boardrooms than in classrooms and the principal's office, and they take their status from approval by those they advise rather than from the respect of those whose lives their advice most directly affects.

If the members of this new elite are not themselves employed by foundations, government agencies, legislative staffs, quasi-government agencies, or lobbying groups, it is likely that these organizations and agencies will be primary clients of those who do employ them. Therefore, the skills this elite is most likely to develop are less likely to have to do with scholarship than with salesmanship, marketing, and persuasion. Planning and producing what they call "deliverables" in accordance with arbitrarily prescribed time lines are their priority concerns. Managing budgets often takes precedence over the pursuit of ideas and the disciplining of ideas with facts. A record of scholarship is less important than a record as a consultant, advisor, and a procurer of grants and contracts.

Because this is so, these rising elites tend to frame their problems as bureaucrats frame them, and they assume others think and work as they do. Indeed, they do not know or understand any other style of work or any other discipline than that of bureaucracies. They are driven not by ideas but by agendas. They are motivated not by questions and uncertainties but by answers and certainties. They do not seek to reframe issues and develop new insights. Rather they seek to solve problems as these problems are presented to them by their clients.

THE CONSEQUENCES OF BUREAUCRATIZATION

Over time, these policy elites have formed networks, cliques, and sometimes even professional associations. (More often they seek to dominate the agendas of existing professional organizations.) In addition, their institutes and centers function as training grounds for the people who staff many of the emerging positions in the growing federal and state bureaucracies, as well as administrative positions in the foundation world. Some are also employed as directors of research and development in public schools, especially in large urban schools and in the offices of the newly consolidated county school districts that have been developing around the nation.

Because the agencies that provided funding are themselves embedded in bureaucracies, the grants use bureaucratic terms and bureaucratic language. And so the language of bureaucracies has come to confuse even further the already jargon-ladened language of educators, further encouraging teachers and school administrators to use language in ways that exclude participation from any but the initiated.

It should come as no surprise that this bureaucratic language has become a part of the language of teachers and administrators. Those who teach the teachers, especially in schools and departments of education, are likely to have mastered the language as a necessary part of their induction into the role of research assistants and grant writers. Thus, teachers learn to speak about "IEPs (Individualized Education Programs), at-risk youth, and 'brain-compatible learning.'" (I have always been curious to learn about the nature of brain-*incompatible* learning, but to date no one has been able to give me an example.)

School buildings are no longer schoolhouses; they are "facilities." Those who teach in these "facilities" are no longer teachers; they are "employees." Principals have become "supervisory personnel" and central office staff a part of the "management team." Parents and other members of the community have become "stakeholders."

Bureaucratic language has become such a hindrance to communication between parents and teachers that some university-based institutes have taken it on themselves to develop special training programs for parents so that they too can "speak the language." This is an especially common practice in special education—leaving one to wonder why so few think of trying to speak to parents in language they can understand without special training.

The bureaucratization of educational thought and the rise of policy elites has had many additional consequences[14] Among the more obvious are the following:

- They have created a cluster of academic bureaucrats who have a vested interest in moving the control of educational policy from local communities—and sometimes even from the state—to the federal level, for this is the arena in which they prefer to operate. Academic statesmen and intellectual managers have much more to gain from alliances with the powerful in Washington, D.C., and in the statehouse than they do from alliances with local educators, whose only source of repute is in the local community. Academic statesmen and intellectual bureaucrats thrive on national repute. Local reputations have little meaning or significance to them.

- This new breed of bureaucrat has formed or is forming into cliques and schools of thought, and each school is vying for the attention of shakers and movers. Political ideology is becoming a primary determinant of whose advice will be taken and who will be asked for advice. Those who advised the Clinton administration are not the same groups that advised the Bush administration or will advise the Obama administration. Regardless of ideology, however, almost all of the policy elite are persuaded that local communities no longer deserve to have the level of autonomy that local school districts enjoyed prior to 1950, and increasing numbers of these persons are also doubtful about the extent to which states should be autonomous with regard to schooling.

- There is a growing chasm between local educational practitioners who are called on to implement policy and the policy elite who are primarily interested in creating policy. It may be true, as Thomas "Tip" O'Neill, former Speaker of the House of Representatives, said, that "all politics is local," but when it comes to education policy, it seems increasingly the case that all policy is national, including policies administered by the states.

---

[14]I know of no systematic study of the issues raised here, but I am convinced it is a study worthy of pursuit. Unfortunately, those most likely to be equipped to conduct such a study and those with the resources to fund such a study may not find it in their personal interest to do so, and those who do find it in their interest would be likely to so slant their study that only those who are ideological soul mates with the researchers would believe the results.

- In a recent study of who influences educational policy, not a single local leader was mentioned—no teacher leaders, no school board members, and not a single superintendent.[15] Moreover, only the American Federation of Teachers and the NEA were noted among all the professional organizations that might have been mentioned, and these two organizations were well down the list of influential organizations. The result is that not only are local citizens increasingly estranged from their schools, but also so are those who teach in those schools and try to lead within the bureaucratic context in which they must work. Even more distressing is that many of these local leaders and local teachers feel helpless to do anything about their plight. Their fate, many feel, is in the hands of people who occupy offices in the state capital and in Washington bureaucracies.

- Given the fact that professional status is determined more by national reputations and reputation among policy elites than by local sources, many local educators orient their actions to gain the approval of policy elites located outside the local community rather than respond to the expressed needs of local constituencies. This leads to increasing estrangement between local civic leaders and those they hire to manage local schools and school districts, especially in large urban school districts. Such a condition must surely account for at least some of the conflicts some superintendents have with their local school boards.

- It is becoming increasingly difficult to disentangle research findings from the ideology and interests of researchers and sponsors. Recent controversies regarding which reading programs have received favorable treatment in the federally sponsored Reading First program is a clear example of this problem. Accusations, some of which seem to me well grounded, are so widespread that funding under this initiative is at best suspect.[16]

- Since the National Governors Association conference in 1989, there has been considerable conversation among the policy elite regarding the creation of

[15]Swanson and Barlage, *Influence.*
[16]See, for example, Michael Grunwald, "Billions for an Inside Game on Reading," *Washington Post,* Oct. 1, 2006, p. B1. In part this controversy stems from the fact that programs that have gained preference in these initiatives are those that fit most easily into existing bureaucratic patterns and purchasing strategies. And of course there is the very real possibility that some of these programs were favored because top-level bureaucrats in Washington offices found it in their interest or the interest of those they served to do so.

"break-the-mold schools" and similarly radical notions, like the creation of charter schools. When one views the research that receives official approval, however, and considers the official insistence that improvement efforts be based on "the research," it seems unlikely that the kinds of reform sponsored by the federal government and large foundations are likely to crack a cup, let alone break the mold. If one insists on using empirical research to determine the innovations to be installed in schools, then "what works" may turn out to be what works best in schools that are not working very well at all.

THE NEED FOR GRASSROOTS ACTION

Clearly the growth of the bureaucratic ethos and the policy elites that accompany this development have done much to move the locus of educational policy from local communities to Washington, D.C. At the same time, the attitudes that accompany the assumption of expertise and the language that accompanies those attitudes have done much to estrange local constituencies from the schools in their communities—and to estrange them from teachers and local school leaders as well.[17] It is becoming clear that education policy is now primarily controlled by an interlocking directorate of policy elites housed in think tanks, staff members in private foundations, state and federal bureaucrats, and corporate managers, all of whom give advice and direction to governors, state legislators, and members of Congress.

The reaction to the No Child Left Behind (NCLB) initiative expressed by policy elites, legislators, and most political pundits and editorial writers leaves little doubt that the transformation of America's schools from community institutions to government agencies is seen by many as a positive move. Even leading members of the business community who once were appalled at the idea of federal aid to education now stand prepared to defend and strengthen NCLB, including its most intrusive accountability measures. The National Chamber of Commerce, which once argued vociferously for local control, has formed a coalition in defense of NCLB. The National Business Roundtable is similarly inclined. Many in the policy elite see standards-based school reform and the creation of state-controlled accountability systems as the solution to what ails America's schools.

---

[17]See Sam Wineburg, "Maintaining the Vitality of Our Irrelevance: Preparing a Future Generation of Education Researchers," *Education Week,* Apr. 6, 2005, p. 35.

Governmental agencies are, however, inherently bureaucratic, whether they operate at the local, state, or federal level. Unlike the politicians who set goals and establish priorities, those who work in government bureaucracies are not expected to set direction; their job is to provide expert advice to those who do set direction (legislators, governors and so on) and to respond to priorities set by these outside actors.

It therefore behooves these advisors to work closely with others in the policy world, so that the advice they give will have the effect they intend. This leads to a certain distrust of teachers and others who work in schools, a distrust that leads some members of the policy elite to want to ensure that "practitioners" have limited influence on the thinking of their chosen clients: the legislators and other political leaders. It is not unheard of, in fact, for members of this policy elite to try to persuade legislators to pass laws limiting the conversations local school officials can have with legislators who are considering new laws. (Such legislation was proposed in Texas, and perhaps in other states as well.)

If local civic leaders and educational leaders are to be successful in transforming schools, they must learn to mobilize communities so that their voices are as loud and clear from the bottom of the well as are the voices that are currently shouting down the well. It is equally clear that some of the policy elite do not believe ordinary citizens have much worth listening to regarding these matters. My experience, however, is that most teachers and most school administrators are more oriented toward serving the children in their classrooms and their local communities well than they are in challenging the elites who now dominate the argument about schools and standards. The consequence is that most of the reform movement has bypassed local leaders or treated them with disdain. Equally unfortunate is the fact that too few educators see themselves as community organizers as well as educators, so they seldom effectively assert themselves into the policy debate. Indeed, rather than being viewed as part of the solution, those who set educational policy often view local educators and local civic leaders as a part of the problem.

The transformation of schools into learning organizations will have to be a grassroots movement, for there is not a great deal of sentiment at the top for increasing the power of local communities with regard to our nation's schools. This means that those who lead the transformation of schools must be prepared to lead a counterrevolutionary movement at the same time they are launching a revolutionary one. They must be willing to confront many who have an investment in the continuing bureaucratization and nationalization of America's schools, not the least of whom will be textbook publishers and test makers, as well as many who see bureaucratization as a means of reinforcing the authority of those members of the educational establishment who want to control local decisions without being forced to build local sentiment behind the decisions their professional judgment leads them to favor.

To launch such a grassroots movement, educational leaders who are committed to public education as a community-building as well as a child-focused endeavor—and who believe that their job is building a public for public education—need a deep understanding of the nature of the impulse against which they will be contending. It is especially important to understand how and why a bureaucratic mind-set has come to dominate the thinking of America's business leaders and the education policy elite and the impact this is having on the sentiments of local citizens. In the chapters that follow, I have a great deal to say about how the conditions I describe in this chapter might be dealt with.

Reassessing Standards

I n recent years, the term *standards-based school reform* has been
added to the lexicon of education. This movement is based, at
least as it is being played out at the state and national levels, on
assumptions derived from manufacturing industries. Therefore,
the standards-based movement is quite consistent with the bureaucratic mental models that underlie much of the American schooling
enterprise. The only real change is that it moves power and authority away from local school districts and lodges it more firmly in state
and federal agencies.

Ironically, many proponents of standards-based education view standards as a
means of breaking the power of bureaucracy and liberating local school leaders
to be more creative.[1] Nonetheless, in the standards-based approach, students are
viewed as products to which standards are applied, as contrasted with participants
who are involved in upholding the standards. Teachers are workers whose primary
responsibility is ensuring that students meet standards set by outside customers.

   As things now stand, the effort to impose standards on schools is only exac-
erbating the problems that schools face due to their bureaucratic nature. So long
as this image prevails and evaluative authority is located in the state and federal
bureaucracy and as long as local citizens do not feel ownership for the standards

[1]See, for example, National Center for Education and the Economy, *Tough Choices for Tough Times:
The Report of the New Commission on Skills for the Workforce* (San Francisco: Jossey-Bass, 2006).

that are to be upheld, the disabling effects of bureaucratization of schooling cannot be avoided.

As David Mathews, the author of *Reclaiming Public Education by Reclaiming Our Democracy*, puts the matter, "People don't believe they 'own' the standards that schools use to document their accountability. And Americans don't think that current efforts at 'engagement' as called for in the No Child Left Behind Act restore broad ownership of the schools."[2]

AN UPSTREAM STRUGGLE

The standards-based movement is a powerful tool in support of bureaucratic centralization. Many consultants and providers of services to schools have a major stake in promulgating the idea of standards-based education. This is so not only because their careers and reputations have been made by advancing the idea that the key to improving schools is to develop clear performance standards for students but also because centralization of authority reinforces their status as experts. Textbook publishers and producers of tests also stand to make millions, if not billions, of dollars by supporting the standards-based movement.

In addition, many political leaders have become persuaded that there is no better way to achieve quality education for all children than the imposition of a bureaucratically administered accountability system. Similarly, some civil rights advocates see the standards-based movement as a tool to address the disparities that have existed for too long between the quality of education provided children from poor families, especially poor minority children, and children from more affluent circumstances.

The consequence is that anyone who challenges the standards-based movement will face the possibility that he or she will be perceived as indifferent to the demand for quality education for all children or, equally damaging, wanting to escape the public accountability the standards-based reformers hope to provide. It will therefore involve some risk for local leaders to suggest that the existing efforts to improve America's schools are wrong-headed.

Is the risk is worth taking? It certainly is for those who believe, as I do, that the continuing transformation of America's public schools into government

---

[2]David Mathews, *Reclaiming Public Education by Reclaiming Our Democracy* (Dayton, Ohio: Kettering Foundation Press, 2006).

schools is a major threat to both the quality of education provided all children as well as a threat to democracy more generally.

The fact is that state-mandated standards, especially as they are being enforced through standardized testing, are becoming the primary vehicles through which public schools are being transformed into government agencies. This results in the standards-based movement becoming a fundamental threat to the link between the public and the schools. It drives a wedge between the parents and teachers, and in the long run it will remove from local environments one of the most powerful sources for a sense of belonging and a sense of community among local residents. It is therefore not only the education of children that is at stake. The long-term health of American democracy is at stake as well, as is the vitality of the local communities on which democracy depends.

There is no way to transform schools into learning organizations without running head-on into some of the interests served by the standards movement. Some local leaders may be accused of trying to escape accountability, and others will be accused of being insensitive to the disparities between the educational opportunities of the poor and the affluent. But whatever the risks, they are justified, for the stakes are very high. It is possible to reduce the risk by ensuring that leaders are well informed about the nature of the condition they must confront. Ensuring all children equal access to a mediocre education is not the same as ensuring all children are inspired to achieve excellence in an environment that honors equity as a primary value. This chapter provides some of the information leaders might need if both equity and excellence are to be our goals and if a just democratic community is to be our aim.

THE PROFIT MOTIVE

Many proponents of standards-based education, perhaps because of their susceptibility to influence from traditionally oriented business interests, make frequent reference to what they call "the bottom line." The intended parallel is between profit and learning—between profit and loss statements and test scores.

It is in fact commonplace for critics of education from the business community to complain that educators are not accountable for the bottom line and to argue that the imposition of state-mandated tests is the way to remediate this problem. They assume, of course, that this will also result in products (students) that are more in conformance with the requirements of the end user—especially the requirements of prospective employers for a "world-class workforce" and institutions of higher education for "college-ready students."

It may be that measures of learning in schools and measures of profit in business can be usefully compared when trying to think of new ways to improve schools. It is important, however, for both educators and the business leaders who advise them to be attuned to the fact that it is the misuse of financial data and overattention to the "bottom line" that accounts for the decline and demise of many American businesses. The leaders of Merrill-Lynch were clearly focused on the bottom line—so clearly focused that they lost their business and hurt many others along the way. The leaders of Enron were not insensitive to the bottom line—that is, profit—as were many other American business leaders who are now in bankruptcy courts or in jail. Apparently many advocates of standards-based reform are unaware of the problems a misguided loyalty to a bottom-line mentality has caused and is causing in the world of business.

Peter Drucker, the reputed father of management studies in America, tried all of his life to help business leaders understand the problems associated with a fixation on profit and measures thereof. According to Drucker, the business of business is to produce products and provide services that the customer values enough to pay a price that yields a profit. Profit is what happens when businesses do their business right—and when they are in the right business—but *profit is not the business of business.* Profit and loss statements are nothing more than management tools that help to validate the business and verify that one is in the right business and doing that business right. Drucker observed: "Profit is not the explanation, cause, or rationale of business behavior and business decisions, but rather the test of their validity. . . . The root of the confusion is the mistaken belief that the motive of a person—the so-called profit motive of the business-man—is an explanation of his behavior or his guide to right action."[3]

Some business leaders have followed Drucker's lead, but many others continue to insist that the bottom line is the only thing that matters in business, and the bottom line is profit. Such thinking is especially prevalent among old-style managers struggling—without much success, I might add—to fix their own bureaucracies and who have yet to become conscious of the new requirements the global economy and the information society impose on every sector of American society.

[3]Peter F. Drucker, *The Essential Drucker: The Best of Sixty Years of Peter Drucker's Essential Writings on Management* (New York: HarperCollins, 2001), pp. 19–20.

For new-style leaders—where knowledge work rather than manual work is the norm—growth, innovation, and development—rather than short-term measures of profit—are the bottom line. In the view of these leaders, it is only when one gets the top of the line right that the bottom line will respond.

Business leaders who manage by profit and for profit rather than by a focus on customer needs and customer values get their businesses into trouble precisely because their first reaction when profits are unsatisfactory is to get profit back up by whatever means are readily and easily available. Among the customary approaches are cutting the cost of production by cheapening the product provided the customer or putting more pressure on employees to produce more products, faster, which often leads to deteriorating quality. Another favored strategy is to cut back on human resource development and the development of leaders.

What Drucker said about profit in business can be said as well about learning in schools. Just as profit is important in business, learning is important in schools, but learning is no more the business of schools than profit is the business of business. As in a well-run business, educators must understand that their first obligation is to meet the needs and serve the values of those who are most directly affected by them: customers in the case of business and parents and students in the case of schools.

Learning is not the explanation, cause, or rationale for school behavior or for decisions made in school. Students are not motivated by learning; they are motivated by characteristics of the tasks that call on them to learn. It is the quality of the work teachers provide for students, along with the quality of support teachers provide to students in the conduct of that work, that should be the bottom-line concern. Teachers do not cause students to learn; teachers design tasks that they assume will call on students to learn, guide them to sources of instruction so that they can learn what they need to learn, and lead them to the successful completion of the work assigned.

This argument is not intended as an effort to escape accountability. Rather, it is intended to embrace accountability at the deepest level possible—accountability in the classroom and accountability for the performance of every student and every teacher. Evidence of intended learning results is a test of the validity of the theories and rationale on which schools are based and from which decisions regarding school and teaching practices emanate. Measures of learning are nothing but artifacts left behind as a result of the prior experiences of students. Artifacts are good for teaching history lessons, but they say little about needed future actions. What teachers need and what they feel they need are ways to more fully assess the quality of the experiences they are providing to students and ways of improving that quality when it is lacking.

Failure to understand this fact can lead school leaders to provide students with an increasingly shoddy education—as illustrated by some of the current misguided efforts to improve test scores. Even worse, when their misguided strategies fail, school leaders put increasing pressure on teachers to do more with less, resulting in further deterioration in the quality of teachers and of school performance.[4]

School leaders need therefore to be clear about the fact that the business of schools is creating engaging experiences for students and ensuring that these are the right experiences. The fact that they are the right experiences is validated by evidence that students learn what it is intended that they learn, but producing this evidence should not be the end in view for schools and teachers. The end in view should be the quality of the learning opportunities provided to students.

When schools do their business well, students do learn, and test scores, if the tests are well designed and are testing for the right things, will indicate that this is so. However, test scores no more indicate how schools should do their business than profit and loss statements indicate how business leaders should do their business.

WHO ARE THE CUSTOMERS?

As things now stand, the business leaders and higher education—rather than teachers, school leaders, parents, and students—are the customers for school standards. Teachers, local school leaders, are judged by standards but they have little ability to influence them. Parents and local citizens are informed about standards, but it is not assumed that they must be satisfied by or with them. Parents are expected to be an appreciative and supportive audience rather than active participants. Students are nothing more than the products to which standards are to be applied. Sad to say, many members of the policy elite and the academic elite hold local educators, many parents, and citizens in local communities in low regard. Indeed, I have been in meetings where persons in positions

---

[4]See Linda Perlstein, *Tested: One American School Struggles to Make the Grade* (New York: Holt, 2007). If one needs more evidence that this is so, all one needs to do is to keep abreast of newspaper reports regarding corrective actions being taken in such school districts as Chicago, Illinois, and Charlotte, North Carolina, where a variety of punitive strategies are being developed to force teachers to teach harder in inner-city urban schools where teaching is already quite hard enough.

to provide advice to governors and legislators clearly indicated their belief that ordinary citizens have no business setting standards for students and that even parents were probably not to be listened to very much in this regard. Indeed, some argue that it is the low standards of local communities and parents that cause the problems in our schools, and it is because this is so that outside experts need to intervene.

The consequence of this view is that rather than developing strategies for getting local communities heavily involved in discussions about the standards that should be used to judge their schools, the more common strategy is to form some sort of "stakeholder" committee made up of official representatives of various interest groups and charge them with setting standards. Usually those appointed to such committees already enjoy a relatively elite status in some interest group organization or hold some position in one or the other of the government bureaucracies and foundations that have an interest in the affairs of schooling.

The job of these groups is to create a list of standards or to endorse a list created by an expert staff employed by the state education agency. Once this committee has done its work, there may be some perfunctory hearings in local communities, but by the time these hearings are held, the deal is pretty much done. Eventually this committee, or some other committee or agency, will be empowered to contract with a qualified testing agency to construct tests to assess the extent to which students meet the standards that have been set. Because real dialogue at the local community level does not occur, such actions provide at best the facade of democracy. It does little to ensure community involvement in the life of the schools and does little to assure parents that their voices are being heard.

Even then, some critics among the policy elite complain that the standards generated in this way are watered down. Although these standards may have been developed by a state-level elite, apparently the elite that develops them is not quite elite enough to meet the standards of some folks. It seems that what is really needed to develop these higher standards is the presence of true experts who know what students need to know and be able to do and who are not afraid to say so.

As an example, Chester Finn of the Fordham Foundation regularly comments on the fact that the standards promulgated in most states are at best mediocre. He attributes low-quality state standards to the fact that progressive educators, members of teachers' unions, and other representatives of organized interest groups are far too influential in setting standards. According to Finn, states where the standards in fact "meet the standard for standards" have found a way to ensure that the standards were developed by knowledgeable experts, many of whom lived outside the state.[5]

To be sure, the wishes and desires of parents and local citizens are sometimes parochial and narrow, and sometimes the thinking of professional educators is shallow and overly concerned with being politically correct. Certainly experts should be involved in the setting of standards. The interests of ordinary citizens and ordinary educators should not, however, be without meaning and significance in the development of standards.

In public schools operating in the context of a democracy, the more parochial interests of ordinary citizens are as critical to the debate regarding what children should know and be able to do as are the opinions of the most informed scholar. This is, in fact, the nature of democracy. It is assumed that through such debates, error can be revealed and purported truths verified or refuted. In a democracy, the marketplace for ideas is extended to the public forum. It is not limited to the academy or any other self-anointed elite.

The fact that many citizens are not as informed as they should be or are ill informed does not justify denying them the right to participate in setting the standards for their schools. Moreover, the fact that the opinion of the common citizen is not always consistent with expert opinion does not mean that expert opinion should be given the force of law. The response should be to educate the public so they can make informed decisions on these matters.

When it comes to matters of values, experts are no more entitled to speak than are other citizens. Standards inherently involve values and value judgments. Juries in murder trials, for example, often hear expert testimony, but the juries are usually not experts themselves. They are, however, expected to render a judgment about the merit and worth of the testimony of experts. More important, we have sufficient confidence in these judgments to condemn men and women to a lifetime of incarceration or even take their lives from them. Surely if ordinary citizens can be entrusted with such power, they can also be trusted to be involved in the debate about what the young should learn.

---

[5]For a comprehensive statement of the view of a relatively representative group of experts, see Chester E. Finn Jr., Michael J. Petrelli, and Liam Julian, *To Dream the Impossible Dream: Four Approaches to National Standards and Tests for American Schools* (Washington, D.C.: Thomas Fordham Institute, 2006).

In a democracy, experts should not rule without consulting with the citizenry. Experts should be required to demonstrate the superiority of their views on matters of values in the course of community arguments, not simply in legislative committee hearings and bureaucratically appointed study groups. If the expert's opinion is more meritorious, then this voice should be inserted into the community argument, and the expert should stand his or her ground in the community forum. Those who do not agree with the experts should have the right to say so in a forum where their opinion can be heard and made to count. Even if the opinion of the ill informed and misinformed goes down in flames (and democracy assumes this will usually occur), he or she will have had the right to speak and be heard. If the expert's opinion is not honored, the expert needs to learn how to be more persuasive or perhaps reexamine his or her own views about the way the world should work. If ignorance prevails, then the solution is the eradication of ignorance rather than the denial of liberty.

It is in this way that the community comes to be educated regarding matters before them. This is all democracy can guarantee, and it is the reason that public education is so essential to the survival of democracy. Imposing expert views by legislative mandate may satisfy the bureaucrats who run government agencies, but it is also a near-certain way to estrange ordinary citizens and increase their feelings of powerlessness and alienation from the institutions that are supposed to serve them.

It is, in fact, one of the ironies of our time that many educators, who should be at least as concerned about the link between education and democracy as they are about the link between education and the economy, spend much more time figuring out ways to make local schools more accountable to the state and federal government than they spend figuring out ways to make the schools, as well as the state and federal government, more accountable to local citizens. It is time for educators to recognize that part of the reason for the growing estrangement between educators and those the schools are intended to serve has to do with the growing estrangement of the citizenry from government agencies more generally. Making local schools more accountable to agencies that the citizens distrust does not increase trust in the schools and those who run them. Educators must learn to trust those they serve just as they ask those they serve to trust them.

Even if one puts aside ignorance and parochialism, as well as religious and ideological concerns—and these are not trivial matters—what parents want from schools and what the experts believe they should want are not always the same. Even the much-vaunted strategy of giving parents the option of transferring their children out of schools where standards are not being met has met with only limited success.

Moreover, when parents in so-called failing schools do not take advantage of the opportunities policymakers have provided, there is a tendency to explain this away by the suggestion that parents, after all, do not have a very refined sense of quality. It may be, however, that parents have other standards in mind when they decide where their children will go to school. Maybe the standards the experts most value are not the ones of concern to many parents.

Whatever the case, if the public does not own the standards by which their schools are judged, it is but a short step until they no longer own the schools. When this happens, the prospects of building a sense of community around them is lost, and it is the loss of community, along with the loss of public education, that constitutes the greatest threat to the future of America.

Certainly leaders in business and higher education have an interest in what students learn in schools. That interest is, however, a stakeholder interest (which translated into business terms is a stockholder interest), not a customer interest. The first-line customers of schools are students and, through students, parents.

Educators know, and bureaucratic experts should know, that both parents and students are concerned with much more than scores on tests—at least this is so with many parents and many students. Indeed, there is some evidence that as schools place greater pressure on children to score well on tests, parents of students who would do well without such pressure are becoming increasingly dissatisfied with schools. Consider the following statement by a parent who chose homeschooling for her children:

> I've been very concerned about the increasing emphasis on standardized testing in schools, as well as the desperate attempts by some states to force homeschoolers to take them. I've always suspected that part of the power of homeschooling is that we have the right to teach our children to think. As schools become increasingly dependent on tests to determine educational content, they become increasingly unwilling to allow students to think. Thinking teachers don't have the time or encouragement to include anything in the curriculum that isn't on the test. There is no room for creativity, for

analysis beyond what the test creators think should be there, or even for reality.[6]

Considerable controversy surrounds this matter. Some empirical studies indicate that parents are generally satisfied with the standards-based movement, and others indicate the contrary. I believe there is growing dissatisfaction, and as the pressure mounts as 2014 approaches, the year set by the federal government as the time when all children will have achieved grade-level proficiency, the dissatisfaction will increase. Whatever the case, citizen disaffection from schooling and the collapse of a sense of community around the schools is a more than trivial concern.

THE MEANING OF STANDARDS

Standards suggest measures of quality. To say that something or someone has met a standard is to say one of two things:

- The product or service meets some technically described condition—for example, machined parts meet specified tolerances.
- The product or service meets or exceeds the requirements of the intended customers—that is, the product or service possesses the qualities or attributes valued by the customer in sufficient quantity.

Clearly, technical standards and market-based standards often interact. For example, if too much variance is permitted in machined parts, the reliability of an automobile may be compromised. Although the customer does not particularly care about this variance, he or she does care about reliability and therefore has requirements in this regard. Too much variance in a machined part can lead to lack of product reliability, just as lead in the paint on toys is intolerable.

Those who set product standards must be clear about who the customer is and what requirements the customer might impose. To set technical standards requires clarity about the technical requirements of the item to which the standards apply.

The first question to be addressed therefore is this: Are the standards called for, in the standards-based approach, customer-focused product standards or

[6]Terry Lynn Bitner, *Homeschooling with Attitude.* http://homeschoolattitude.blogspot.com/, May 21, 2005.

technical standards? If they are technical standards, then what is the condition that must be satisfied? If they are product standards, who are the customers who must be satisfied?

THE TRIVIALIZATION OF STANDARDS

Setting standards is not a simple matter, and deciding who must be satisfied by them is not a trivial concern. Standards that will satisfy progressive educators will not satisfy a more traditionally oriented academic, for example. And those that might motivate parents and drive students to higher levels of performance may not be those that satisfy some business leaders.

Even within the standards movement, there are substantial disagreements about what the standards should be. Although members of the business community insist on new standards of learning appropriate to the twenty-first century, these skills—such things as critical thinking and the ability to work in groups to solve problems—are difficult, if not impossible, to measure with tests that satisfy the requirements of bureaucrats for objectivity and standardization. The need of bureaucracies for standardized test scores, however, drives the reduction of powerfully stated standards toward the trivialization of the content to be tested, and thereby trivializing what will be taught. Given the bureaucratic ethos that governs so much thinking about schools, it is standards that are easily measured by standardized tests that are gaining ascendance in evaluation of schools and even the performance of teachers. Twenty-first-century skills may be the aim, but early nineteenth-century notions of what is worth learning and how students learn appears to dictate what gets measured.

To date, no state has come up with a standardized test that provides data on the power of schools or teachers to generate an environment where students become more creative than they might otherwise have been, more able to use technology than they were before attending the school, more adept at solving real problems, or even more disciplined in the way they approach problems. What is being tested for today is precisely the things that educators assumed they were teaching fifty years ago, such as basic reading skills and computation skills, with perhaps some attention to basic knowledge in some of the academic disciplines. Short-term memory and an encyclopedic grasp of unrelated concepts seems to be that which is of most value.

It is ironic that educators, especially those known as progressives and constructivists, have long pursued results similar to those now called twenty-first-century skills. There is good evidence that they have sometimes been quite successful in their quest. Unfortunately, the evidence they produce is not convincing to those who insist that scores on standardized tests are the only "hard evidence" that is acceptable. Authentic assessments, portfolios, and demonstrations may persuade local audiences, but only scores on standardized tests seem to convince the universal audience that a centralized and remote system of evaluation assumes must be convinced. Business leaders who want their employees to demonstrate critical thinking skills, skills in collaborative work, and leadership skills must be brought to understand that they will never get what they say they want if they continue to support those who insist on measuring the wrong things.

Moreover, the fact that ability to work as academics work is more highly valued in the academy than it is elsewhere in our society sometimes escapes proponents of standards-based school reform. In the world outside the academy, teamwork and leadership are at least as highly valued as is the mastery of academic content, especially content that has no use beyond demonstrating the ability to recall isolated items for a short period of time. What business leaders say they want are students who are creative and know how to access information when they need it. They are not especially impressed with young men and women with encyclopedic knowledge, unless these young people also know how to put that knowledge to use in situations other than a test or a quiz.

Unfortunately, when academics think about standards, few are immune to the parochialism of the academy, a parochialism that insists that the only way to truly demonstrate mastery of academic content is the way academics do these things: through writing papers, oral examinations, and paper-and-pencil tests. Concrete demonstrations in authentic settings are rare in the academy except as students approach the doctoral level.

Even more to the point, proponents of the standards-based movement have yet to come to grips with the relationship between standard setting and the requirements of democratic communities. For many parents and citizens, and certainly for most students, the argument about standards is one among political elites, business elites, and academic elites. The standards that many parents are most concerned about are moral standards, cultural standards, and standards that have to do with the way their children are treated in school. Proponents of a standards-based approach usually steer clear of such standards because to become involved in this discussion would be certain to uncover the fractures that lay beneath the surface of many communities.

As an example, I have recently taken up the practice of asking—or causing others to ask—parents to list ten things they would like to be able to say about their children's teachers and schools. Concern for academic standards almost always shows up on these lists, but generally academic matters have less potency than do matters of the heart—such things as, "My son's or daughter's teacher really cares about him or her as a person." A common response by high school parents and students can be summarized as follows: "Some adult or some adults in the school really care about me [my son and daughter] and it shows in the way I [he or she] am treated."

It is certainly true that many public schools have not been as attentive to enforcing academic standards as they should have been. Moreover, locally governed schools have not always been as accountable to the local communities as should be the case. These are common problems in a bureaucracy, and making the schools even more bureaucratic and locating the authority center of that bureaucracy even further from local communities will not solve this problem.

If the problem is to be solved, a means must be found to embed academic standards into the values system that shapes the sentiments of parents and students toward schools. Rather than fixing the problem, today's reform strategies simply relocate it and thereby make it even more likely that the schools will continue to decline in their ability to satisfy the needs of our society. Bureaucracies are not good with matters of the heart and of sentiment, and standards are as much matters of the heart and sentiment as they are technical concerns. That is one of the reasons that transforming schools into learning organizations is so important.

Put differently, the problem is the system. Currently standards are located primarily in the context of the power and authority system. If standards are to have meaning, they must be embedded in the directional system, and both students and teachers must be inducted into the system so that they will embrace and own the standards that are to be applied. Moreover, standards should be understood to be separate from whatever tests are used to determine progress toward the standard; otherwise the test becomes the standard—and that way lies disaster.

NO TESTS FOR STANDARDS

For the most part, the standards set for schools are focused more on the needs and expectations of assumed "customers" than on technical requirements. In education as elsewhere, however, there are those who view standards more from a technical perspective than from a product perspective. For such people, standards and the ability to meet them should serve as a predictor of future performance. Thus, the ACT and the SAT, two tests often used for college admission, make claims of predictive validity: that those who score well on these tests are more likely to succeed in college than are those who score poorly.

One of the more interesting facts about the standards-based movement is that only a few states have concerned themselves with the predictive validity of the tests they have developed. Indeed, although state tests are used to evaluate the performance of schools, it is uncommon to link student scores on these tests to the students' later performances. There is, for example, little research that would help educators understand whether improvements in reading scores in the early grades that are attributed to "programs that work" have persistent effects, since most of these studies do not follow cohorts of students over time.

Furthermore, only a few states use tests that purport to have predictive validity (for example, the SAT and the ACT) as part of their accountability system. Moreover, few colleges give credence to student scores on state standardized tests when making college entry decisions, and even fewer businesses bother to review high school transcripts. This suggests that although higher education and business leaders have an interest in states' establishing standards—and some are pleased with the standards that have been established—few have enough confidence in the tests used to measure performances against the standards to use these test scores in any meaningful way.

As a practical matter, the tests used to verify the achievement of state standards have not proven relevant to anything other than a narrow slice of information related to standards developed by experts far removed from schools. Whether the standards set by the state really matter in the later life and later performance of students has yet to be demonstrated.

THE EFFECTS OF STANDARDS

If standards are to inspire excellence as opposed to minimum compliance, they must have intrinsic value in the context where they are being applied. With regard to schooling, this means that parents and teachers, as well as other concerned citizens, must understand the standards to be applied well enough to embrace them and to know when they are being met and when they are not. More than that, if standards are to be compelling, they must be assessed by means that are believable and credible to those to whom they apply.

Such understanding and commitment can be gained only when parents, teachers, and community leaders are involved, and feel they are involved, in the development and enforcement of standards. Indeed, the fact that standards must be enforced from the outside through threats of punishment and promises of reward is evidence that the standards are not compelling to those to whom they are applied.

The full long-term results of the standards movement and No Child Left Behind are yet to be seen. In the shorter term, however, the effects are not difficult to see. The following sections describe some of the more prominent repercussions of these policies.

Profound Learning Versus Superficial Learning

As suggested in Chapter Three there are at least two types of academic learning: profound learning and superficial learning. *Profound learning* affects and shapes habits and worldviews; it is learning that involves the ability to evaluate and create, as well as to compare, contrast, and remember, and can be used in a variety of contexts.

Superficial learning involves short-term memory. It provides little in the way of application in novel contexts. Superficial learning is compartmentalized rather than embedded in worldviews and habitual ways of thinking and doing. It does not require much in the way of commitment, meaning, persistence, or voluntary effort. All that is required is student compliance and a means of inducing students to spend sufficient time on task to "master" the involved operations well enough to respond appropriately on paper-and-pencil tests.

Because academic learning is so central to schools, it is understandable that academic standards are the primary standards with which schools should be evaluated. Bureaucratically organized schools are ideally situated to produce superficial learning, focused as they are on compliance. Paper-and-pencil tests are easy to administer and simple to score, thus meeting bureaucratic standards for efficiency. Such tests are also best at assessing skills associated with short-term recall—that is, they are best at testing for superficial knowledge, but ill designed to test for profound understandings and insights. This is the reason that many critics argue that the standards-based movement can result in a narrow and truncated curriculum.

Bureaucracies are not, however, proficient at fostering the conditions that promote profound learning. Profound learning requires a certain tolerance for ambiguity, an acceptance of uncertainty, and a degree of playfulness not found in a bureaucratic system. It is for these reasons that I argue that if schools are to serve society well, they must be transformed into learning organizations. Rather than simply ensuring that students comply with meaningless (to them) tasks that result in sufficient superficial learning to improve test scores, schools must provide students with intellectually engaging experiences that result in profound learning. This is learning that lasts and has meaning beyond the classroom in which it was learned or the test to which it was oriented. Learning organizations provide such conditions. Bureaucracies do not.

Content Standards Versus Performance Standards

In addition to differing with regard to being focused on the superficial or the profound, academic standards also differ in other ways. As any review of the literature on standards will reveal, it is common when discussing standards to place them into two categories: *content standards* and *performance standards.* The two-part question, "What do we want students to know, and what do we want them to be able to do?" has become prominent in the language of school reform in America. What we want students to know has to do with content standards. What students are to be able to do involves performance standards.

Using a score on a paper-and-pencil test as the primary indicator of whether one has met a standard is an effort to combine content standards and performance standards. What students need to know is whatever information is required to perform on the test in question—thus, test performance becomes the primary performance of concern.

It seems not to occur to some who are adamant about using test scores as a standard that this is circular reasoning and may have little to do with the ability of students to perform in anything other than a test setting. More than that, the evidence is mixed regarding the predictive validity of paper-and-pencil tests, even within the context of the academy. For example, persons who score high on college entrance exams are more likely to do well in college than do those who score low. However, the performance of any single person can never be predicted based on a single test score. Some people who score high on the SAT fail in college, and some who score low—if given an opportunity to attend college—do quite well. Probability statistics are appropriate only if one is prepared to accept the prospect of error in any particular case.

Paper-and-pencil tests have considerable power in measuring knowledge of content and some other processes essential to academic performance—for example, the ability to compare and contrast, spot logical fallacies, and read complex passages with comprehension. Paper-and-pencil tests, especially those that are easy to score in a reliable way, are not, however, particularly useful in measuring creativity, the ability to imagine, the ability to work with others to solve problems, persistence in the face of perplexity and difficulty, the ability to pursue a line of inquiry independently and produce a product as a result of that effort, habits of reading with purpose, and myriad other things one might wish to find embedded in any reasonable set of state standards.

Tests as Standards

Clearly, if standards are to have any meaning, then some means of testing, assessing, and evaluating performance against the standard is required. Moreover, when performances fail to meet standards, some means of ensuring corrective action must be present and available.

Unfortunately, across the nation, students' ability to perform on a test has become the standard, thereby trivializing what might otherwise be a standard that could serve to encourage profound learning. I heard one superintendent say, I am certain in jest, "We know why so many schools are not meeting the standard. Too many students are marking the wrong answers. All we have to do is figure out some way to get them to mark more right answers." This is a classic case of goal displacement and is typical in organizations dominated by a bureaucratic ethos.

Some states have tried, and continue to try, to use other means of assessment—for example writing samples, essays, and portfolios. These alternative procedures are, however, under constant assault on the basis of being both too subjective and too expensive. Furthermore, as states have gained experience with mass testing, they have found that one of their major problems is returning test scores in a timely fashion. When tests or even parts of tests must be scored by people rather than machines, the time problem is compounded. Simplicity and ease of administration are important in an organization where standardization is a prime value.

The result is that within the context of bureaucracies, the substitute measure for demanding standards is likely to become test items that call on students to recall tidbits from books they have supposedly read at some point in their academic career. Such sampling is assisted by state-specified curriculum guides that suggest—if they do not prescribe—which books all students should have read, thereby making the chore of the teacher and the tester at least a bit "easier."

The problem is deciding which books should be included in the list and why they should be included. Such decisions are usually made by a committee appointed by bureaucratic officials. As a consequence, the literary tastes of students are likely to be narrowed rather than broadened in order to reflect the collective judgments of a bureaucratically appointed and anointed curriculum committee, leaving little to the judgment of the teacher or the student. Among other things, teachers become limited with regard to the range of literature they can offer as a way to invite students into the wonderful world of modern novels or classical literature, and students are limited with regard to the variety of content to which they might be exposed.

It is not surprising, therefore, that students are increasingly finding ways to go outside the boundaries prescribed by adults in order to access knowledge. Moreover, these outside forms of instruction often present information in ways that are more engaging than bureaucratically constrained schools can provide. Students are, for example, increasingly exploring digital resources, which, among other things, often provide random access and easy access to data they might otherwise need to commit to memory. This often causes those who lead bureaucratically organized schools to become even more coercive; for example, fearing that students will use cell phones to cheat on tests, educators sometimes attempt to exclude student cell phones from schools. Students are warned not to consult Wikipedia on the grounds that this source contains too much erroneous information, while at the same time textbooks that are sometimes loaded with dubious generalizations appear on state textbook adoption lists.

The one-right-answer curriculum is more appropriate in the artificial environment of the bureaucratically dominated classroom than it is in the real world youngsters experience every day when they watch television or use the Internet. Great teachers make the use of the errors that these outside sources might introduce to help students learn to evaluate information. Teachers in bureaucratically organized schools are often encouraged to try to control the flow of knowledge so that students receive only the one answer required by the test.

If students are to be prepared adequately for their future, they need to learn to pull information from their environment. Schools organized as bureaucracies are platforms for instructors to push information at students. Instead, they need to be organized as platforms for learning rather than platforms for instruction.

Using a standardized test in the context of a pluralistic and multicultural society, where free access to varieties of information is readily available, is not the way to verify whether standards are being met. Standardized testing requires standardized teaching and standardized content. When standardization replaces standards, it is not enough to say that students will read historical fiction; one must specify the fiction to be read. In the area of mythology, should the student know about Pecos Bill, John Henry, or Paul Bunyan? Or is Hercules a more fitting figure for a test item? The test cannot be constructed unless and until the mythology is specified. Or, do we use the content of the test to specify the curriculum?

In many schools, curriculum alignment has been pursued as the solution to this problem: first, determine what is to be tested; then determine what to teach. The argument, of course, is that state tests are aligned with state standards, and so the decision as to what to teach precedes the test.

All of this is supported by a burgeoning emphasis in schools on what is often called test prep, which is nothing more than a mandatory rehearsal for performance on the most important stage of a young life: the theater of the high-stakes test. Students who muff their lines will fail, and those who have mastered their lines will succeed. This is certainly not the way to a first-class education or to twenty-first-century skills.

A Narrow Set of Values

Academic learning is important, and all students should be able to meet reasonable academic standards. It is likely, however, that those who are able to deal with academic matters in a truly creative way are limited to a relatively small proportion of the total population—perhaps 25 percent, give or take a bit. However, the ability to pursue advanced graduate study in one of the academic disciplines should not be the only indicator of success in school. It is certainly not the indicator of success in the world outside the schools.

Schools must find ways to nurture multiple talents, not just those that satisfy the interest of the academy. Even the academy, at least as represented by higher education, must find ways to nurture multiple talents in multiple ways. This is a challenge, because the academy tends to be dominated by those who were successful in it and have a tendency to define success in terms that their own experiences can verify.

Many educators and parents, and increasing numbers of politicians, understand these arguments, at least intuitively, and this is the reason for their growing uneasiness with much that is going on in the name of school reform. Sir Ken Robinson put the matter this way:

> People in education want to pursue a more sophisticated agenda but feel hemmed in and often demoralized by political pressures to raise particular standards. Politicians say that this pressure comes from business and is essential to national economic survival. The popular press promotes a tireless antagonism between traditional and progressive teaching methods and campaigns against liberal education. They know that parents are sleepless with worry about the quality of education that their children are receiving. Yet . . . parents . . . often want a much broader and more sensitive style of education for their own children than politicians seem to promote for everyone else.[7]

One of the major difficulties with the standards movement is that in the effort to spotlight the deplorable performance of some schools in developing basic reading skills and skills in arithmetic, it has emphasized academic standards to the point that other areas where schools should be developing talents are being overlooked or looked past. Because academic talent, like all other talent, is not equally distributed, relatively few students will experience the exhilaration that comes with true success. Equally important, many will come to devalue the academic talent they do possess, for no matter how hard they try, they can never meet the standards of excellence that their more academically talented peers seem to attain so easily.

Even worse, the less academically able are more likely than their more able peers to be put through rigorous, tedious, and meaningless preparatory activity to help ensure that they will score well enough to meet minimum standards on a test that is without meaning or challenge to their more able peers. And because bureaucratically organized schools often employ batch processing techniques (everyone does the same thing at the same time), these rituals of test preparation are likely to teach both the more able and the less able that academic work is meaningless work, good only for ensuring test scores and satisfying some present or future boss.

Ironically, the major complaints of the business community often involve the concerns that too many high school graduates lack creativity, imagination, the ability to work effectively in groups, the ability to organize and lead others,

[7]Ken Robinson, *Out of Our Minds: Learning to be Creative* (Mankato, Minn.: Capstone, 2001), p. 15.

the ability to think critically, and so on. Yet when such claimants turn their minds to standards, the only ones they know to talk about are academic standards. Moreover, when educators suggest other standards of concern, which must be assessed by something other than standardized tests, "hard-nosed" business leaders are likely to see this as a sign of soft-headedness and a lack of willingness to be accountable for results. What nonsense!

It is, for example, clear that we need many more people who find inspiration in the sciences and mathematics than we now have, and perhaps we could find more if we understood that what we want in scientists and mathematicians is creative intelligence rather than slavish mastery and imitative intelligence. To be sure, mastery and the ability to imitate and replicate are important aspects of creative intelligence, but to be creative requires going beyond imitation and replication. Albert Einstein, for example, developed his theory of relativity by imagining himself riding on, or beside, a beam of light.

If all that schools really encourage and reward is academic intelligence, the supply of creative high school graduates, or for that matter college graduates, will never meet the demand, and it will not only be the economy that will suffer—so will our cultural and our civic life. The standards movement limits the kind of intelligence that schools are encouraged to nurture.

DIFFERENT CONSTITUENCIES, DIFFERING STANDARDS

When viewing a proposition regarding the merit and worth of an educational practice, members of the research community apply very different standards than do the classroom teachers who are considering the same proposition. The researcher wants to know the extent to which the proposition can be generalized to all cases that fit the class of phenomena to which the proposition applies. The classroom teacher wants to know the extent to which the proposition can be applied in his or her particular situation.

The standards that must be met to convince academic elites are quite different from the standards that must be met to persuade the classroom teacher.[8] The standards applied by academic researchers are not, however, higher than those applied by the classroom teacher; they are simply different. This matter is often overlooked by those who make policy regarding school improvement.

[8]Ernest House, *Evaluating with Validity* (Thousand Oaks, Calif.: Sage, 1980).

One of the assumptions underlying the No Child Left Behind initiative is that the standards of major concern to most parents are academic ones. The idea of parental school choice therefore is introduced on the assumption that, provided the opportunity to leave a school that has notably low performance on tests, most parents will choose to send their children elsewhere. Moreover, when parents do not make such choices, it is assumed that they fail to choose to transfer their children because they do not sufficiently value academic performance or because they are uninformed and have low standards.

It is rarely acknowledged that in addition to academic standards, parents may be even more concerned about other standards—for example, standards having to do with whether their children will be well treated and respected in the schools available for choice. Parents whose children are well treated and respected in a low-performing school and are safe as well may choose to stay with that school rather than choose a high-performing school, especially if the parent has reason to believe that his or her child may be stigmatized or mistreated in the higher-performing school.

Physical safety is important to parents, but parents want their children to be psychologically and socially safe as well. Such standards apply to all schools. A school of choice that does not attend to the psychological and social safety needs of students whose parents chose the school will not be chosen for long or by many. Moreover, given a physically safe school that is conveniently located, academic standards must compete with these other standards in ways that policymakers sometimes little understand or take into account.

The Complexity of Standards

Another problem is that even within one category, standards can be very complex. The following, taken from the Indiana state standards, is illustrative of this problem:

STANDARD 2

READING: Comprehension and Analysis of Nonfiction and Informational Text

At Grade 12, in addition to regular classroom reading, students read a wide variety of nonfiction, such as biographies, autobiographies, books in many different subject areas, essays, speeches, magazines, newspapers, reference materials, technical documents, and online information.

STRUCTURAL FEATURES OF INFORMATIONAL AND TECHNICAL MATERIALS

12.2.1   Analyze both the features and the rhetorical (persuasive) devices of different types of public documents, such as policy statements, speeches, or debates, and the way in which authors use those features and devices.

Example: Evaluate a famous political speech, such as Abraham Lincoln's "Gettysburg Address" or John F. Kennedy's 1960 inaugural address, and describe the rhetorical devices used to capture the audience's attention and convey a unified message.

ANALYSIS OF GRADE-LEVEL-APPROPRIATE NONFICTION AND INFORMATIONAL TEXT

12.2.2   Analyze the way in which clarity of meaning is affected by the patterns of organization, repetition of the main ideas, organization of language, and word choice in the text.

Example: Analyze speeches of Winston Churchill to examine the way his language influences the impact of his message.

12.2.3   Verify and clarify facts presented in several types of expository texts by using a variety of public or historical documents, such as government, consumer, or workplace documents, and others.

Example: Verify information in state and federal work safety laws by checking with an employer about internal company policies on employee safety.

12.2.4   Make reasonable assertions about an author's arguments by using hypothetical situations or elements of the text to defend and clarify interpretations.

Example: Read General Dwight Eisenhower's June 1944 "D-Day Pre-Invasion Address to the Soldiers" and evaluate the validity of his arguments for succeeding during the Normandy Invasion (World War II).

12.2.5   Analyze an author's implicit and explicit assumptions and beliefs about a subject.

Example: After reading excerpts from British physicist Stephen W. Hawking's *Black Holes and Baby Universes and Other Essays,* evaluate how the author conveys explicit information to the reader. Analyze the author's unstated philosophical assumptions about the subject.

EXPOSITORY (INFORMATIONAL) CRITIQUE

12.2.6   Critique the power, validity, and truthfulness of arguments set forth in public documents; their appeal to both friendly and hostile audiences; and the extent to which the arguments anticipate and address reader concerns and counterclaims.

Example: Evaluate campaign documents from different candidates for a local or school election or opposing position papers on a policy issue, such as a citizen's right to privacy or raising taxes, and critique the arguments set forth. Address such issues as how candidates/supporters of an issue try to persuade readers by asserting their authority on the issues and appealing to reason and emotion among readers.[9]

This is but one of seven standards in one subject (English). Standards in other subjects are equally demanding and equally complex.

I have no difficulty believing that such standards are valuable and that pursuit of them is worthwhile. I am also persuaded that if teachers and students could be brought to embrace and pursue standards such as these, our world would be a better place and students would be well served.

I am not persuaded, however, that the best way to inspire performance oriented toward these standards is by developing a bureaucratic accountability system that insists on using a paper-and-pencil test as a proxy for such profound standards. Nor is holding teachers and students accountable for guessing what

[9]Indiana Department of Education, "Indiana's Academic Standards and Resources." 2006. http://dc.doe.in.gov/Standards/AcademicStandards/PrintLibrary/docs-english/2006-06-ela-grade12.pdf.

short-term things need be memorized in order to convince an external agency that the standard has been met.

In addition to the obvious temptation for teachers to teach to the test or, worse yet, to cheat, those aspects of the standard that are likely to gain emphasis will be those that can be measured by paper-and-pencil tests in a formal test setting. Those that are more difficult to measure will not be emphasized.

Standards such as Indiana's require students to demonstrate profound understandings. To meet some of these, students need the ability to engage in persistent inquiries over sustained periods of time and to go down blind alleys and recognize these as early as possible. Such abilities can be observed by teachers and nurtured by them, but they cannot be tested on one bright morning in February of one's senior year. Such standards require continuous pursuit by students and therefore continuous assessment, coaching, and guidance of students by skilled teachers. This kind of teaching should be encouraged and rewarded in schools rather than the sporadic and disjointed instruction that sometimes passes for test preparation. Standards like those set by Indiana might make a significant difference in the performance of students, teachers, and schools if they were used to guide and assess the performances of teachers and students rather than to control and evaluate those performances. In a learning organization, standards would be built into the directional system and the induction system. In a bureaucracy, standards are built into the power and authority system by transforming evaluation into an exercise of authority rather than a means of maintaining direction and work orientation.

Unfortunately, in spite of good intentions, the standards-based school reform movement does not challenge the basic assumptions on which schools are organized. Indeed, the movement simply reinforces the bureaucratic tendencies of schools and school leaders and provides bureaucratic managers with a new set of coercive tools to regain control over a system that seems to some to have spun out of control. The inherent flaws in the standards-based approach are, however, likely to make the performance of existing bureaucratically organized schools even worse than is now the case.

Another Way to Look at Standards

The challenge in setting academic performance standards might better be addressed as is the setting of performance standards in golf. The primary standard in golf—usually a par score of seventy-two strokes over eighteen-holes—is difficult enough to attain that even very good golfers do not routinely achieve it without special effort or discipline. Yet an average golfer should have a reasonable prospect of achieving par from time to time on any given hole. In sum, for standards to be inspiring, they must be achievable by persons of ordinary ability yet challenging to persons with extraordinary talent.

In golf adjustments are made that take talent into account, but these adjustments have to do with the difficulty of the course to be mastered rather than the standard itself. Senior citizens do not have to use the same tees as the club professional, but given this adjustment the senior citizen and the club professional still calculates his or her score relative to par.

High performance standards can be inspiring and motivating, even for golfers of limited ability. There are, in fact, few golfers who expect to score a par on every hole, but most golfers believe that par is possible on any given hole even on a championship golf course. Therefore, every golfer starts on every hole with the assumption he or she can meet a standard of excellence. If the golfer fails, he or she moves on to the next hole to try again, using the same standard—that is, par. Indeed, most golfers know that on any Saturday morning they will be fortunate to have three or four pars, and they will also be lucky if they do not have eight or ten double bogeys (two over par). Furthermore, golfers are not judged on any single performance, and they are provided as many chances as they can want to learn the vagaries of a particular course or hole, so that they can develop greater mastery and more success. The cumulative score one achieves depends on the application of a variety of skills over multiple performances—driving, chipping, putting—and on demonstrating power, finesse, judgment, control, memory, and adaptability in unique environmental conditions.

As the game of golf is organized, high common standards can inspire low performers as well as excellent performers. All players play against a common standard, but past performance against that standard provides the golfer a personal benchmark by which to judge his or her own performance. A handicap system provides a mechanism for including all sorts of players in the game, while at the same time providing incentives for improvement by golfers of all levels of ability and performance. The extremely proficient golfer is inspired to maintain a low handicap, whereas a high-handicap golfer is inspired to lower his or her handicap. Even terrible golfers may experience a sense of pride and accomplishment when their handicap goes down from thirty to twenty-nine. If such a player happens to be playing in a tournament on the day the improvement first shows up, he or she might even win a trophy or be celebrated for making a major contribution to a team effort. Golfers who are masterful putters and whose short game excels can compensate for lack of length in the drives and fairway woods.

The question that must be answered is this: Are we interested in our schools' producing winners and losers or are we more interested in developing in our students the will and skills to succeed? Do we want students who are lifelong learners and who enjoy learning even though others learn more quickly and perhaps even more or do we want to ensure that the vast majority learn that while they can learn, what they learn is not worth all that much? Equally important, do we want to limit valued learning to learning that is only academic or can we imagine a school in which the meaning of learning is expanded to incorporate the wide range of abilities present among students?

Multiple Standards, Not Lower Standards

Organizing schools so that multiple standards come into play—so that a student's past performance is a benchmark against which later performances are judged, and so that improvement on past performance can become the subject of honor—should not be difficult to achieve if educators set their minds to the matter. Almost all students have some extraordinary abilities, if they can only be identified, nurtured, and developed and if meaningful performance standards and performance measures can be established to support their development. (By "meaningful," I mean meaningful to the students, in contrast to being meaningful to others but of no meaning to the students.) Furthermore, if these abilities can be identified and developed, creativity can also be developed and will flourish, for the fact is that creativity is more likely to occur in areas where one has clear talent than in areas where talent is limited.

It should be the mission of schools to help students identify their extraordinary talents and develop them to a level of excellence. At the same time, it is essential to ensure that students' more limited talents are developed to levels at which they can experience personal satisfaction, enjoyment, and a sense of participation in the full range of life that is available in the school and in the larger society as well.

Restoring Civic Capacity and Building Social Capital

Two Keys to School Transformation

*C*ivic capacity refers to the ability of business leaders, union leaders, civic leaders, educational leaders, and leaders of other signifi-cant organizations to work together on behalf of common goals.[1] *Social capital* refers to the presence of trust, norms of reciprocity, feelings of mutualism, and common identity, and community.[2]

A considerable body of research indicates that the ability of leaders and their organizations to generate and exercise civic capacity is a significant factor in the ability of schools and school systems to successfully install innovations.[3] The presence or absence of social capital has similarly been shown to be directly related to the success of schools in installing innovations.[4] When civic capacity

[1]Clarence N. Stone, Jeffrey R. Henig, Brian D. Jones, and Carol Pierannunzi, *Building Civic Capacity: The Politics of Reforming Urban Schools* (Lawrence: University of Kansas Press, 2001).
[2]See, for example, Robert D. Putnam, *Bowling Alone: The Collapse and Revival of American Community* (New York: Simon and Schuster, 2000).
[3]Stone, Henig, Jones, and Pierannunzi, *Building Civic Capacity*.
[4]See Anthony S. Bryk and Barbara Schneider, *Trust in Schools: A Core Resource for Improvement* (New York: Russell Sage Foundation, 2002).

and social capital are present, the likelihood of success is increased. When they are absent, the likelihood of success is diminished.

Unfortunately, special interest groups and the organizations that have been created to represent their interests within communities, as well as groups and agencies that have been created to serve a specific public good (for example, the public health system, the justice system, and the schools), often seem to lack the ability to work together in the cooperative pursuit of the public good. Even more devastating is the fact that large numbers of men and women perceive themselves to be isolated and alone.

Educators can look on these matters as a problem, lament that it is so difficult to mobilize communities in support of schools, and complain about the absence of community support, or they can look at these matters as opportunities to learn how to build communities around the schools and new ways to promote collaboration among groups and agencies that have an interest in the welfare of children and youth and are committed to local control of schools. The former alternative threatens continuing decline and social disaster. The latter offers hope and inspiration.

SCHOOLING AND THE DECLINE OF COMMUNITIES

After more than thirty years of campaigning against local control of schools by much of the national media and members of the expert education policy community, nearly half of Americans still believe that local school boards should retain control of their schools; only 20 percent would have the federal government play a major role in deciding what is taught in school.[5] This constitutes a continuing shift in public views. In 1980, 68 percent of respondents believed that the majority of control in these matters should reside in local communities. In 2007 that number had dropped to 49 percent.

For those who believe, as I do, that local control is important to high-quality democratic education, there is considerable reason to believe this trend can be reversed. The authors of *Applebee's America,* for example, observe that many politicians and religious leaders are discovering that two of the most important motivators for many Americans are the quest for community and the

---

[5]Ibid, p. 39.

desire to be associated with a cause that is greater than themselves.[6] According to these authors, Americans are tired of sloganeering. They no longer respond well to bureaucratic jargon and symbols.

Rather, Americans respond to leaders who appeal to "gut values" having to do with a sense of belonging and to a compelling invitation to contribute to the common good. Americans are therefore increasingly less likely to respond to leaders who are fixated on such instrumental concerns as test scores and who see students as data points or even as products to be shaped to meet the needs of multinational corporations. They are more likely to respond to leaders who appeal to their core values—values that are often quite different from those that bureaucratic experts bring to the argument about schools. Those who would transform schools into learning organizations that serve as the bedrock on which communities can be built need to understand and take advantage of these facts.

In spite of expert criticisms of public schools, the majority of American parents are generally satisfied with the schools their own children attend. Fifty-two percent of parents (as contrasted with 32 percent in 2002) believe there is too much testing in schools. In spite of this sentiment, the U.S. Department of Education is recommending even more testing.[7] Increasingly parents seek options to public schools, at least in part because they do not believe they have any ability to influence what goes on there and believe as well that schools are becoming too much like many of the other government agencies they have come to distrust.

Educating the Public

If local citizens are not sufficiently informed to make decisions about what children should learn in school, the answer is to educate the citizens rather than take power from them. The debates surrounding what schools should teach and what standards should prevail, could, if properly framed, serve as a primary means by which communities can be educated about the condition of education. It is through such education that trustworthy communities might be created and defined and through such discussions that the common ground that binds communities could be discovered.

[6]Douglas B. Sosnik, Matthew J. Dowd, and Ron Fournier, *Applebee's America: How Successful Political, Business, and Religious Leaders Connect with the New American Community* (New York: Simon and Schuster, 2006).

[7]Lowell C. Rose and Alec M. Gallup, "The 39th Annual Phi Delta Kappa/Gallup Poll of the Public's Attitude Toward the Public Schools," *Phi Delta Kappan*, Sept. 2007, p. 37.

Building schools into the fabric of community life by involving them in the building of communities, as well as involving communities in establishing standards for their schools, will satisfy the needs of both adults and children. Indeed, I would argue that given globalization and the revolutions that are occurring in the way information is transmitted, processed, and communicated, if we do not move quickly to build a sense of community at the same time that we dramatically improve our schools, the blessings that the information revolution promises can quickly turn into a hell that even George Orwell could not predict. Absent the kind of communitywide conversations needed to define standards for schools and meaningful local input into the way those standards are to be assessed, the community-building potential of schools is dramatically decreased, if not totally nullified.

These conversations cannot occur if the meaningful and influential conversations about standards take place only among experts in offices far from local school districts. These conversations almost certainly will not occur if schools are made into the government agencies they are becoming under current policy.

It is time that state legislators and members of Congress are awakened to the fact that the best chance we have of significantly improving the quality of education is to revitalize local control of schools. Rather than entrusting the future of education to bureaucrats at the state and federal levels, regardless of how expert these bureaucrats may be, we must give our attention to building trustworthy local communities. I discuss strategies for bringing this about in later chapters.

School Consolidation and Busing

It is commonplace to assert that the schools should serve the community. One of the fundamental problems confronting many school leaders, however, is that it is difficult to figure out which community is to be served. Sometimes it is even difficult to figure out whether there is an identifiable community.

Community involves a sense of common identity, feelings of belonging, and feelings of affiliation—of shared values and shared destiny. Community is not a place. It is an orientation and a source of personal identity, as well as group affiliation.

Schools have clearly suffered from the weakening of a sense of community, and some efforts to improve the schools have probably contributed to this weakening. For example, in the effort to create comprehensive high schools and increase administrative efficiency, reformers in the 1950s and 1960s argued successfully for school consolidation. In many instances, these efforts had the effect, as critics said they would, of eroding local community identity.

Court-ordered busing also affected the way citizens felt about their schools. The decision in *Swann* v. *Charlotte-Mecklenburg Board of Education* (1971) mandated busing as a remedy to the continuing segregation of schools in Charlotte-Mecklenburg, North Carolina. One of the implications of the decision was that for many Americans, black and white, students no longer attended school with their neighbors and friends—or persons with whom the students or parents commonly associated or about whom they had personal knowledge. Moreover, in too many instances, too little attention was paid to building a sense of community around these newly integrated schools. Rather, the effort was to make the schools work in spite of the fact that there was little sense of community in them or around them.

In most major cities, for example, there was usually at least one traditionally black high school that stood as a beacon and a source of community pride. One of the effects of court-ordered busing was to cause many of these schools to be closed or to lose their historic identity. This loss too seldom was compensated for by efforts to truly integrate both parents and students and creating a new common identity around which all could rally. Even today many large urban high schools reflect the racial tensions that have their origin in unresolved issues dealing with race and ethnicity. These issues have their origin in the larger community and that is where they must be resolved. The school house and the boardroom of school districts, however, are probably the best place for such a reconciliation to begin. The now nearly cliché statement that "it takes a village to raise a child" has considerable appeal among all racial groups. Using the common interest we all have in the future and the role of children in that future can be a powerful resource in community building.

THE NEED FOR COMMUNITY BUILDING

There is certainly much more involved in the decline of American communities than school consolidation and court-ordered busing. (District consolidation involves issues of governance, whereas comprehensive high schools are more associated with school size and the complexity of the curriculum.) The reason I focus on these two events in the history of education is not to lament that they happened; I am not suggesting that education would have been better served if consolidation had not occurred, or if the *Swann* decision had not happened.

School consolidation and court-ordered busing do, however, clearly demonstrate the linkage of communities, community identity, and the schools. They also demonstrate the ways in which communities can be developed—and the ways in which they can be harmed—by policy initiatives that seem aimed at improving the education of children. The symbolic power of schools and education to unite divisive forces should not be underestimated. At the same time, one should never underestimate how the forces that would divide communities can use this symbolic power to achieve their ends.

The comprehensive high school is not a bad idea. The problem is that those who designed this school were often so fixated on increasing the services provided to students that they forgot to attend to building a sense of community and belonging among adults and students. Although the sense of community exists in some comprehensive high schools, many of them, especially in urban areas, have come to be seen as the impersonal and segmented schools that are the center of attention of advocates of small high schools. In some rural areas, the comprehensive high school has come to mean nothing more than a long bus ride and fewer opportunities to play varsity sports.

Court-ordered busing also has had many positive effects on the education of children, as well as on relationships among the races. In Charlotte, for example, one of the side effects of the implementation of the *Swann* decision (at least in the first twenty years following *Swann*) was an increase in the level of support and pride evidenced by various civic and cultural leaders. Indeed, as pressure mounted to dismantle busing, many of these African American and white civic leaders who had earlier joined together in support of court-ordered busing have found themselves bound together defending the gains they felt were made under *Swann*.

Similarly, in Louisville (Jefferson County, Kentucky), where the local school board only reluctantly accepted a court-ordered busing plan, the school board recently took the lead in an unsuccessful effort to resist court actions intended to undo much that had been accomplished in response to earlier busing decisions. A similar situation developed in Charlotte, North Carolina.

Even in Charlotte and Louisville, however, the community-building effects of court-ordered efforts to desegregate schools have probably not been as widespread or as deep as some of the veterans of the implementation battles might want to believe. And the unfortunate fact remains that it is still in the boardroom of school districts like the Charlotte-Mecklenburg Schools and the Jefferson County Schools where the drama of the racial divide and lack of common ground is most likely to be acted out.

POLITICS, ECONOMICS, AND THE MORAL ORDER OF COMMUNITIES

Civic capacity is dependent on the will of the leaders of community groups, local organizations, and public agencies to work together on behalf of the common good—and on the skill these leaders have, or develop, in pursuing such cooperative efforts. In brief, civic capacity has to do with the ability of agencies and groups that exist in a community to collaborate. Sometimes these collaborative efforts may focus on improving health care, sometimes they focus on schools, and sometimes they have to do with other areas of civic concern, for example, race relations or public safety.

Implicit in the idea of school boards as community leaders is the corollary notion that these boards should be responsible for building and maintaining civic capacity. Because they are a part of the political fabric of the community, however, the short-term interests of factions, groups, and parties necessarily influence schools more than does the notion of the common good. For example, parents living in one area may find their interests best served by having a new high school built close to them, whereas senior citizens would prefer to have the high school located elsewhere. Local contractors want the school to give preference to purchasing from local providers, and the taxpayers' union wants the school district to seek the lowest bidder, wherever the lowest bidder may be.

As a part of the economic system, schools and school boards are peculiarly vulnerable to being co-opted to serve the needs and interests of the more powerful members of the economic community, sometimes at the expense of those who are less powerful (such as students). Similarly, those who would foster social change in the community sometimes try to co-opt the schools to serve their ends and to achieve their goals with little or no concern for the impact these efforts might have on public support for schools more generally.

For example, as the directors of one of the largest employers in the geographical area that defines the school district, school boards are likely to be under considerable pressure to make sure that their hiring practices and promotion policies are responsive to the patronage needs of various local factions and local groups. At the same time, there is pressure to ensure that those who are hired are the most able and most qualified of all the available candidates. Sometimes the patronage interests of groups and factions overwhelm an interest in the common good that might result from ensuring that all employees of the district meet high standards.

School boards are usually very good at responding to the political and economic pressures exerted by the community, and when they fail in this regard, the electoral process usually corrects this problem. Where school boards often fail is in looking out for the long-term interests of the community generally—and in ensuring that the decisions they make to satisfy the short-term demands of factions and groups also reflect the deepest beliefs and abiding values and aspirations of the community at large. Put bluntly, school boards are good at balancing the short-term needs of the interests, factions, and groups that exist in the community; they are not necessarily good at building a larger sense of community among those diverse, competing, and sometimes antagonistic forces. It is as moral leaders that school boards are most likely to fail.

In Search of Community

A common assumption is that those who are elected to the school board will have a strong sense of the common good and will transcend the demands of the factions and groups that supported their election once they are in office. This is an unrealistic expectation. Altruism, like heroism, is in short supply. Because this is so, school boards are more prone to reflect the divisions that exist in the community than they are to represent the common good. Indeed, if the common good is attended to, such attention results from heroic—and often self-sacrificing—efforts on the part of individual school board members.

In communities with elected boards of education—most American communities—individual school board members are accountable to the citizens through the process of election. The school board as a collective body is, however, accountable to no one other than the state that grants them the right to exist and the government agencies that fund the programs they oversee. Yet it is only when the board acts as a collective group that its actions have any real effect.

Unfortunately, in most communities no organization has sufficient moral authority to uphold the claim that it represents the common good. Moreover, the common good has no vote, and it seldom has an organized constituency group to represent it. Local newspapers sometimes try to exercise such moral authority, but usually they fail because they too are likely to be identified with particular interests in the argument.

Philanthropic groups are becoming increasingly aggressive in this arena. In Pittsburgh, for example, three foundations withdrew funding from the schools in an effort to focus the school board's attention more clearly on what the foundation leaders held to be the common good. Though widely praised by many as a step in the right direction, this effort is not without critics who argue that foundations too have agendas, and such agendas are not always aimed at the common good as it might be construed locally.

The failure of boards of education to reach consensus on the community values that should guide the schools is the primary reason that schools have abandoned the expressive functions they once served and have embraced ever more tightly instrumental functions alone. Apparently they assume that the best way to deal with competing values is to avoid dealing with values at all.

Values and their competing expressions are, however, at the heart of communities—and communities are at the heart of American democracy. Unless school boards develop the capacity to put the general good and the long-term interests of children and the community above the concerns of the interest groups that often shape their election, the future of public education is not bright. This is the reason I have argued that school boards must become community builders rather than simply reflectors of the will of the electorate. They must be clear on the beliefs and values that guide them as a collective entity. Once they are clear, they must engage the constituencies that elected them in serious dialogue about what they believe and why. In such conversations and dialogue, the community-building functions of school boards can begin to be realized.

THE NEED FOR SCHOOL BOARD LEADERSHIP

Over the years local school boards have been criticized on many grounds, not the least of which is that they tend to be provincial and ill suited to providing the kind of intellectual and moral leadership one might want in a vital educational institution. Mark Twain's famous statement, "In the first place God made idiots. This was for practice. Then he made School Boards," is illustrative of such a sentiment.[8]

In larger school districts, especially in large cities with a complex set of high schools and relatively large administrative staffs, school boards have often been viewed by the citizenry with suspicion. The consolidation movement has also made many school districts larger and usually more bureaucratic, thereby

[8]Mark Twain, *Following the Equator*. http://www.twainquotes.com/Idiots.html.

increasing the numbers of local districts subject to the criticism of being nonresponsive to parents and students.

Through the 1950s, most who criticized school boards did so because they perceived the boards were cultural monoliths that represented primarily the needs and interests of white, middle-class Protestants or the needs of the business community. Indeed, some were prepared to argue that the reason the National Chamber of Commerce supported local control and local school boards was that it made it easier for business to control the schools. Stewart McClure, then chief clerk of the Senate Committee on Labor, Education, and Public Welfare, said about school boards at the time of the National Defense Education Act (1958), "In the real world the business community dominates the school boards in every damn town in the country."[9]

Rather than representing the common good, many school board members view their roles as representing the factions and groups that have elected them, and these factions quite often form their own "communities," based on race, ethnicity, religious identification, or social class interests. The result is that local school boards are often viewed as centers of community conflict rather than places where conflicts are negotiated and worked out. This has led some critics to suggest that school boards, especially those in larger school districts, are so dysfunctional that they are beyond repair and should be abandoned.

To abandon local school boards, in my view, is to abandon any prospect that public education has of becoming a community-building force. I do agree, however, that as they are constituted now, school boards have many more incentives to behave in dysfunctional ways than in ways that are functional. Furthermore, unless the incentive system can be changed in fundamental ways, the way school boards operate is as likely to lead to the demise of public education as to the preservation of the ability of local communities to control their own destinies and the destinies of their offspring. I also believe that local school boards provide the last best hope America has of maintaining vital schools in vital communities.

If school boards are to serve the community-building functions that are required for school districts to develop as learning organizations, they need to reorient their actions. Rather than concerning themselves primarily with the internal operations of the schools, they need to be more concerned with setting

[9]Stewart E. McClure, Oral History Interviews, Senate Historical Office, Washington, D.C., Jan. 1983, pp. 110–111.

and articulating the direction of the district—and with ensuring that leaders inside the district and in the community understand and support this direction. Rather than lead the schools, a task they should entrust to superintendents and principals, school boards must learn to work with the superintendent as part of a leadership team and to assume, as a part of that team, the role of community leaders and educators of the community about the schools.

This means, among other things, that the school board as a collective body will need to be guided by a clear and compelling set of beliefs regarding the direction of the schools and a vision of the schools that these beliefs suggest. They must learn to use this vision to create communitywide conversations about the direction of the district, the beliefs that should guide the schools, and the standards by which school and student performances should be judged.

This vision must be articulated in ways that inspire commitment from all who participate in the life of the schools. It must invite all who participate in the life of the school district to participate in a cause that is bigger than they are. It must describe a place where people are valued and where important work is being done.

The board will also need to ensure that the various constituencies, factions, and groups that have an interest in the operation of the schools are involved in conversations concerning the beliefs and vision that drive the system, the results that are being achieved, and the kind of community actions that will be needed to more fully realize those beliefs and pursue the vision.[10] This is not a call for endless hearings. Rather, it is a call for the development of strategies for continuously involving citizens in serious conversations about the nature of schools and schooling, as well as the hopes and dreams they have for their own schools.

To serve effectively as leaders of schools organized as learning organizations, board members need to be especially attentive to their roles as community leaders. They need to be builders of consensus around programs of action intended to strengthen the ability of the school district to maintain (or regain) local authority over decisions affecting the direction of the district and its schools. They especially need to assert the use of evaluation systems within the district as a means of providing direction as opposed to a means of surrendering control to external authority. This means that boards need to establish partnerships with community groups and agencies, as well as leaders from other school districts,

[10]See Sosnik, Dowd, and Fournier, *Applebee's America.*

for the purpose of influencing state and national policies that impinge on the ability of local communities to transform their schools from bureaucracies to learning organizations.

The Issue of School Vouchers

It is very hard to judge how much public support there is behind the notion of vouchers. Religious considerations, issues related to race and ethnicity, and the desire for some relief from private school tuition fees are among the primary motivations for supporting vouchers. Some who support vouchers as a general proposition are not in favor of using them for children to attend parochial schools. Others are not enthusiastic about providing vouchers to supplement tuition for private school students.

Quite often proponents of vouchers argue that the public schools are not teaching the young the things they need to know to take their place in the workforce, and that a privatized system would be more likely to coordinate effort so that the product of the schools would be more closely aligned with the demands of the marketplace. Milton Friedman argued, for example, that the choice and competition introduced by vouchers would be beneficial in their own right. In addition, they would make the management of schools more accountable to the market economy and therefore more consistent with the values that govern other enterprises in America.[11] These arguments fail to take into account that the primary rationale for public support of public schools is the notion that this education should be a common education—as implied in the term *common school.*

The only safe statement that can be made regarding the voucher debate is that there is much more support for the notion today than there was twenty-five years ago, the support is growing, the courts are becoming friendlier to the idea of using vouchers to support children attending something other than public schools, and few advocates of vouchers seem concerned about the community-building potential of public schools. Rather than viewing education as a common good, advocates of vouchers generally view education as a commodity, a property right, and an entitlement. Some politicians, for example Mitt Romney, have gone so far as to argue that the quality of the education afforded youngsters

[11]See Milton Friedman, "The Market Can Transform Our Schools," *New York Times,* July 2, 2002.

is the civil rights issue of the twenty-first century, just as equal access to schools was the civil rights issue of the twentieth century.[12]

PUBLIC EDUCATION AS A MORAL IMPERATIVE

Education in a democracy is neither a property right nor a civil right. It is a moral imperative and a cultural requirement. Public education is provided to promote the common good and the general welfare. Just as individuals benefit from the protection provided by the military and the laws to protect the environment, they benefit from education. Public schools are not, however, provided solely for individual benefit, so it is a mistake to think of them solely as instruments to make life better for individual children. Child benefit is certainly intended, but it is also intended that public education make communities more livable and the culture more vital and stimulating.

The widespread use of vouchers will almost certainly serve to confirm the view that schooling is a private commodity rather than a common good. Education vouchers will embody the idea that all citizens are entitled to an education, and that they are entitled as well to choose the form this education will take. Once the notion that education is a property right and an entitlement has been accepted, it is but a short step to turn education into a commodity for sale on the open market, subject to the same market forces that regulate the purchase of any other commodity.

The provision of vouchers for education will also challenge the notion that a community has a serious interest in the nature of the education its youth receive, beyond the idea that each child is entitled to learn basic skills in reading, writing, and arithmetic. The community-building and culture-building functions of schools, in the case of vouchers at least, will likely be seen as relatively unimportant, if not altogether irrelevant.

Once general community interest in education is set aside—that is, "the common good" argument is considered irrelevant—public support for public schools will be increasingly hard to maintain. Once vouchers become widespread, one will need to argue for public support for education on the same grounds that one argues for support of food stamps and other social welfare programs rather than on the traditional grounds of the common good and general welfare.

---

[12]See for example, Mitt Romney in 2012 "Raising the Bar on Education." http://myclob.pbwiki.com/Raising+the+Bar+on+Education.

When this becomes the case, quality for all will no longer be a public issue. Welfare programs are intended to ensure minimums rather than excellence and maximums. Protestations to the contrary, education vouchers will no more ensure equal access to high-quality education than food stamps now ensure that the poor will have equal access to steak and caviar as opposed to bologna and rice.

Although vouchers may empower parents to an extent, they will take power away from those who pay the major portion of the taxes that support education. Indeed, vouchers will make even clearer to nonparent citizens what many are already coming to suspect: "Unless you have children in school, you have no right or ability to influence how your education dollars will be spent." Those who have no ability to influence how their dollars are spent will in the long run seek to provide fewer dollars.

With the widespread use of vouchers, it will no longer be assumed that senior citizens and other nonparent citizens can put their stamp on the future by engaging in the debate about what children should be taught and how they should be taught. Vouchers assume that these are matters best left up to parents and teachers. The role of the citizen—especially the senior citizen—will be to provide funding to the young to use as they will for whatever purposes they decide are appropriate. This will lead to the view that vouchers are a form of wealth transfer.

In addition, because increasing numbers of those who receive vouchers will come from the ranks of the poor, especially the racially and ethnically identifiable poor, it is likely that public support for public education will meet even greater resistance. This seems even more likely to be the case if the debate over social security and health care becomes transformed into one regarding the obligation of the relatively young to ensure support for the relatively old. If vouchers become widespread, senior citizens may well turn this argument around and ask why the relatively old should help pay education costs for the relatively young, especially when senior citizens and other nonparent taxpayers have no voice in how that money will be spent.

Given the fact that senior citizens are increasingly estranged from the schools and given the growing presence of senior citizens in American society, it is difficult to see how vouchers will contribute to public support for public education. Vouchers may even serve to exacerbate the growing divide among retired citizens and the relatively young. This is a matter of considerable significance as the post–World War II baby boom generation moves into retirement and the digital natives move into the workforce and their childbearing years. This is certainly one of the reasons that the Gray Panthers (an organization of senior citizens and younger people interested in building civic capacity) has taken a stand in opposition to vouchers and critical of No Child Left Behind.[13]

BUILDING SOCIAL CAPITAL

Bureaucracies are distrusted because they are impersonal, and they are impersonal because they are distrusted. They substitute objectivity for fairness and the uniform application of rules and standards for informed and disciplined judgment. Bureaucracies are more concerned with what is doable than with what is hoped for, more concerned with measurable goals than with dreams and aspirations.

When a direction leads into uncharted waters, where standards for performance have yet to be established, bureaucrats retreat to that which they know, understand, and can control with certainty. Rather than trust individuals to make sound judgments based on shared values, they assume that individuals do not share values and can be controlled only through well-articulated and rigidly enforced rules. Trust is not a part of the bureaucratic ethos. In fact, it is lack of trust and trustworthiness that makes bureaucracy seem so necessary and so appealing to those concerned with the possibility of loss of control.

Because bureaucracies assume a lack of trust and trustworthiness, they rely on the exercise of rational authority supported by evaluation mechanisms that are deeply embedded in the power and authority system. They depend as well on rigid definitions of boundaries, within which responsibilities are clearly defined, tasks are assigned, and duties are specified. The questions "Who is inside?" and, "Who is outside?" are clearly answered, and the link between status and authority is clearly understood.

Learning organizations, in contrast, require trust, so their leaders necessarily attend to systems most likely to build trust: the directional system, the knowledge development and transmission system, and the recruitment and induction system. It is not that they are unconcerned with the way power and authority are exercised, evaluations conducted, or social boundaries established and maintained. They are concerned with these matters, but they consider these matters to

[13]See http://graypanthers.org/index.php?option=com_content&task=blogcategory&id=7&Itemi d=49.

be of secondary concern. The primary concern of leaders in learning organizations is with direction, knowledge, and matters of staff and skill, for social capital resides in these systems. Building social capital and civic capacity is at the heart of the public school system as a learning organization. Those who would transform schools into learning organizations, especially superintendents and their staffs, principals, union leaders, and boards of education, must be particularly attentive to building community trust and confidence. In an age when public institutions are increasingly distrusted, school leaders must give priority to building trust—trust among themselves and trust in the organizations they lead.

Such trust cannot be created by public relations efforts, though a sound public information program is essential to trust building. Neither can it be built overnight or by a targeted campaign. It must be done almost one person at a time and face to face. The following are some suggestions regarding ways in which such trust might be built:

- With leadership from the superintendent and in cooperation with the board of education, a compelling statement of beliefs must be articulated, consistent with the notion that schools are learning organizations, students are volunteers, and engagement (rather than simple compliance) is the aim of school activity. Once this statement of beliefs and a vision derived from it have been created, they could become the focus of community forums, discussions in civic groups, and so on. Business leaders who have had experience with marketing a new vision could be invaluable allies in developing a strategy for gaining community buy-in for such a vision. Businesses with strong marketing departments might be induced to donate some of their services to this endeavor as well.

- Based on an assessment of the capacity of the district to support a transformation effort, a document might be prepared that accurately describes the current situation in the school district with regard to performance and capacity to support change. This document should be especially attentive to demographic trends, mobility patterns, economic trends, and evidence that bears on community cohesion or disintegration. Such a document could serve as a major resource in developing other materials and presentations for involving the community in understanding the condition of education in the community.

It is essential that such a document be developed with honesty and written in language that is understandable by the general public.

- The board of education might consider developing a weekly television show focusing on local education issues. To do this it would probably be useful to find some a moderator of sufficient stature to command an audience. It would also be necessary to get local sponsors for the show.

- A weekly column for the local newspaper could focus on the beliefs, vision, and goals of the district and provide concrete examples of how the beliefs are being pursued in the school district. This must be candid and without fluff or pretense.

- A speakers' bureau might be developed and provided with training in making formal presentations as well as talking points for community presentations and conversations. Likely candidates for such a group are teacher leaders, principals, school board members, central office staff, and the superintendent. Over time, involved and informed community leaders might be invited to be members of this group.

- A "key communicators" group, based on models often used in political campaigns, might be developed with an eye toward making this structure a permanent feature in the community. A reasonable goal for such an endeavor might be to develop one such person per fifty adults in the community and to make special opportunities available for these key actors to gain access to information and have opportunities to participate in policy discussions that occur in the district.

- The school board might encourage the use of regular surveys, focus groups, and other forms of market research intended to assess the images of the school district, as well as other aspects of community life. It would also ensure that data drawn from these sources are made available to decision makers in the school district and elsewhere in the community—and to the board itself.

- School principals and school faculties should be oriented to understand their critical role in building community understanding of educational issues. They should be provided training to assist them in working with parents and others who interact with the schools in ways that build trust and increase feelings of ownership of the schools.

Initially most of the conversations regarding the beliefs that would guide an endeavor such as this would probably need to be focused on the official leaders of critical groups in the community. Among these are groups and organizations whose active support is essential if a significant educational change effort is to move forward—for example, organizations that represent the interests of minorities, the business community, local political leaders (especially the mayor), significant leaders in the faith community, and leaders in local philanthropic groups.

A second set of groups to be concerned with would be those whose resistance would be harmful and whose support, while not essential, would be of value. The editorial board of the local newspaper, for example, and the leadership of the local electronic media fall into this category.

Such activity would undoubtedly require the superintendent and the board to convene important community figures to discuss the vision and intentions that gave rise to the strategies being developed. The intent of such meetings would be to increase communitywide ownership of the vision that drives the system and educate the community regarding support for developing the systems that are envisioned. This process of involvement and discussion would also undoubtedly provide useful data to further discipline action within the school district; assumptions about community concerns and interests could be clarified and modified as a result.

CAN IT BE DONE?

Can a program of action such as the one outlined above really be accomplished? The answer is a qualified yes. It will require courageous and strong leadership. It will require superintendents capable of leading by vision rather than by programmatic mandates and principals and teachers who inspire trust among those they serve as well as among themselves.

There is no question that the strategies I have thus far suggested would be more easily put in place in school districts of more modest size (fewer than 100,000 students) than in large districts (of more than 100,000 students). Indeed, as size and complexity increase, the tendency to impose bureaucratic solutions to the problems that beset schools seems to increase as well. It is, in fact, urban schools, especially urban high schools, that provide the image most Americans have when they think of "America's troubled schools." It is these schools that critics are quick to label as "dropout factories." They are not characterizing high schools in the small towns and villages of Ohio, Indiana, North Dakota, or Pennsylvania. It is in fact one of the ironies of the school reform movement that those who are most adamant about the desirability of more firmly embedding public schools into the state and federal bureaucratic structure for the most part have as their point of primary reference schools that have long suffered most from the adverse consequences of the bureaucratization of schools—that is, schools located in America's largest urban school districts.

I am not convinced that the quality of education provided children in urban schools, or any other type of school, will be much improved by transferring the bureaucratic authority of the local board of education to the bureaucratic office of the mayor or the state capital. I also know that transforming schools in large urban districts will require different strategies from those applied in smaller school districts where there is at least a residual sense of common identity and a sense of common destiny. Nevertheless, such modifications are possible, and some examples give hope. Consider the case of Houston Independent School District. In spite of notable flaws in the models it produced, the experience in Houston between 1995 and 2003 clearly demonstrates that strong and imaginative school board leadership can bring about fundamental changes in the way school districts—even large urban districts—go about their business.[14]

The critical point here is that change must be focused on creating systems that make it less likely that the errors made in the past will be made in the future. Current problems must, of course, be resolved, but they are best resolved when they are reframed so that new opportunities emerge and new solutions are presented.

School board members must be prepared to act in ways that the incentive system for board members now sometimes discourages them to act. To ensure the presence of such persons, it may even require a means of electing board members that provides more protection from the pressures of interest groups and is more clearly fastened on concerns having to do with direction and the future. I once proposed the idea of a charter school board that involved the systematic

[14]See Donald McAdams, *What School Boards Can Do: Reform Governance for Urban Schools* (New York: Teachers College Press, 2006), for a detailed description of aspects of the Houston experience. This book presents one of the most thoughtful treatments of issues related to school governance available.

use of community involvement strategies as a means of building charters that would serve as platforms on which slates of potential school board members might compete for the right to operate the school district for a period of years.[15] Another idea might be to use regional or even national accrediting agencies to establish standards for school board operations (note I did not say the operation of schools) and to articulate the standards in such a way that school boards would be obliged to be attentive to acting in ways that built communities and encouraged ongoing communication about performance standards and the means of assessing these standards.

The common good and posterity, rather than the short-term interests of the constituencies and coalitions that are brought together in the typical school board election, need to be the standards that guide action. The future of schools and of communities depends in large measure on the ability of local civic leaders to find ways to ensure that men and women of character, vision, and wisdom are elected to the board of education, and once they are there, that they are protected from the vagaries of interest group politics.

A CONCLUDING COMMENT

There are no matters more important for those who would lead the transformation of schools than those associated with the building of civic capacity and social capital. And there are few other matters related to the improvement of education that are so heavily dependent on the presence of courageous, informed, sensitive, and responsive moral leaders who have their egos under control—leaders who are capable of giving away success and absorbing failure, leaders whose primary goal is building great schools as opposed to simply building great careers.

Without such leaders, school transformation cannot happen. With such leaders, entire communities can be mobilized in support of public education that once again is linked to the common good as well as to the personal benefit of individual students and the needs of the American economy and the body politic.

---

[15]Phillip C. Schlechty, *Inventing Better Schools: An Action Plan for Educational Reform* (San Francisco: Jossey-Bass, 1997).

PART THREE

Taking the First Steps

How Transformation Can Happen

Painting a New Image of Schools

T he image of the little red schoolhouse continues to stir the
hearts of many Americans. The fact is, however, that most of
America's children attend school in a building that is a subset
of other buildings; all are linked together by systems of power and
authority that have their locus of control outside the building
and often outside the community in which the building is located.
Increasingly, the image that Americans are developing of their
schools is that of a government agency with about as much emotional appeal as the local post office.

This image of schools and school systems must be transformed in ways that
inspire communities to once again own and take pride in their schools. To do so,
school leaders need to abandon old ways of thinking about schools and embrace
new ways of describing what they are about.

THE USES OF METAPHORS AND MENTAL MODELS

Learning organizations do not happen by chance; they are invented. School leaders
must make a conscious choice to transform their schools from bureaucracies to
learning organizations. The superintendent, teacher leaders, and principals must
have the insights and skills needed to develop in others the commitments and
capacities required to move this agenda forward.

209

Make no mistake, transformation is not as simple as installing a new program, a new process or new procedure. Unlike efforts to improve the operation of existing systems, transformation requires more than changes in what people do; it requires changes in what they think and what they feel about what they do. It requires changes in the images people have of the organizations in which they work and live, as well as changes in the way they envision the roles they play in those organizations.

To bring about such changes, leaders must be adept at painting vivid word pictures of the world as they see it and as they think it should be. This requires that they learn to think metaphorically as well as systemically. It requires that they tell compelling stories as well as present convincing data and persuasive arguments. In brief, leaders must master the discipline of mental models as well as the discipline of systemic thought.[1]

The Power of Mental Models

The power of mental models, as discussed in Chapter Four, is clearly demonstrated by the manufacturing model that informs the thinking of many American business leaders, reform advocates, policymakers, and educators. This model is well understood and respected by many in the business community because of the marvelous results it produced for so many years. Indeed, the rise of American industrial dominance in the world can be attributed to the application of the assumptions on which this model is based.

Although business leaders might prefer that I use the label *rational system* as opposed to *bureaucracy,* the fact is that the mental model that has shaped American industry is strikingly similar to the bureaucracy ideal type (see Chapter Three). It assumes that most important elements of human action can be managed through a rationalized system of controls (complete with clearly specified job descriptions and patterns of delegation of authority), the application of rationalized management tools, and the strategic use of systems of rewards and punishments. In addition to informing leaders in business, this model has also been embraced by many American educators, sometimes consciously and sometimes unwittingly.

[1]See Peter Senge, *The Fifth Discipline: The Art and Practice of the Learning Organization* (New York: Doubleday, 1990).

Many business leaders are beginning to suspect that the models that the manufacturing giants of the twentieth century used do not fit the realities of the twenty-first century. Among other things, the nature of the workforce and its members' motives are different than they were in the past, and the nature of the work that is being done is different. In the past, increases in productivity were dependent on finding more ways to get a relatively unsophisticated workforce to more efficiently apply muscle and sinew to highly regimented tasks aimed at producing a relatively well-standardized product.

Today productivity is more likely to be increased by motivating and directing the activity of members of a relatively sophisticated workforce to use their minds and to apply theories and concepts to solving problems associated with the continual invention and production of new and customized products. In brief, manufacturing has moved from an emphasis on manual work to knowledge work.[2] Creating the conditions in which people work more with their minds than with their hands requires a different type of organization. It is out of this understanding that the idea of the learning organization has been—or, more accurately, is being—developed.

The American businesses that have been most successful with the application of these new assumptions tend to be those that have emerged since 1960, businesses like Apple, Cisco, and Microsoft, along with many of the smaller and less well-known companies that have developed around the creation and production of hardware and software related to the information technology revolution. America's established businesses such as the automobile industry initially resisted the notion that their management strategy was flawed. When they were confronted with threats from corporations like Toyota, their leaders tried to explain the successes of these foreign companies away by reference to such myths as, "Japanese workers are more docile and their unions less adversarial." Only recently have many of the leaders of established American businesses begun to embrace the notion that their problems may be based in their assumptions about how the world works (or should work). Today, many of these leaders are struggling to throw off old organizational models and embrace models more closely resembling the idea of a learning organization. They are not finding this an easy task.

[2]See for example, Peter Drucker, "The Age of Social Transformation," *Atlantic,* Nov. 1994. http://www.theatlantic.com/politics/ecbig/soctrans.htm.

With regard to schools and schooling, numerous critics have shown that the old rational systems manufacturing model is not now, nor has it ever been, appropriate to schools and schooling.[3] The fact that this is so, and the increasing evidence that the old model is no longer appropriate even in the manufacturing sector, has not, however, dissuaded many business leaders from insisting that these antiquated principles are applicable to schools. Furthermore, it has not dissuaded some policymakers and educational reformers from believing what their business advisors tell them. Moreover, even as some business leaders are coming to discover how inappropriate these old models are, many continue to insist on the relevance of these old frameworks for improving education.

The result is that policymakers and educators are receiving mixed messages from the business community. On the one hand, the leaders of the newer enterprises, and a few of the established ones, are insisting that there is a need for critical thinking skills, collaborative skills, and a long list of understandings that in a bygone era were thought to be reserved for the academic elite.[4]

On the other hand, when the business community provides advice regarding how these new demands are to be met, the voices still speak from the old manufacturing paradigm: of students as products to which standards should be applied rather than as active participants in the life of schools, which are themselves directed by standards; of the need to strengthen the power of outside inspectors to ensure quality as opposed to the need to develop the means of ensuring that students and teachers, as well as school leaders, develop personal commitments to common standards of excellence and maintain those commitments without the presence of an intrusive system of inspection.

Business-oriented writers and speakers cling stubbornly to the idea that teachers are motivated by extrinsic rewards such as merit pay and that their performance can be improved through rationalized monetary incentives. As they sometimes do in their own businesses, these leaders often overlook the subtleties of human motivation and the power of the human group to shape sentiment and reaction. They overlook, for example, the fact that when workers feel relatively deprived, as is often the case in school, any differential in rewards that

[3]See, for example, Raymond Callahan, *Education and the Cult of Efficiency* (Chicago: University of Chicago Press, 1962). See also Linda Darling-Hammond, *The Right to Learn: A Blueprint for Creating Schools That Work* (San Francisco: Jossey-Bass, 1997).
[4]For a comprehensive statement of this perspective, see *21st Century Skills Framework*. http://www.21stcenturyskills.org/index.php?Itemid=120&id=254&option=com_content&task=view.

involves judgments of merit is likely to create resentment and hostility. Rather than establishing the recipient of merit pay as a model who inspires others, the recipient becomes a target of group sanctions. If students are to receive the uniformly high quality of support that professional educators are ethically expected to provide, it is first necessary to ensure that most teachers feel they are being fairly compensated for doing a difficult job.

Of course, some jobs and some types of workers (for example, salespeople) respond to extrinsic incentives. Other jobs have their incentives built in. These usually require high levels of skill and dedication or perhaps unusual courage or personal sacrifice. The task of leaders of persons in these types of jobs is to make the job sufficiently rewarding (both financially and symbolically) to encourage the right kind of talent to apply for the job.

Albert Shanker, the former president of the American Federation of Teachers, suggested to me that lion taming was an example of a job with the incentives built in. For those of us who fly a great deal, I suspect we hope that pilots feel as Shanker suggested lion tamers might feel. I also would be uncomfortable if I needed brain surgery and found out that my surgeon was on a behavior reinforcement schedule—which is what most merit pay plans turn out to be.

It is only partly in jest that I have sometimes observed that any person who enters teaching with the expectation of great financial reward is probably too ignorant or too stupid to teach in the first place. I want those who teach my grandchildren to be paid enough that they do not feel that they must behave as martyrs and mistreat their own families for the honor of serving others. Moreover, I want their jobs to be such that whatever financial sacrifices they must make are truly compensated by the intrinsic values built into their work. The kind of talent needed to be a highly qualified teacher can never be competitively compensated in financial terms within the context of a public service job. Therefore, it is imperative that teaching be organized in ways that are more rewarding and ennobling than is now the case in bureaucratically organized schools. Unfortunately, many policies aimed at improving school performance within that structure demean the role of teacher even more than is now too often the case. I do not want my grandchildren taught by teachers who need merit pay to ensure that they will perform as well as they know how to perform.

To break through a mental model that has such a strong grip as the manufacturing model and counter the negative effects of this model on both policy and action, educational leaders must learn to imagine the schools and school systems they lead as if they were organized as places where creativity and critical thought were valued. They must paint pictures that describe what a school might look like if it were a learning organization and how this might contrast with the school as a factory, a warehouse, a prison, or even a hospital. (See Chapters Four and Five.) They must learn the art of telling stories, and must use this art to paint a vivid description of the organizations they live and work in, as well as the organizations they intend to build. Through such storytelling and the imagery stories convey, the urgency for change and visions of the future are created.

Metaphors as Makers of Meaning

As George Lakoff and Mark Johnson have shown, metaphors reveal much about the way people think and act.[5] Negative images of school (the school as a factory, as a prison, or as a warehouse) are commonly used by critics to help reveal the weaknesses of our system of education. Positive images (the school as a nurturing family, the school as a community, the school as a hospital) are used to convey the warmth and tenderness that are sometimes associated with the development of children.

Perhaps the most important function of metaphors in the life of schools, as well as in other organizations, is to frame events and define situations.[6] The same circumstance, event, program, or activity can have very different consequences and can be regarded very differently depending on how it is framed. Metaphors are often used to provide the framing.

Consider *in-school suspension,* for example. This practice, common in many schools, involves removing misbehaving students from the regular classroom and placing them in a special room where they are carefully supervised by an adult. If the guiding metaphor of a school is the hospital, in-school suspension might be seen as the emergency room or the intensive care unit. If the guiding metaphor

---

[5]See George Lakoff and Mark Johnson, *Metaphors We Live By,* 2nd ed. (Chicago: University of Chicago Press, 2003), for a brilliant discussion of the power of metaphors in shaping everyday life. For other examples of metaphorical expressions applied to schools, see Phillip C. Schlechty and Anne Walker Joslin, "Images of School," *Teachers College Record,* 1984, *86*(1), 156–170; Phillip C. Schlechty, *Schools for the 21st Century* (San Francisco: Jossey-Bass, 1990).

[6]For the seminal book on framing and frame analysis see Erving Goffman, *Frame Analysis: An Essay on the Organization of Experience* (New York: HarperCollins, 1974). There is in fact little difference between what Goffman means when he uses the word *frame* and what Peter Senge means when he uses the term *mental model.*

is that of the factory, warehouse, or prison, it is more likely that the suspension room will be seen as the rework room (for remediation), the holding pen, or the prison cell. One principal I worked with kept track of what he called the "recidivism rate" (a term commonly used in criminology to designate the frequency of repeat offenders) in the in-school suspension room, using this rate as an indicator of the effectiveness of the practice in modifying student behavior. He also viewed the deprivation, humiliation, and isolation of the suspension room as the primary means of shaping behavior. He was so convinced of the efficacy of this strategy that he assigned a particularly unpleasant teacher to monitor the room. He reported that this strategy reduced the recidivism rate rather dramatically and that more students were effectively integrated into the "general population" (another prison designation).

How Policy Shapes Metaphors

Policymakers sometimes overlook the fact that the policies they enact often encourage the use of some metaphors and discourage the use of others. For example, when a principal is held accountable for attendance rates but provided no resources to make it possible to provide intensive treatment for misbehaving students, the principal and staff are encouraged to view the in-school suspension room as a punitive device or as a storage area where "bad kids" are sent and contained so they can still be counted as in attendance. Given resources, training, and encouragement, however, the principal and staff might view the in-school suspension room as a place where students can develop the skills they need to participate more fully in the intellectual life of the school; in that case, the room should have a different name.

Similarly, when policymakers present teachers with tightly scripted lesson plans and train principals in the skills needed for tight supervision, the images conjured up in the minds of teachers are more likely to be those of the assembly line worker in a factory, with the principal as a shop foreman, than they are to be those of a knowledgeable and creative professional working in an environment where creativity and imagination are required and expected. Teachers who are high in anxiety, possess a weak self-concept, and have little need for creative expression will likely comply with the expectation such an image would suggest. Teachers who are inner directed, creative, and less risk averse are likely to rebel or engage in bureaucratic scapegoating, passive compliance, quiet sabotage, or concealment of deviation from the prescribed norms and procedures. Many of these teachers will likely wind up leaving bureaucratically organized schools and school systems. The less creative and more security conscious will be more likely to stay, leading to an overall decline in the quality of teaching and teachers.

LESSONS LEARNED ABOUT THE USE OF METAPHORS

I have been engaged in efforts to reform schools for over forty years. During that time, I have used, studied, and thought about the ways metaphors inspire action, as well as the ways they can serve to inhibit action. Here are some of the lessons I have learned:

- *In any school or school district, different persons may carry quite different images of what "school" is.* These differences are likely to be reflected in the metaphors they use and the way they respond to metaphors presented to them. For example, an elementary school teacher is more likely to embrace the image of school as family or community than is a high school history teacher. For many high school teachers, the preferred image is that of the theater, in which the teacher is a star performer and the students are a duly appreciative audience. Many other secondary teachers prefer to see themselves as highly trained and specialized members of a profession organized along the lines of medicine or law.

- *Metaphors are often used to describe troublesome issues.* For example, many of the recent efforts to move school reform in the direction indicated by the No Child Left Behind legislation have resulted in teachers' increasingly seeing themselves trapped in the metaphor of the factory. Similarly, in schools beset with severe discipline problems, teachers complain that they have little time to do what they thought they were hired to do because they have to spend so much time playing the role of prison guard. They sometimes suggest as well that the reason they are having trouble in their classroom is that the principal is ineffective in the role of warden.

- *Individuals often mix metaphors, reflecting a lack of clarity regarding the way they see their school or school system.* For example, it is not uncommon to hear a high school teacher describe his or her preferred role as a service delivery professional (law, medicine), and at the same time suggest that the proper role of administrators should conform to the more bureaucratic expectations associated with the school as a factory, a warehouse, or a prison.

- *Metaphors that are clearly defined can as easily result in division as unity.* I recall one school district that had created a center for teachers that they referred to as the Teaching and Learning Center (TLC), and the metaphors they used to describe this center, as the initials TLC might suggest, conveyed warmth, nurturing, care, and concern. This worked well for many elementary teachers and for some high school teachers, but for many high school teachers, the softness suggested by the nurturing metaphors also conveyed a lack of attention to intellectual rigor, standards, and proper concern for academic matters. As a consequence, many high school teachers avoided the TLC, even though there were objectively many things there that could have been of value to them.

- *Over time, there is a tendency for metaphorical expressions to become consistent.* As larger visions become clear and more widely shared, consistency increases. Indeed, one of the indicators of a shared vision is that the metaphors participants use to describe a preferred future represent a relatively coherent and patterned view of the world as the participants would want it to be.

- *A vision that is clear and shared is important, but clarity of vision and consensus on the vision are not enough.* Sometimes the vision participants share is also the nightmare they are experiencing. It is therefore especially important that visions intended to provide future direction be morally defensible as well as clear and widely shared. The notion that students are products, often advanced by business leaders concerned with the quality of schooling as the source of a well-prepared workforce, is an example of a clear image of dubious moral and aesthetic value. Indeed, it is probably because so many business leaders speak of schools in images reminiscent of the factory that many educators, including some sophisticated reform leaders, become nearly apoplectic when it is suggested that the study of well-run businesses can provide useful insights for educators.[7]

---

[7]It is ironic that the idea of the learning organization grew out of the business sector rather than out of education. In my view schools should have all along been the archetype of the learning organization. If this had been the case, businesses would now be learning from public schools regarding the ways the affairs of people who value critical thought, creativity, disciplined dialogue, collaboration, and so on should be conducted in the context of formal organizations.

- *To be morally defensible, metaphors must express beliefs that are ethically defensible and congruent with the way the school—or the organization—defines its core business.* Most important among these beliefs are those that define the direction of the organization and the ends that are to be obtained in pursuit of that direction. Indeed, it may well be that the most important work for top-level school leaders is to identify what they hold to be the superordinate goals of the systems they lead and to find persuasive ways of expressing these goals to others. In skillful hands, metaphors are powerful tools in support of this task. (See Chapter Six for a further discussion of this matter.)

- *Metaphors are powerful tools in helping one to understand just how deeply embedded an ideal type has become and the variety of ways the principles of the ideal type are manifest in the organization.* The earlier discussion regarding the power of mental models illustrates this point. Most educators reject the idea that schools should be organized in the same way as factories, but many embrace the notion that schools should be organized like hospitals. What they overlook is that hospitals, like factories, are often organized on bureaucratic assumptions. Thus, it should not be surprising that teachers sometimes insist that they should be viewed as service delivery professionals (such as physicians) but continue to insist on viewing their students as products to be "modified." Nor should it be surprising that the clinical language of special education is often accompanied by many precise indicators regarding how students are to be placed, categorized, and sorted, as though they were items in a factory or a warehouse.

SELECTING METAPHORS TO AID IN TRANSFORMATION

Those who would be transformational leaders must learn to select the metaphors they use in ways that will most clearly illuminate the dimensions of organizational life they want to more clearly understand or bring to the attention of others. If, for example, one wanted to better understand how schools and classrooms are led and coordinated or how they might be led and coordinated, one might consider imagining how a school is like a symphony orchestra, a jazz band, or a marching band. By contrasting images of school as different musical groups, the fundamental principles of a school's organization and its patterns of leadership can become clearer.

Among other things, the examples provided by the orchestra, the jazz band, and the marching band can help clarify that different tasks require different types of leadership. The visible leader of the marching band (the drum major) is usually leader in name only; the real leader is the band director. The conductor of the symphony orchestra, however, who is equally visible, is the focus of the attention of all orchestra members and is both a literal and symbolic leader. The leader of the jazz band blends into the group so as to be hardly distinguishable from all the other members—at least to the naïve outsider. Disciplined discussions of the possible parallels between these forms of leadership and the type and style of leadership observed in schools and classrooms can yield powerful and useful insights.

There is no science that can prepare leaders to select the right metaphors. By understanding how metaphors work, however, leaders can become increasingly disciplined in one of the most critical arts of leadership: the art of creating and sharing new mental models and revealing the debilitating effects of the mental models that are so often unconsciously embraced.

A SUGGESTED EXERCISE

Mental models affect both attachment and estrangement, involvement and alienation. The ways men and women and boys and girls are treated in school are shaped by the images that are held regarding the roles of students, parents, teachers, and others who work in and around the school. When these images are ennobling, people are treated well. When they are degrading, they are treated poorly.

School leaders interested in encouraging faculties to consider the need for school transformation might find it useful to engage their staff in conversations regarding the mental models they currently hold of their own schools. Table 4.1 and the metaphors in Chapters Four and Five can be useful in supporting such discussions. I recommend, however, that before proceeding with such discussions, participants be encouraged to reread Chapters Four and Five as well as Appendix B so that they can consider the future while reflecting on the past and present.

OTHER USES OF METAPHORS

In addition to providing insight into the assumptions being made about the nature of a school, attention to metaphors can serve other valuable ends:

- Through the intentional application of metaphorical reasoning to school life, participants in the life of the school can be encouraged to take a few steps back from day-to-day realities and gain enough distance to see a bigger picture. Once the picture comes into focus, it becomes more possible to think about ways the picture would need to change to make it more pleasing for all who participate in the life of the school.

- The use of metaphors can cushion the threat value of discomforting but important facts that must be communicated if a sense of urgency is to be developed and real change is to occur. For example, characterizing the school as a warehouse can make more obvious the dysfunctional aspects of labeling and categorizing students, or it can make clearer how misused in-school suspension programs can have negative effects throughout the school. Indeed, using metaphors is one of the most powerful tools I know to reveal in a relatively nonthreatening way the tendency of schools to seek compliance over engagement—and thereby to cause discussions of this matter. The picture of students as products or inmates does not inspire support, even from those who operate on assumptions that are consistent with the view that students are, or should be treated as though they were, products or inmates.

- Metaphors can be used to convey messages about what schools should be and could be. They can express unrealized possibilities and can be used to raise "what if" questions: What if we thought of students as volunteers or as knowledge workers, and parents as genuine partners? What if we thought of teachers as leaders, and principals as leaders of leaders?

- Metaphors offer a way for people to talk about school reform that is powerful and incisive but less likely to be pointed at individuals. Participants can become trapped in certain roles, in schools and in the rest of life. Sometimes metaphors can help them understand the traps they are in. Sometimes the metaphors people have already adopted to understand who and what they are can become traps, holding them in outworn and unproductive circumstances. When individuals become aware of the assumptions their chosen metaphors reveal, they are sometimes made uncomfortable, but it is in such discomfort that one finds the seeds of change.

A CONCLUDING COMMENT

Metaphors and stories are among the primary tools in the tool kit of effective transformational leaders. This is becoming increasingly apparent to business consultants who are trying to communicate transformational messages. For example, there has been a spate of books written by business authors that use extended metaphors and analogies to make points.[8] Educational leaders must learn to use such storytelling devices, drawing on not only the written word but also powerful television productions and digitized games to convey ideas. To move the schools into this century, educational leaders need to learn how to fully use twenty-first-century tools as well as storytelling skills that have served as culture building tools since prehistoric times.

[8]See, for example, John Kotter and Holger Rathgeber, *Our Iceberg Is Melting: Changing and Succeeding Under Any Conditions* (New York: St. Martin's Press, 2005), or David Hutchens, *Shadows of the Neanderthal: Illuminating the Beliefs That Limit Our Organizations* (Waltham, Mass.: Pegasus Communications, 1999).

Creating the Capacity to Support Innovation

I f the performance of America's schools is to improve, it is essential that the schools have the capacity to innovate on a continuous basis and in a disciplined way. Bureaucracies lack this capacity. Continuous innovation is the lifeblood of learning organizations.

Bureaucracies are, of course, capable of installing innovations, but only if the innovations do not require fundamental changes in the way critical social systems are organized—that is, as long as the innovations are sustaining innovations. As I have suggested in earlier chapters, the introduction of innovations that call for rearranging the relationships within or between social systems usually creates a crisis in a bureaucracy.

It is the inability to smoothly incorporate innovations requiring systemic changes that makes bureaucracies incapable of continuous innovation, and it is this failing more than any other that leads to the need to transform schools from bureaucracies to learning organizations. Thus, this transformation requires, among other things, capacity building, the topic of this chapter.

CAPACITY BUILDING: A POINT OF VIEW

In the most generic sense, the word *capacity* has to do with potentials and limitations: what a person, group, or organization is capable of doing if called on to act. It also has to do with the limits beyond which performance should not be expected. To say that a jar has a one-quart capacity is to say that the jar can hold up to one quart of a liquid but no more than that.

The word *capacity* is meaningless without some referent. The question to ask about capacity is, "The capacity to do what?" The most critical capacities in organizational life are those needed to innovate on a continuous basis and to adjust critical systems in ways that are supportive of the innovations that are installed.

Because schools are usually organized as bureaucracies, their capacity to install dramatic innovations is limited by a lack of nimbleness with regard to systems change; indeed, it is that lack that makes certain innovations disruptive in the first place. If schools were organized as learning organizations, there would be few innovations that would be disruptive, because the drive to innovate would be built into the DNA of the learning organization itself.

It is therefore incumbent on leaders to focus attention on transforming their schools into learning organizations. Only through such transformation can schools develop the capacity to support continuous innovation. Without that capacity, the ability to improve schools is limited to improvements that can be accomplished with sustaining innovations alone. Thus, capacity building is both the end and the means of school transformation.

Over the past twenty years, I have spent considerable time identifying and describing the characteristics of schools and school systems that are successful in managing innovations and undergoing the types of systemic changes that powerful innovations require. Over these years, I have identified three general capacities that schools and school systems must have in place if they are to be successful at supporting and sustaining systemic changes and introducing disruptive innovations:[1]

- The capacity to establish and maintain a focus on the future
- The capacity to maintain direction once a clear focus has been established
- The capacity to act strategically by reallocating existing resources, seizing opportunities, and creating a new future

SYSTEM CAPACITY STANDARDS

In my work with many school districts and a dedicated staff, I have created a set of standards that will help to describe the nature of the capacities that must be

[1]For a more detailed discussion of my views on these matters, read Phillip C. Schlechty, *Inventing Better Schools* (San Francisco: Jossey-Bass, 1997), and Phillip C. Schlechty, *Shaking Up the Schoolhouse* (San Francisco: Jossey-Bass, 2001).

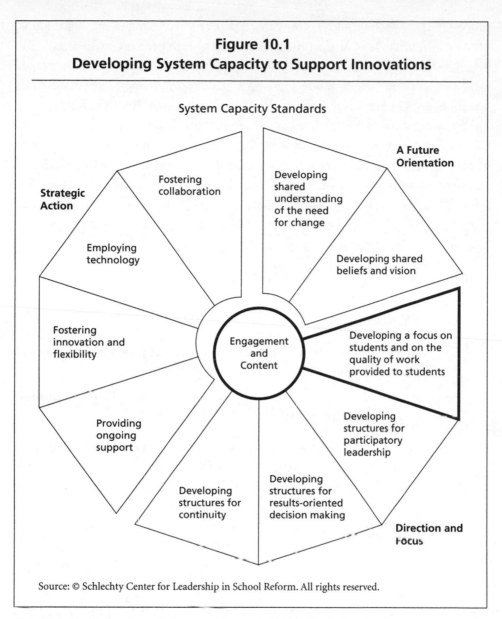

Figure 10.1
Developing System Capacity to Support Innovations

System Capacity Standards

A Future Orientation

Developing shared understanding of the need for change

Developing shared beliefs and vision

Fostering collaboration

Strategic Action

Employing technology

Fostering innovation and flexibility

Engagement and Content

Developing a focus on students and on the quality of work provided to students

Developing structures for participatory leadership

Providing ongoing support

Developing structures for continuity

Developing structures for results-oriented decision making

Direction and Focus

developed within the social systems that define schools (and other organizations as well). Figure 10.1 summarizes those standards.

A Future Orientation

The capacity of a school, or any other organization, to be oriented toward the future depends on the ability of the organization and its leaders to develop a shared understanding of the problems that give rise to the need for change and the ability to communicate a clear vision of the direction that change will entail. Too often leaders try to sell a solution to a problem long before they have persuaded others that there is a problem for which the actions they are proposing is a solution. In a bureaucracy where compliance is assumed, it is relatively easy to maintain initial action aimed toward implementation, but as the dimensions of the solutions become clearer and the pressure of the solution on existing systems becomes more obvious, it is most likely that the solution will be abandoned unless it requires little in the way of systemic adjustments. For this reason, it is imperative that the organization have the capacity to develop and sustain a clear vision and sense of direction, as well as the ability to communicate the need for the types of systemic changes that will be required for the innovation.

Developing Shared Beliefs and Vision   To focus on the future, leaders must be able to articulate a vision of the future. To articulate a vision they must be able to answer two questions:

- What business are we currently in, and to what extent do our customers and clients value what we do?
- If we want to become highly valued by our customers and clients, what business do we need to be in?

The key to school transformation lies in understanding that the existing system was designed to produce attendance and compliance and to harvest whatever engagement happens to occur. If public education is to survive and thrive, it will be necessary to focus on nurturing student engagement.[2] Schools and school systems must be positioned to be in the student engagement business rather than the compliance business. Rather than demanding and commanding compliance without commitment, they must attend to creating work that commands attention as well as commitment.

If this view is accepted, it is clear that schools of the future must be organized in ways that are at substantial variance with the way they are now, and teachers must learn to do things only a few teachers have ever done purposefully and consistently, as opposed to simply learning to do what "good" teachers have always done.

---

[2]Much that I am suggesting here is discussed in more detail in my book *Working on the Work* (San Francisco: Jossey-Bass, 2002).

Today most teachers, even good teachers, place heavy reliance on the fact that their tradition-based role as adults entitles them to expect students to look to them for instruction, direction, and guidance. In the opening chapters of this book, I suggested that the assumptions underlying these expectations are increasingly suspect. It will, therefore, become necessary for teachers to rely less on the status claims that have been embedded in the role of teacher and to rely more on the expert authority that derives from a deep understanding of student motives. It also means that schools must be organized to support teachers who are intent on changing their roles and to shed obsolete expectations that come out of the past but have no place in the future.

Teachers need to focus on creating work that gains the attention and commitment of students. Although they must ensure that the work students do calls on them to learn things that the adult community values and sees as important, the primary job of the teacher can no longer be that of instruction and ensuring that students are on task simply because the teacher demands that it be so. The title of Marc Prensky's article on the new expectation students have regarding their learning—"Engage Me or Enrage Me"—is not too far off base.[3]

Developing Shared Understanding of the Need for Change   In addition to being capable of leading by vision, leaders must be able to determine whether the innovations required to move the vision into reality require one or more sustaining innovations—or innovations that go beyond the capacity of the existing system. Put differently, leaders must determine whether the innovations they are trying to install call for changes that are systemic in nature.

This means that leaders need to be able to assess whether the existing system has the capacity to support the proposed innovation. If it does, then the job of the official organizational leaders (for example, superintendents and principals) is to ensure that those who are charged with installing the innovation have the authority needed to command the resources they require. If the needed capacity is lacking, leaders must involve themselves in the much more difficult (and less well understood) process of capacity building.

---

[3]Marc Prensky, "Engage Me or Enrage Me: What Today's Learners Demand," *Educause Review*, Sept.–Oct. 2005.

Building the Capacity to Focus on the Future   Assuming that key leaders—the superintendent, key central office personnel, and the majority of principals and teacher leaders—share a common understanding of the need to install disruptive innovations, they will also need to envision the kinds of changes that will be necessary to support these innovations. This means that the school district and its leaders must have the capacity to do the following:

- Communicate the beliefs that give rise to the effort in a way that is compelling to those whose support will be needed to bring about the changes required to act on these beliefs.

- Develop among key leaders and relevant constituencies a shared vision of what schools and the school system would look like if these beliefs were acted on and develop a bias toward action relevant to these beliefs.

- Assess the current status of operations at the classroom, building, and district levels and, based on these assessments, develop plans for moving each of these units toward a condition in which the guiding beliefs are more and more fully realized in the district.[4]

- Create consensus around the plans that are developed as well as a shared commitment to act on these plans, including a commitment to provide or locate the resources (time, people, space, information, and technology) needed to support these actions.

This means that it is essential for leaders to ponder what they believe about the business of schools and how schools go about doing that business. It also requires that they make clear decisions regarding their willingness to commit to and support what they say they believe, even when the going gets tough. Without such clear commitments, the likelihood of successfully installing a disruptive innovation is quite modest.

If the school district is envisioned as a school system rather than a system of schools, all schools in the district should be guided by the same beliefs about the nature of the core business of schools, the role of teachers, and so on.[5] This

---

[4]The Schlechty Center has developed a variety of tools to support such assessments. See www.schlechtycenter.org.

[5]It is my view that much harm has been done to public education and to the ideas of excellence and equity by confusing decentralization of decision-making authority with the decentralization of values, commitments, and beliefs. Devolving decision-making authority to the level of the schoolhouse and the classroom is essential to school transformation. If this occurs without serious attention to the central values and beliefs that will guide decisions, however, the likely result will be mediocrity for the masses and excellence for the few, rather than excellence for all students.

means that leaders must have considerable persuasive skills to move followers from beliefs to vision.

It is also essential that this vision, which is necessarily a district-wide vision, be translated into missions that can drive action in the schoolhouse, the classroom, each department, the superintendent's office, and the school board itself. Each of these operating units might have a different mission, reflecting both their unique condition and unique capacity to contribute to the overall good of the district, but all would be disciplined by the same vision and be committed to a common direction anchored in shared beliefs. Indeed, another way to think about mission is to conceive of it as an operating unit's version of the overall vision that drives the enterprise. (Visions differ from missions in the sense that visions cannot be accomplished; they can only be realized. Visions set direction; missions determine action. Missions can be accomplished, and it is in the accomplishment of missions that visions are realized.)[6] For example, a compelling mission for a large urban high school might be very different from the mission that would guide a small elementary school in the same district, but both missions would derive from the same vision, and each would be consistent with the beliefs and standards that guide the district as a whole.

Direction and Focus

Transforming schools from bureaucracies into learning organizations means first developing a clear sense of direction. This can be done only by centering attention on those elements of the system that have to do with the means by which direction is maintained in an organization where creativity and inventiveness, rather than routine and control, are prime values.

Focus on Students and Quality Work   Two general conditions must be ensured if direction is to be maintained:

1. Leaders must have a clear image of where they are going.
2. Leaders must have a clear understanding of where they are now—and some appreciation of what it is going to take to get from where they are to where they want to go.

In part, the development of a clear image of where leaders intend for the system to go is addressed in the visioning process. It is essential, however, that this

[6]See Schlechty, *Inventing Better Schools,* for further discussion of these distinctions.

process be informed by a clear understanding of the nature of the core business of schools as well as an understanding of the available means of conducting that business. There must be some general consensus on answers to such questions as, "What do we do around here, and what does it mean?" Consider the image of the old story about the two workers in the marble quarry: "Are we building a temple, or are we just breaking up rocks?"

If leaders accept the premise that the core business of schools should be designing educational activities for students that command attention and commitment, as well as leading and supporting students in the pursuit of such work, then it should be clear that the focus of schools should be on students and their motives. In other words, the business of schools is designing engaging work for students. It should therefore be clear that engaging work is the primary product of schools and that students are the first-line customers of schools. Given clarity on these matters, one of the first results that should be assessed is the ability of school leaders and those who teach to focus attention on creating engaging work for students.[7]

Regardless of the vision that guides schools, the goal should be to ensure that all students are learning at high levels. Assessing the quality of student learning therefore becomes a key consideration and must be done on a continuous basis using many measures and tools. The question of whether annual assessments using standardized measures are appropriate depends on the judgment of local educators and the desires of parents and other members of the local community, but regular and continuous assessment of student learning is essential if internal processes are to be disciplined.

The kinds of assessments I have in mind are aimed at continuous improvement, rather than to increase the power of persons outside the system to control internal operations. There are clearly many other factors that an educationally sophisticated community might want to consider as well. Among these is the capacity of the system to support continuous innovations that result in continuously improved performance of systems as well as of students.

Developing Structures for Participatory Leadership Another critical component of the capacity to maintain direction has to do with participatory leadership. Disruptive innovations interrupt habits and often create fear and uncertainty. Participatory leadership may not reduce uncertainty, but it

---

[7]I provide a framework for such an assessment in *Working on the Work*.

can help to transform fear into heroic collective action by making it possible to exploit the power of what anthropologists refer to as the *shared ordeal.*

Knowing that others are as frightened as you are often generates courage. After all, courage is nothing more than behaving as you need to even when you are scared to death. It is only through participatory leadership that one is likely to create the level and type of commitments necessary to generate the courage to sustain disruptive innovations.

Rosabeth Moss Kanter observes,

> My favorite maxim of management, if not of life, is "Everything can look like a failure in the middle."
>
> Predictable problems arise in the middle of nearly every attempt to do something new. Almost inevitably, innovation projects encounter shortages of time or resources because forecasts were overly optimistic. Unexpected obstacles have to be removed for the project to proceed. Momentum is lost because of staff turnover. Morale dips because of setbacks or sheer fatigue. Or critics attack because they start to notice the project when it looks like it might succeed. Before that, it was not enough of a threat to arouse antagonism.[8]

It takes a great deal of courage and commitment for those who are associated with the change to ride through these rough spots. Such commitments are more likely to happen when the change has been introduced by leaders who know how to involve others in decisions, are strong enough to absorb failure on behalf of others, and are strong enough to give away success to others. Without such leaders, system change will not occur.

In summary, people who have committed to a common vision based on shared beliefs are more likely to persist with their efforts when they confront difficulties than are those whose only reason for participation is compliance with a directive from above. Enhancing the capacity of leaders to lead in a participatory way and developing policies and procedures that encourage participatory leadership are essential capacity-building activities. Without this capacity, few will be willing to take the risks that must be taken to invent new systems.

[8]Rosabeth Moss Kanter, *On the Frontiers of Management* (Boston: Harvard Business School Press, 1997), p. 11.

Developing Structures for Results-Oriented Decision Making   Consciousness of intended results and a disciplined approach to assessing them are essential to maintaining direction, especially in an environment where innovation is encouraged. Otherwise what starts out as an innovation ends up as a fad, and what begins as vital movement becomes directionless meandering.

But a view of results that is too narrow or truncated can stifle innovation and creativity. Indeed, one of the unfortunate consequences of the standards-based reform movement and the governmental drive to make schools and teachers accountable for learning outcomes is to create the impression inside many schools that test scores are the only results that matter and that the only data that matter are those that can be derived from standardized tests and submitted to statistical analysis. This is nonsense, but it is a type of nonsense that must be confronted by school leaders who are sincerely committed to enhancing the capacity of the districts they lead to use results as a means of disciplining action and maintaining direction.

Schools, like other formal organizations, produce many results—some intentional and some unintentional, some recognized and some unrecognized, some that are desirable and some that, if recognized, might be unwanted. Only by attending to all of these results can leaders maintain direction while they install the kind of disruptive innovations that are required if the quality of student learning experiences is to improve.

Leaders must have a clear understanding of the causal mechanisms that result in students' being willing to do the things they must do to learn those things schools are designed for them to learn and that will lead students to invest the effort they must invest to learn. For example, students are more likely to be engaged if their teachers are as well, so it is as important to be as concerned with results for teachers as it is to be concerned with results for students. Schools are more likely to be successful when the communities support them and when the results produced enhance the quality of community life as well as student success. Thus, one of the results that should be assessed is the level and quality of community involvement and support. Assessing these kinds of results is as important as, if not more important than, testing every child every time there is an opportunity to do so.

Developing Structures for Continuity   Continuity is dependent on two features of organizational life: induction and executive succession. Effective induction programs must attend to inculcating in new members the beliefs that guide action, as well as ensuring that individuals new to the organization possess the technical skills needed to act in the way the culture requires. Too many induction programs in education attend only to technical matters. Moreover, when transformation is occurring and new social systems are being installed, it becomes equally necessary to provide for the induction of members of the old system into the new. Indeed, the failure to provide for such induction often leads to failed transformation efforts.

Executive succession planning, which is virtually absent in most school districts, is also essential to the maintenance of direction. Indeed, the absence of such planning leads teachers to the view that "this too shall pass," a view that not only decreases commitment but also engenders cynicism. Leaders who are committed to building capacity therefore must attend to executive succession planning almost before anything else.

People who are asked to make the sacrifices that transformational change requires need to be assured that a leadership structure to sustain them is in place. In an organization that is already in the process of transformation, a new leader with a vision different from the vision that is motivating the initiative is as likely to generate cynicism about the prospects of improvement as to inspire new hope. Being a visionary leader has its merit, but it is more important to be a leader who leads by vision. The most difficult work in any transformation may not be in establishing a vision but in sustaining it over time. Critical to school transformatiom is ensuring that when leaders change, the vision that inspires action remains constant.

Leaders who are committed to the creation of organizations that have the capacity to support disruptive innovations do have different characteristics from those who lead change-inept organizations:

Leaders in Learning Organizations	Leaders in Bureaucracies
Are clear about their core business and can communicate this understanding to others in clear and persuasive ways.	Have only a vague understanding of their core business, or define their business in terms of the peculiar interests of their department or operating unit. This results in leaders' holding competing views and therefore sends unclear messages to others regarding what they should be about and what matters should be given priority.

Treat change as an ongoing, expected, and normal process.

Treat each change as an independent event.

View new technologies and shifts in the external environment as opportunities for growth, improvement, and continuing development.

View new technologies and shifts in the external environment as threats to internal stability and problems to be managed and dealt with.

Ensure that systems are in place to support changes once they have been initiated.

Fail to attend to the support systems needed to sustain changes that have been initiated.

Invest in the creation and maintenance of support systems in the same way they invest in programs and projects intended to produce substantive improvements in performance.

Invest in programs and projects intended to improve performance but fail to invest in the support systems needed to sustain these programs and projects.

Confront uncertainty with ease and "thrive on chaos."[8]

Are overwhelmed by uncertainty and seek to impose a traditional order on situations that are not fully understood or are particularly threatening.

Introduce innovations as a means of improving performance or expanding service rather than use innovations as tools to appease critics.

Introduce innovations primarily as a means of accommodating outside threats and protecting the control exercised over the core operations of the enterprise.

Often incorporate multiple changes simultaneously, and sometimes introduce changes that create unusual demands on the system and the people on whom these systems depend.

Seek to limit the number and types of changes introduced.

Place a high value on innovation and novelty.

Place a high value on stability and predictability, and to ensure those qualities, they seek to limit the impact of the environment on day-to-day operations by creating boundary systems that protect internal operations from external influences.

[8]See Tom Peters, *Thriving on Chaos: Handbook for a Management Revolution* (New York: Knopf, 1987).

Strategic Action

Strategic action, which focuses on the future, seeks to bring into existence some desired end state that has yet to be realized. It is not the intent of strategic action to solve immediate problems. Rather, the intent is to seize opportunities and invent new futures for the organization.

Schools face a number of significant barriers to strategic action:

- The way schools are governed, especially the tendency of boards of education to anchor decisions in short-term constituent interests as opposed to strategic goals

- The tendency to allow efforts to keep things from getting worse (mainte-nance interests) to overwhelm efforts to make things better (developmental interests)

- The lack of an understanding of and support for the experimentalism that is involved in innovative efforts, especially innovations that require the disrup-tion of existing systems

- The tendency to try to domesticate emerging technologies rather than incor-porate such technologies in ways that exploit the full power that they might otherwise bring to the task

- The limited capacity of most schools and school districts to develop and sus-tain actions that call for collaboration within the system, for example, among departments, grade levels, or schools, as well as between the system and other organizations that have a stake in the way the schools operate, such as teacher unions and advocacy groups

If schools and school systems are to develop the capacity to act strategically, lead-ers must be prepared to address these issues in the following way:

- Ensure that appropriate support systems are in place—especially human resource development systems and political and financial support systems.

- Create a culture that drives out fear, encourages responsible risk taking, and separates unsuccessful tries from punishment

- Assess the system requirements presented by innovations and ensure that these requirements are responded to at the same time that the other require-ments of the innovation are being addressed

- Support and encourage the development of relationships within schools, among schools, and between the school district and the larger community to create conditions of trust and perceptions of competence and community

Providing Ongoing Support Providing support is essential, whether the innovation to be installed is a sustaining or a disruptive one. The kind of support needed when an innovation calls for systemic change, however, is likely to be quite different from the support needed when the innovation is a sustaining one, for several reasons:

- Sustaining innovations build on preexisting competence. Innovations that require systemic changes often require persons to do things they have never before done, which force them to act in areas where they may have limited competence. This means that leaders, especially top-level leaders such as superintendents and boards of education, must work hard to provide assurances that initial failures will not be punished and that honest efforts—even when immediate results are not evident—will be rewarded.

- The type of training that can be provided to support disruptive innovations is often quite different from that required when the innovation is sustaining in nature. In the case of sustaining innovations, it is likely that the demands of the innovation are well known, codified, and subject to demonstration and modeling. Disruptive innovations are usually more uncertain in their demands, less clear in their requirements, and less easily demonstrated and modeled. This requires a much more collegial approach to implementation, in which all who participate do so as learners and in which there are no clear models to master. Rather than mandates for implementation, disruptive innovations involve invitations to invention.

- Because disruptive innovations introduce so much uncertainty and static into existing systems, the intentions, motives, and commitments of leaders, especially top-level leaders, become critical to successful implementation. When innovations are disruptive, the integrity of leaders and the perception that leadership commitments can and will be sustained over time are critical determinants of success. Furthermore, in the case of disruptive innovations, the time line in which success can be measured is likely to be much longer than would be the time line appropriate to measuring the success of a sustaining innovation.

To provide support to disruptive innovations, leaders must have or must develop the capabilities these issues suggest. Among other things, they must do the following:

- Develop strong and personal bonds of trust and feelings of common destiny with those whose support they want and need in order to make the innovation work as it is intended to.

- Be prepared to make themselves vulnerable and proceed as a learning leader rather than an expert leader. Like those they are leading, they will often be on the cutting edge of ignorance rather than on the cutting edge of knowledge, and they need to learn to be comfortable with this condition.

- Like Caesar's wife, they must not only be virtuous but must appear to be virtuous. The slightest dissembling can destroy credibility. Unlike bureaucratic leaders who sometimes absorb success and give away failure, leaders who are committed to the installation of disruptive innovations must learn to absorb failure and give away success. Fixing the system is very different from "fixing the blame" or solving the problems that the present system has created.

Fostering Innovation and Flexibility Although encouraging innovation is essential to strategic action, schools are peculiarly ill equipped to encourage innovations, especially disruptive ones. Although they regularly install innovations, they seldom stick with them long enough to ensure that their intended effects will be realized. The result is that many see schools as fickle and given to fads. But the fact is that schools too often lack the system capacity to support innovations through the difficult stages of implementation.

Fostering Collaboration Collaboration and the ability to engage in collaborative action are becoming increasingly important to the survival of public schools. Indeed, without the ability to collaborate with others, the prospect of truly repositioning schools in the constellation of community forces is not likely. And schools that are not repositioned are unlikely to have the capacity to support the kind of disruptive innovations that will be needed to ensure a healthy future for public education in America. Here is what schools and school leaders must do to ensure that the organizations they lead will have the capacity to collaborate with others. First and foremost, leaders must ensure sufficient cohesion within the school and the school district that cooperation with others does not needlessly threaten the internal integrity of the system. Sharing authority with others is essential to collaboration, but sharing authority is not the same as giving up authority. Only organizations that have clear beliefs to which most members are committed can collaborate without fear of compromising their mission and their integrity.

Second, the social boundaries of the system must be sufficiently permeable that interaction with others can be encouraged and supported without aimless wandering about, attempting to satisfy so many competing interests that nothing of substance develops. This means that leaders must lead rather than simply manage, and they must provide direction rather than seek to control.

Finally, the ability to collaborate is dependent on all who are parties to the collaboration having a clear sense of the mission they are pursuing and the vision they want to realize. Failing this, the most politically powerful parties to the collaboration will almost certainly dominate the action and co-opt the resources of other members. They are likely to serve their own ends with limited attention to the collective ends to which the collaborative effort should be addressed.

Employing Technology   Introducing and effectively using new and emerging technologies, which I have defined as the means of doing the job, whatever the means and the job may be, requires the capacity to evaluate the technologies to assess the demands they will put on the operating systems in place. It also means that leaders will be prepared to reallocate resources (time, people, space, and information) and make the system changes required to support these technologies. In my view, the greatest threat to the survival of public education is the inability of the schools to use new and emerging technologies in the ways they have been designed to be used. Rather than use them to provide students with new forms of schoolwork, for example, too many educators use them to do old forms of schoolwork in new ways.

PERSISTENCE OF EFFORT

One of the most fundamental problems confronting those who would transform schools from organizations that produce compliance to organizations that nurture and develop engagement is that of persistence of effort. As Rosabeth Moss

Kanter has observed, "To convert imagination into useful ideas requires persistence, which is also helped or hindered by the organization."[9]

Competent leaders who display courage and strength of will are essential to the transformation of schools. But competent, courageous, and strong-willed leaders will fail if the schools and school districts they are trying to transform do not have the systems in place that are needed to support and sustain innovations over time. For example, school districts that do not create the means to protect developmental activity will not be able to sustain efforts at continuous improvement because the needs of the maintenance systems will overwhelm developmental needs and lead to the co-optation of developmental resources. (See the discussion in Chapter Three regarding goal displacement.) Persistence of effort is an organizational capacity issue as much as a question of competence, courage, and will.

Thus, leaders must work first on those things that enhance the capacity of the schools they are leading. This enhanced capacity will make it possible to invent schools where nearly every child learns at high levels and no child will be left behind—because every child will have a genuine opportunity to get ahead.

[9]Kanter, *On the Frontiers of Management,* p. 11.

Standards as Sources of Direction

One of the fundamental differences between schools organized as bureaucracies and schools organized as learning organizations is the position that performance standards occupy in the constellation of social systems defining the organization. In a bureaucracy, standards serve as a primary link between the evaluation system and the power and authority system. In a learning organization, standards link the directional system to the knowledge development and transmission system and the recruitment and induction system. In bureaucracies, standards are rules, and compliance is expected. In learning organizations, standards define preferred states to be realized and serve as guideposts on a continuous journey. The intent of most of those who advocate the use of standards as a base for school reform is to use the standards as a source of direction. But because standards are usually installed in the context of a bureaucratic structure, they most often constrain creativity and impose external controls.

My intent in this chapter is to suggest some ways that standards might be repositioned in schools so that they serve more effectively as tools to set and maintain direction, and as a source of inspiration for creative solutions to the problems that beset America's schools.

REFRAMING THE PROBLEM OF STANDARDS

If standards are to be used as powerful tools for transforming schools into learning organizations and building community, state governments must change the way they approach the business of setting and enforcing standards. Rather than setting many standards, the state will need to be concerned with setting only a relatively few of the right standards.

The only student performance standards that states should develop are those for graduation. As spokespersons for the taxpayers, state officials should be expected to assert what they, in consultation with constituent groups, believe the outcomes of schooling should be. Setting performance standards for graduation is a powerful way of meeting this expectation.

It is a mistake, however, for states to go beyond stating outcome measures associated with the expectations of high school graduates. Moreover, the state should not include in its list of standards the means by which local communities are to produce these outcomes; for example, states should not specify courses to be taken or hours of attendance. The standards should have to do with what a reasonably well-educated high school graduate needs to know and be able to do. All other student performance standards are matters best left up to local communities and local educators.

Variances between and among children and differences in expectations within communities are too great to impose unreasonable consistency on what necessarily requires highly flexible processes. It is, for example, unreasonable to expect a child who has had little language experience at home to perform at the same level as a child of the same age who is born into a language-rich environment. Moreover, the academic performance of both children has less to do with school programs than with nonschool experiences, and neither the students nor their schools should be blamed or credited for the differences that show up on tests. It is only over time that school effects should be expected to be measurable on a basis that makes between-student and between-school comparisons meaningful. (The so-called value-added assessment process is an effort to deal with this problem, but these efforts usually rely on standardized tests, which still confuse value added by family and community to value added by school.)

What is more important is to recognize that if the child who has language deficits is ever to meet reasonable graduation standards, he or she needs high-quality and intensive language experiences. Testing and retesting this child to prove what an observant teacher would already know does no good for the child or the teacher. Moreover, asking such a child to take a test that will simply reinforce the child's understanding that he or she cannot do the same level of work as the student in the next seat may do some real harm to that child. (Diagnostic testing, customized to meet the needs of individual children, can be a powerful tool, but such tests cannot be administered en masse, as most of the standardized tests administered by state mandates are.)

The argument I am making can, of course, be used to support what some have called "the soft bigotry of low expectations." This must not be permitted to occur. Schools must, however, have many different types of standards, including those having to do with clear commitments to excellence and equity. Such standards pertain to the values embedded in the culture of the school rather than in the technical aspects of student performance standards.

High expectations should not be confused with unrealistic performance standards. The soft bigotry of low expectations can be avoided only when the values of the school and the community insist that every child should be challenged every day, but that no child should be without success on any given day.

This leads to a second observation—one having to do with the enforcement of standards. In the daily lives of students, there is considerable evidence that evaluations by teachers, parents, and peers are likely to have more impact on student performance than evaluations done by the state. Dornbausch and Scott, for example, carried out studies in which they found that evaluations done by people who are significant in the lives of those being evaluated and are believed to be in a position to observe performance have more effect than do evaluations conducted from afar or on an impersonal basis.[1] This should not be surprising, but its significance sometimes escapes those who operate from a bureaucratic mind-set.

If state standards are to be enforced local communities are going to have to do the enforcing. To ensure that this happens, states need to go well beyond administering standardized tests, counting dropouts, reviewing teacher credentials, and administering punishments and rewards for noncompliance with specified standards. The bottom line is that states must find ways to encourage local communities to develop standards in which the community believes and the state can support as well.

---

[1]S. M. Dornbausch and W. R. Scott, *Evaluation and the Exercise of Authority: A Theory of Control Applied to Diverse Organizations* (San Francisco: Jossey-Bass, 1975).

Developing Student Performance Standards That Orient Action

One of the first tasks confronting a school leader intent on transforming schools into learning organizations should be to review state graduation standards and endeavor to reduce them to a few powerful statements that focus on action while at the same time addressing the areas of concern in the state standards.[2] Rather than asking how we get students to perform on a test, the question becomes, "What kind of authentic performances would one expect of a student who could meet these standards, and what would those performances need to demonstrate to ensure that the standards are being met?" The answers to this question would need to be stated in ways that are understandable to students as well as to their parents and teachers. For example, a history department might state a standard as follows:

> Graduates will be able to carry on an intelligent conversation with a knowledgeable expert regarding what the graduates consider to be defining events in the history of the United States, and they will be able to justify why they include some events and exclude others.

Similarly a science department might frame a standard as follows:

> Students will be able to read with understanding the lead article in the journal *Nature* [a sophisticated science journal] in the month of their graduation and carry on an informed discussion about its contents with a person who is known to have expertise in science.

Given such statements, students would know from the time they enter high school that before they graduate, they will be expected to carry on informed conversations with persons who are knowledgeable about history, read journals like *Nature,* and so on. They would know that in these conversations, they should be prepared to make a reasonable case about why some historic events are more important than others. They would know that they need to have a science vocabulary to read *Nature* and therefore could engage in self-assessment by trying to read such a journal.

[2]Douglas Reeves refers to such standards as power standards. See Douglas B. Reeves, "Power Standards: How Leaders Add Value to State and National Standards," in *Educational Leadership*: *The Jossey-Bass Reader on Educational Leadership,* 2nd ed. (San Francisco: Jossey-Bass, 2007). What I am suggesting here has some parallels to Reeves's argument, though I am not certain Reeves would agree with all that I suggest. For example, I am interested in reframing state standards, whereas my understanding is that Reeves's concern has more to do with prioritizing than with reframing.

Students would, of course, need to be able to identify historic events and understand the language of science but identifying historic events and science vocabulary lessons is not what history and science standards are about. The standards are about understanding history and science, not simply knowing isolated facts and being able to identify isolated events.

When standards are stated in the way suggested here, teachers will be in a better position to use them as guides to their design of work for students and as tools to help them assess the progress of students. Such standards could be enforced in casual conversations with students, as well as in conversations among students and between students and their parents. Standards stated in this way also have increased potential to become compelling simply because they suggest activity that might become part of the intellectual life of the school and part of the conversation and dialogue that should go on in school. For example, as part of their work in schools, students might be encouraged to create electronic discussion boards dealing with topics relevant to the standards. Teachers, students, parents, and other members of the community could be invited to share views about the subjects that are the focus of the standards.

State standards are necessarily designed to satisfy audiences external to the school who must be satisfied, as well as to provide direction to those who work in schools. They are therefore stated as universal propositions. To compel action, standards must focus on particular situations at a given time. Standards stated in the manner suggested above are designed to satisfy students, teachers, and parents. They are intended to motivate and give direction in a specific context rather than simply serve as a basis for evaluating performances.

For these standards to fulfill the directional functions, parents and other adults must be able to use the standard to test students just as teachers can use the standard. This means that parents and other relevant adults need to be informed about the standards and their intended uses. It also means that the standard must be stated in terms that are clear to noneducators.

Locally developed student performance standards must be operable on a day-to-day basis. They must be clear in the work that teachers design, the tasks that students undertake, and the support that parents and other adults provide the children. Most important, they must be applied every day where they count the most: in every classroom and every school.

The critical point is that if standards are to compel action, students and teachers must be able to visualize what the standard means for them, and there should not be so many standards that teachers and students are overwhelmed. If school faculties took the time to formulate standards something in the fashion suggested here, both teachers and students will have scaffolding around which they can organize their work and their experiences. It is this organization of effort that will give clear direction to schools.

Developmental Standards

The ability of students to meet graduation standards is not determined by high schools alone. What is learned in primary schools, intermediate schools, and middle schools makes a crucial difference as well. Therefore, there should be locally developed standards that apply to earlier school experiences. But as with the high school standards, no single test should be used to assess progress. Such developmental standards should be set in collaboration with teachers from a receiving school: the high school working with the middle school, the middle school working with the intermediate school, and the intermediate school working with the primary school. (I would personally be more comfortable with framing this discussion around age groups—for example, nine-year-olds, twelve-year-olds, fifteen-year-olds, and eighteen-year-olds—but until schools are organized differently, graded discussions are the best we can do.) Furthermore, these standards would not be thought of as exit standards, but rather as entrance standards. The focus of the conversation between high school teachers and middle school teachers might be framed as follows:

> Given the fact that we [the high school faculty] must seek to ensure that all students who enroll in our school can satisfy the state academic standards by the time they are eighteen, here is what we think they need to know and be able to do when they come to us. What do you think about that? Is it reasonable? If not, what can we do about it? Do you think you will have many students who could not meet the standards we propose? If so, why? And is there anything we can do to help them meet these standards before they come?

A similar conversation would need to occur at the other levels as well. It is likely that there will never be complete agreement regarding the issues raised in such conversations. Even if there is agreement, some students will not meet the entrance standards at the next level. Then the conversation would need to turn to the question, "What can be done about that? Is the problem with the standards, the programs, or those students? If the problem is with the students, is it a problem about which something can be done? If not, how should such a case be handled, understanding that the focus must be on the benefit of all children, not simply on the ease by which such a case might be administratively disposed?"

If such a standard-setting process were in place, I seriously doubt that intermediate school teachers would be much concerned with whether nine-year-olds had yet learned the names of the continents (though many students probably would have learned such things) or even whether they had seriously studied science (though most probably would have). What they would want to know and what they would want from primary schools would likely be more along the lines of the following:

- Can these youngsters read well enough to comprehend the material in a science textbook, and do they enjoy reading enough that they can work their way through some tedious material without giving up?

- Will the youngsters you send to us be able to add, subtract, multiply, and divide?

- Have they developed work habits that make it possible for them to be productive alone and in groups?

- Are they excited about learning and willing to risk failure?

These are standards that have meaning to teachers and about which teachers can argue productively. These are standards most parents can understand as well, and because they understand them, they can participate in creating and enforcing them. Whether it is more important to know the names of the presidents when one is nine, or whether that can wait until one is ninety, is more esoteric in nature—interesting, and perhaps important, but certainly not as important as ensuring that every child can read and that all children have as rich and rewarding an educational experience as possible, especially in the first few years of school.

Students who have the basic skills needed to access disciplined knowledge and the work habits needed to pursue difficult tasks independently and with others will learn science in the intermediate school even if they have had no science in primary school. They will know the names of most of the presidents because they can read history texts, even when some are boring or tedious. Moreover, if their teachers are alert, students who have an interest in science as kindergartners will learn a good deal of science, because their interest in science can be used to encourage them to read. Similarly, those who have a love for poetry may learn a bit about poetry as well.

What is more important, however, is that all will learn to read and to enjoy reading before they have to learn that much that one reads in school and in later life really is not worth reading, or if it is worth reading, it is not all that interesting. Learning that reading can be boring can wait until a child is nine or so. First, let's get them excited about reading.

Additional Standards

I assume that a school district that is serious about educating children rather than simply training them would also have some notions about the place of art, music, drama, and athletics in the lives of students, and they would develop standards in these areas as well. As with academic standards, such standards would necessarily grow out of a shared vision of what the educated citizen should know and be able to do. Such standards would be based in a conception crafted by the community that would be molded and remolded over time. It is not assumed that standard setting would ever be set in stone, but it would be one of the primary functions of the board of education to ensure that the argument goes on. Eventually the conditions of dialogue and conversation should be so well established that the kind of shouting and bullying that is often heard in boardrooms—and increasingly in legislative halls—would be kept to a minimum. In fact, arguments about standards might well serve to keep the community and the board focused on what should be the essential questions that should be confronted again and again, and out of such focused and continuing conversations, a sense of community might grow.

HELPING COMMUNITIES HOLD SCHOOLS ACCOUNTABLE

If the recommendations set forth above were acted on, how might legislators, governors, and other state officials would be assured that local communities are carrying out their obligation to uphold state standards responsibly and responsively? Here are the answers I would provide to this question:

- The state should develop an audit process, making it possible to assess whether students who are declared graduates of the local high school meet the state-prescribed performance standards. This process should include in-depth assessments of the performance of a random sample of students as opposed to a more superficial assessment of all students. (Assessing all students would be a local function.)

- The state would make the result of the audit public and would be especially attentive to the number of students who are judged not to meet graduation standards.

- The state should report to the community the overall distribution of graduates by race, sex, and ethnicity. Apparent gaps would be highlighted and addressed in the audit report.

- School officials would be expected to respond in writing to negative findings in an audit report. These responses would be included in the public documents the state makes available to local media and interested citizens through various channels, including the Internet.

One way to implement such a process would be to require that each school district submit to the state a list of the names of all students whom school officials are prepared to nominate as meeting graduation standards. On a random basis, each year between 10 and 20 percent of the school districts in the state might be visited by a board of visitor for the purpose of conducting interviews, reviewing portfolios of selected students, and making other observations appropriate to assessing the performance of a randomly selected group of students whose names appear on the graduation list submitted by the school district. This idea is similar to the notion of the idea of the inspectorate used in many European nations. In the inspectorate model, however, both operational matters and student performance issues are usually of concern. The board of visitors envisioned here would have but one function: to verify that recent graduates in fact know and can do what the state standards say they should know and be able to do. (It might make more sense to use high schools rather than the school district as a unit of analysis, thereby taking into account the fact that the number of graduates in an urban school district would be much greater than in a small rural school district. It might also be necessary to stratify the sample in other ways, for example, using a poverty index or a school size index.)

Prior to the visit, a reasonable random sample of graduates would be selected by state officials, and the school would be notified to have these students available for interviews, conversations, and other such activities as the visiting committee might devise in their quest for data regarding student performance. For example, the committee might examine student work products and portfolios, or they might create team problem-solving situations to determine the extent to which students have developed problem-solving skills and have learned to be members of a problem-solving team. Certainly a great deal of thought would need to be given to the design of the work of such visiting committees and to the kind of preparation they would need before visiting a school system. This would be an intensive activity and would have considerable costs attached—though it would not be nearly as costly in terms of student and staff time and effort as the cost of statewide testing programs.

The important thing to keep in mind is that the intent of the visiting committee would be to provide to the state, the local citizens, and anyone else who cares about the matter assurance that when the school district says a student has met graduation standards, there is every reason to believe that this is so. Therefore, the visiting team would need to be constituted in a way that would take into account the interests of the state, the local community, and the academic community.

The team would almost certainly include a few persons employed by the state education agency who would oversee the working of the team and coordinate the preparation of subsequent reports. It would be important, however, for the team to have a majority of its members drawn from among informed citizens who have credibility among key decision makers in the local community and the media across the state (or who could be presented to the local community in such a way that they would be granted credibility). It is likely that among the team members would be scholars from various disciplines, newspaper reporters and editors, and perhaps members of the state board of education, members of the clergy, and others who might serve as opinion leaders with regard to educational matters.

At the end of the visit, a report would be prepared to be made public regarding the committee's overall impression of the quality of the graduates they interviewed relative to the academic standards of concern. No individual student would be identified in this report, and no student's graduation status would be affected by the judgment of the committee.

If the members of the board of visitors should come to the collective conclusion that there is substantial evidence that the students with whom they have visited are not meeting standards, the school district would be expected to address those concerns. The report would not be made public, however, until district officials had a chance to respond to it. It might be the case, for example, that the school district and the visiting team simply do not see eye to eye on the meaning of the standards. If so, this is a matter that would need to be addressed before the next visit. Or perhaps the school district does not have quality control measures in place to ensure that students who are nominated for graduation in fact meet standards. Such a circumstance would also need to be addressed between visits. This would put tremendous pressure on the school district to ensure that all students who graduate meet standards or to make a powerful case for exceptions.

If a school district persistently failed to meet the standards set—that is, if the number of graduates failing to meet state standards was high, if too few members of the age cohorts graduated, or if there were noticeable discrepancies in the graduation rates of identifiable groups—then, and only then, might it be appropriate for state officials to intervene.

The Case for Exceptions

A major problem with the standards-based movement, especially with versions associated with the idea of high-stakes testing, is that some students cannot be promoted or graduated because they cannot pass a particular test, regardless of the fact that school officials feel justified in passing or graduating them. It is all too easy to argue for uniform application of standards and to allow no exceptions; after all, it is the lack of uniform standards and the uniform application of these standards by local school officials that in part accounts for the rise of the standards-based movement in the first place.

Insistence on the uniform application of standards to all children carries tremendous costs in terms of human suffering, in addition to its cost to society and the economy. A student who has persisted in the struggle to gain a reasonable level of academic competence in spite of limited academic ability, and who has displayed in other areas of school life that he or she understands and is willing to pursue and uphold high standards, must surely be as worthy of walking across the stage with his or her peers on graduation night as is the academically talented student who can clearly meet state academic standards though he or she has invested little in terms of effort or disciplined action. (It is likely that many CEOs of American businesses who are dyslexic would not have met uniformly applied graduation standards. Thomas Edison would almost certainly have had difficulties.)

For these reasons, I argue that school districts should be permitted to submit to the state a list of criteria that would be used to grant exceptions for students whom local educators know will not meet academic standards but who should nonetheless be granted diplomas. These criteria, along with the rationale supporting them, should be officially endorsed by the local board of education and made public prior to their application.

Indeed, I can imagine discussions of standards, and the basis of exceptions to standards, as vital to the community-building conversations suggested in Chapter Eight and elsewhere in this book. Transparency and dialogue are at the heart of schools as learning organizations—not bureaucratic mandates from up high and far away—and it is through disciplined conversations that communities are built and standards are established and maintained. Zoning boards are granted the right to make exceptions. Surely local boards of education should be entitled to the same authority.

Graduation Rates

Another problem that confronts those who would hold schools accountable for student performance is the matter of dropout rates and graduation rates. The following seems to me to be a reasonable way to handle this matter:

- The public schools should be accountable for all eighteen-year-olds who reside in the school district on the one day each year that diplomas are conferred.

- The proportion of these students who are granted diplomas by the school district should be the issue of concern.

- The school district would make public each year the proportions of the eighteen-year-old cohort who (1) graduated from public schools, (2) graduated from private schools, (3) were homeschooled and therefore did not graduate, (4) attended public schools for twelve years and did not graduate, and (5) were afforded diplomas by intentional exception.

- School officials would be expected to prepare a narrative report accounting for the numbers they report.

If a large proportion of students graduate from private schools rather than public schools, it would be necessary to determine whether this is attributable to a quality-of-school choice by students and families or to a lifestyle and cultural choice. Because public schools cannot provide a religious education, for example, some parents choose parochial schools to ensure that religious content is provided. And some parents choose private or parochial schools because they judge the public schools to be inferior. The local school district has an obligation to account for these choices even though they may not reflect either positively or adversely on the overall quality of the schools.

Getting data to support this accounting would cause school leaders to interact with non–public school parents as well as public school parents and dropouts. These interactions would almost certainly provide new insights for a learning organization about its business and its effectiveness. Similarly, the school district would be compelled to justify affording diplomas to students who do not meet state standards, and when the state audit reveals that the number of students who do not meet standards is high, the district would need to account for this fact.

ORGANIZATIONAL PERFORMANCE STANDARDS

A concern beyond the matter of academic standards is whether a school district possesses or is developing the capacities and systems required to support all students and staff in meeting standards. Over the past two decades, I have been able to create, working in cooperation with the staff of the Schlechty Center and many school district leaders around the country, three frameworks within which processes and tools for assessing system performance have been developed or are being developed:

1. Standards having to do with the capacity of the school district to support and sustain disruptive innovations (see Chapter One on disruptive innovations)

2. Standards that have to do with the nature and configuration of critical social systems within the organization

3. Standards having to do with operations at the school level and classroom level

System Capacity Standards

Innovations that are most likely to increase student engagement in schoolwork are also most likely to require changes in the directional system, the knowledge development and transmission system, and the recruitment and induction system. These changes cannot be installed without accommodating changes in the power and authority system, the evaluation system, and the boundary system. Bureaucracies lack the capacity to bring about and sustain such changes.

Therefore, the first step in transforming schools is to build the capacity needed to support and sustain systemic change.

In Chapter Ten, I described three capacities related to the ability of a school district to support and sustain systemic change and innovative effort: the capacity to focus on the future, maintain direction, and act strategically. The descriptors presented in that chapter are in fact standards by which one might assess the capacity of a school district to support and sustain the kind of systemic changes needed to install innovations on a continuous basis—that is, the capacity to become a learning organization.

Having participated in and led numerous efforts to assess district capacity in these three areas, I feel safe in asserting that where most school districts have the most strength is in their ability to introduce innovations (a dimension of strategic action), create collaborative arrangements, and provide initial training to support the installation of innovations. However, because they lack the ability to maintain direction, they are typically unable to sustain the innovations they introduce and maintain the collaborative arrangements they develop. For this reason, I have come to describe schools as "innovation-prone" and "change-inept" organizations. It is also the reason that many teachers complain that they are overwhelmed by changes (by which they mean "innovations"), but we still see few lasting changes in the operation of the schools.

Unless and until school districts and schools develop the capacity to maintain direction and focus on the future, efforts to pursue a strategic course will yield little more than strategic "plans" that are abandoned almost before the print is dry or are discarded as soon as a new board, superintendent, or principal is appointed. Developing these capacities means first knowing what capacities exist at present and where they are weak. This requires both initial assessment and follow-up assessments, for it is only through such assessments that direction is maintained, and it is through the passionate pursuit of a shared direction that improvement becomes possible.

System Standards

Chapter Three presented two ideal types of organizations. Appendix A elaborates on the description of the two types and describes each in terms of the six critical systems discussed in Chapter Two: the directional system, the knowledge development and transmission system, the recruitment and induction system, the boundary system, the evaluation system, and the power and authority system. In this elaboration, the six systems are used as a framework for further describing the differences between bureaucracies and learning organization. These descriptors are easily transformed into standards for assessing the profiles of existing schools and school districts, making it possible to gain a reasonable estimate of the way the school or school district is presently operating. I have found that school districts that take this type of assessment seriously make considerably more progress in developing the capacity to sustain innovations than those that bypass such efforts.

Indeed, because these descriptors are theoretically consistent with those used in the capacity assessment process, it is possible to link changes in these social systems to the capacity of the district to support systemic change and innovations, thereby providing some suggestions regarding possible courses of action. For example, the capacity of a school district to focus on the future and maintain direction directly affects and is affected by the nature of the directional system. In schools where the directional system is more congruent with the patterns suggested for a learning organization, leaders are better able to maintain direction than is the case for schools where the profile is more akin to a bureaucracy. Among the reasons this is so is that in a learning organization, the directional system, rather than the power and authority system, is dominant, meaning that power and authority system will yield to new directions. In a bureaucracy, direction almost always yields to existing systems of power and authority.[3]

Similarly, one of the problems school districts often experience in maintaining direction is the tendency to overlook the importance of ongoing induction processes in ensuring continuity. Quite often when introducing new programs, schools go through a period of intensive training for existing staff but fail to take into account that over the next several years, some of those trained will leave, and new and untrained people will be hired. Unless new staff members are provided the same level of training that initial staff received, the odds are very good that commitment to the new program will wane and continuity of direction will diminish as well.

Building and Classroom Standards

In the appendix of my 2002 book, *Working on the Work,* I presented two sets of standards—classroom level and school level—that have proven to be useful in

[3]A team of educators under my direction is developing tools to assist in the assessment of these six systems. But even now, the concepts are sufficiently well developed that some school leaders are using this framework as a tool to help them gain new insights into the nature of the systems they are trying to change. Readers are encouraged to try their hand at this important work.

working with teachers and school leaders interested in centering the operation of their schools on processes, programs, and activities that show the most promise for increasing student engagement.[4] These standards derive from a theory I worked out in an effort to help teachers become more disciplined in their efforts to design engaging work.

In the context of this theory, I have identified twelve areas where schools and classrooms need operating standards. Although I have not specified the full measurement process necessary to assess performance in terms of these standards, I have provided sufficient specificity to ensure that school faculties can use these standards to inform their work. The following are two examples:

Standard 1: Patterns of Engagement

Nearly all classes are highly engaged, and when they are not, teachers make every possible effort to redesign the pattern of activity in the classroom so that more students are authentically engaged. [Obviously measures of engagement become essential here, and such measures have been and are being developed.]

1. Most classrooms can accurately be characterized as highly engaged classrooms.

2. Teachers intentionally plan the work they provide to students in ways that reflect attention to building in those qualities that show the most promise of increasing authentic engagement.

3. When the pattern of student engagement differs from that which teachers want or expect, teachers analyze the work provided to discover what might account for the difficulty and take corrective action.

4. Teachers commonly work together to analyze the characteristics of the work they are providing students and provide each other assistance and advice regarding ways of making the work more engaging to students.

[4]Philip Schlechty, *Working on the Work* (San Francisco: Jossey-Bass, 2002).

Standard 2: Student Achievement

Parents, teachers, the principal, and the board of education, as well as others who have a stake in the performance of the schools, are satisfied with the level and type of learning that are occurring.

1. The data on which to base judgments regarding student achievement are solid.

2. Central office personnel, parents, teachers, community leaders, and state officials are confident that they have an accurate picture of the level of student achievement.

3. In general, parents are satisfied that their children are progressing the way they believe the children should progress and are learning what they need to learn.

4. Those that receive from this school (middle schools in the case of elementary schools, high schools in the case of middle schools, institutions of higher education and employers in the case of high schools) are satisfied that students from the school learned what they needed to learn to succeed in the receiving environment.

5. Students who have attended the school and have moved to other schools or places of work believe that they learned what they needed to while in attendance here and have an overall favorable judgment of the quality of their experience in the school.

There are ten additional standards. One, for example, centers on the need to ensure physical and psychological safety. Others call attention to patterns of collegiality and peer support, a clear focus on learning standards, and such things as novelty, choice, and variety of activity. The overall intent of these standards is to focus attention on creating operating conditions in schools that are essential to encouraging continuous innovation and the development of engaging experiences for students.

Teachers and principals who have used these indicators in their efforts to develop school improvement plans routinely report that they are very useful and user friendly. More important, they provide a clear framework for disciplining conversations among teachers and between teachers and other school leaders aimed at continuous improvement of student performance and of the capacity of schools and the adults who work in them to support the work of students.

Leadership Development

School leaders in general are much more adept at installing sustaining innovations than they are at leading efforts at systemic change. Efforts to transform schools therefore require a commitment to a different kind of leadership development, as well as to assessing the capabilities of individuals in the district to support systemic change (these characteristics are described in Chapter Ten).

Identifying, recruiting, and developing such leaders require that great care be given to developing an induction system that can provide a reliable supply of necessary leaders. Such leaders cannot simply be hired and put in place. They must embrace and be committed to the direction that the school and school district are headed in and must internalize the values of the system at a bone-deep level.

Leaders in transformation cannot be viewed simply as employees or bureaucratic managers there to do a job. Technical competence is important, but much more is required of transformational leaders. They must be men and women of passion who see the transformation of schools as a cause rather than simply a set of tasks and who see their work as a calling rather than simply a job. This can be accomplished by ensuring first that leaders are selected because they "have the right stuff and the right attitude," and then that they are supported and encouraged to develop the understandings they need to be members of a team committed to going in the same direction.

SOME THOUGHTS ON STATE AND FEDERAL POLICY

The answer to problems that vex our schools may well lie in local political action aimed at convincing Congress and state legislatures to provide incentives to local school districts to transform their schools into learning organizations. Incentives toward this end should not, however, be thought of as mandates for implementation. Rather they should be true invitations to discovery and invention. They might be framed in this way:

1. The federal government should move toward a pattern of block grants rather than categorical funding based on narrowly defined contracts. The language of the 1958 National Defense Education Act that explicitly limited

the federal role in intervening in the affairs of local schools might well serve as a model.

2. These block grants should be specifically targeted toward encouraging local initiatives that address issues like those that are recognized by No Child Left Behind (NCLB) though not effectively addressed. Examples are issues having to do with making the performance of schools and school districts more transparent and understandable to citizens in the local community, issues that emerge out of equity concerns, and issues that have to do with the distribution of resources and talent.

3. States should be required to develop state plans for making the use of these funds transparent to all citizens in the state and for making transparent as well the impact the use of these funds is having on the performance of local schools and the achievement of students. (The federal government would play no role in approving these plans. Its only role would be to ensure that such plans exist and have been made transparent to the citizenry. These would be grants as opposed to contracts.)

4. The type of accountability plan local communities develop should be left up to the local school board. The sole stipulation would be that each school district would conduct an annual survey of all citizens regarding their level of satisfaction with the performance of the schools, as well as their satisfaction with the quantity and quality of the information they receive regarding that performance, and the results of this survey would be made public.

5. Federal funds could be provided to support community efforts to establish standards for school and student performance and create assessment systems consistent with these standards.

6. In support of the concept of market-driven accountability and as a source of technical assistance to local school districts, the federal government might provide funding to each state sufficient to create a virtual school district capable of providing a comprehensive curriculum to any student in the state by electronic means.

ACCOUNTABILITY AND EQUITY

Two of the primary concerns of NCLB are accountability and equity. These are legitimate concerns and should not go unaddressed. It is by ensuring transparency and some market-based accountability that these ends can be achieved. Here is how I would propose addressing these issues.

Transparency

To receive block grants, states could require that local school districts be prepared to present the following evidence on an annual basis:

- Parents are satisfied that they are well informed regarding the performance of their own children and have a reasonable basis for comparing the performance of graduates of their own schools to those of other schools in the state and nation. They also have a basis for comparing the performance of their own children to that of children in their own school as well as other schools in the district.

- Local taxpayers are satisfied with the way the schools are operating and are satisfied that they have adequate information to make an informed judgment regarding the way the schools are performing.

The state could audit the processes by which taxpayer and parent satisfaction data are collected and made public, and then make the results of these audits available to the local media. The standards applied in the audit would be those commonly applied to studies of public opinion and surveys of attitudes. (In case legislators want more standardization than this process would produce, it would probably do no great harm to empower the state to conduct these surveys on an annual basis and return the results to the community.)

Grants might also be made available to local school districts to support actions aimed at developing local capacity to meet the expectations outlined. They would also be made available for local school districts to develop responses to evidence of achievement gaps between and among identifiable groups. The way these funds are used would be made transparent through public reports to the community that would show how and where funds have been expended, as well as the intended and actual impact of this use of funds.

School improvement funds would be made available through block grants, and the targets of these grants would be clearly specified. The law would be written in a way that would make it clear that the local school district is obligated to present evidence that the funds provided are being used to serve the population identified and that data relative to the effects of the expenditure are systematically collected and made publicly available. There would, however, be no predetermined evaluation plan. Rather, the state would specify standards for an evaluation plan to which local communities would need to respond.

Choice

I am sympathetic to the view that market forces can serve as powerful tools in the effort to make organizations accountable. I do not believe, however, that privatization is the only way to bring market forces to bear on local school leaders. Another way is to have the state create competing modes of delivering education to the young that are available statewide and allow parents to choose these alternatives when they are dissatisfied with what the local community has to offer. For example, Florida has created a virtual high school that provides students with an alternative means of meeting the requirements of a high school diploma. There is no reason that a school like this one could not be established in every state (with help from federal funding). Such a school could serve as an accessible choice to any student or parent who found the local school offerings unacceptable. This virtual school alternative has many advantages, especially when viewed as part of an accountability system attached to a statewide school improvement effort.

Any student in the state could enroll in the virtual school at no additional cost to the parent. The school the student would have attended might, however, lose revenue, thus creating an economic incentive to compete for the student's continuing in the local school. The virtual school, which might operate as a local school district, could be made subject to the same transparency requirements applied to locally run public schools, thereby ensuring quality control of the alternative school as well as the locally operated school. This approach would make school choice a viable option in many smaller school districts where population density does not otherwise make choice a reasonable alternative. Virtual schools can be delivered at any time and any place, and funding to make the needed hardware available would be considerably less expensive than the cost of new school buildings. Much of the attention of educational policymakers is aimed at solving the problems of large urban districts (those with more than 100,000 students), but nearly a third of all students attend schools in districts with fewer than 5,000 students K–12, and nearly two-thirds attend schools in districts with fewer than 25,000 students. School choice looks very different from the perspective of a small town in South Dakota than it might in Chicago.

The possibility of the state virtual school's developing partnering relationships with local schools, thereby creating truly blended schools, offers the potential for improving local schools without destroying them and without having the state engaging in a nonvoluntary takeover. Properly staffed, the virtual school could also become a source of technical assistance to troubled local schools that partner with the virtual school.

Homeschool parents could be provided access to the services of the state-run virtual school and might even find new ways of working with local school districts. For example, an effort in Michigan, led by an activist homeschool parent, is seeking new ways for homeschool advocates to work cooperatively and with mutual benefit to public school students as well as homeschool students. Such efforts are deserving of support and study. Given the digital revolution, blended schooling is likely to be critical to developing schools as learning organizations— or so I believe.

Indeed, the state, using the standards it sets for high school graduation for students in local schools, might empower the state virtual school to grant diplomas to homeschool students with the proviso that the state virtual school would be subject to the same auditing process as applied to local school districts.

The number of students opting out of local schools and pursuing their studies through the state-sponsored alternative could be used as data that would be made public in the annual report of each local school district. It would, of course, be up to the citizens of the local community to attach meaning to these numbers and determine whether they were indicative of a problem with the schools or simply a matter of the idiosyncratic preferences of a few parents or a few students.

A WORD OF CAUTION

My proposals are not without risks. They trust state leaders and local leaders to behave well and ethically, which they may not always do. They also assume that local citizens are or can become well informed about the problems that beset their schools, and that they will care enough to respond appropriately to incentives to do something about these problems. There will, of course, be instances in which this assumption will not be warranted, and when this is so, nothing good will happen for children. This is one of the reasons we all should be concerned about the development of leaders for schools. Without strong leaders, there is little prospect that schools can be transformed in the ways they must be if they are to survive and serve this nation well.

It is also likely that some local communities might use funds from block grants to pursue courses of action that policy experts would not endorse. This is, I believe, a risk worth taking. The fact is that the history of the effectiveness of programs developed by experts is not all that impressive—research-based claims to the contrary notwithstanding. Sometimes they have worked, at least a bit, and other times they have failed, and sometimes massively.

There is, of course, something a bit naïve about what I propose, but it is the naïveté of Jefferson, Madison, and many others who believed that in the end, the common sense of the ordinary citizen is more to be trusted than the interest of elites, including the interests of policy elites.

A Theory of Action

chapter
TWELVE

O ver the past forty years, I have had considerable experience with efforts to improve schools. Some of these efforts were more successful than others, but whether successes or failures, I learned from all of them. The most important lesson I learned is that when efforts to install innovations in schools fail or fall short of intentions, it is likely due to the fact that the social systems that define behavior in schools were not transformed in ways that would accommodate the innovations.

In my attempt to understand why efforts to improve schools so often fall short of intention, I have found ideas suggested by sociologists and anthropologists concerned with the study of life in complex formal social organizations of special value. Since the mid-1970s, I have also been informed by the literature on leadership and organizational change produced by those who have studied such complex organizations as corporations, major nonprofit organizations, the military, and religious organizations. Over the years, based on my experiences and observations of the work of others, and disciplined by the ideas suggested to me by sociologists, anthropologists, and students of leadership in organizational context I have worked out what I will call here a theory of action.

FIRST STEPS

This chapter presents a summary of the theory of action indicated previously. The ideas expressed in this theory are presented more as principles for action than as prescriptions. The way actions suggested by this theory are played out will depend on the unique circumstances that exist in the school or school district that is the target of the transformation. My hope is that what I offer here will make the work of transforming schools somewhat less confusing and more disciplined that it might otherwise be, and therefore help make the work of improving the education of young Americans more effective and perhaps even more efficient.

Becoming a Transformational Leader

The first thing that must happen for school transformation to occur is that the top-level leader (in the case of the school district, the superintendent; in the case of the school, the principal) must become convinced that transformation is necessary and that he or she is prepared to undertake leading such an effort. Unlike more modest improvement efforts, in which leadership can be delegated, transformation requires the sustained, dedicated attention of the top leader.

Transformation requires changes in the moral order of schools as well as the technical order. It requires repurposing as well as restructuring. Technical changes can be led by persons other than top-level leaders, but changes in the moral order require changes in beliefs, values, and commitments and changes in definitions of superordinate goals and the core business—and this requires the attention of top-level leaders.

Transformation is threatening—much more threatening than the minor adjustments required to introduce sustaining innovations. Only top-level leaders have the moral authority necessary to sustain effort in the difficult times that are almost certain to occur during the transformation process. Unless others in the organization perceive that these leaders are fully committed and will not waver in that commitment, transformation will not occur. Thus, the first transformation that must occur is a transformation of the top-level leader's role—of the superintendent to that of moral and intellectual leader and of the principal to leader of leaders.

What, in practical terms, does this mean? Among other things, it means that the superintendent or principal who is committed to school transformation must be (or must become) a student of the literature on change and leading change in the context of formal organizations. Furthermore, it means he or she must not limit what is being read to books and articles written for educators. *Fast Company* articles are as likely to be on the reading list of a transforming superintendent as are articles from *Educational Leadership* or other education journals. Books by Peter Drucker are likely to be as familiar as the writings of John Dewey.

Furthermore, transformational leaders do not limit their reading to professional literature. Because much of the work of a transformational leader involves storytelling and the conscious use of metaphors, those who would lead transformation must seek experiences that get them outside the world of education. They must seek out opportunities to discover images and metaphors that will enrich their thinking about the task before them. They might, for example, read historical accounts and biographies of leaders who have led in times of organizational transformation. They might look to the history of art and music to find examples of how repurposing might affect sentiments and styles.

In addition to being committed to a rich and varied intellectual life, leaders of transformations need to become actively involved in networks of other leaders who are similarly inclined and similarly situated. Superintendents, for example, need to join or help create networks of superintendents who believe, as they do, that schools and school districts need to be transformed into learning organizations and who are committed to making this happen. Principals need to be in such networks as well.

Leading transformational change is hard and demanding work. It is likely to become overwhelming if done alone and without outside support. Disciplined conversations with like-minded colleagues, undertaken in a safe environment where uncertainties can be exposed without fear of repercussions on the local scene, are essential to transformational leaders. Leading the transformation of schools without such conversations and absent such networks can be a debilitating personal trial. With such support, the experience can be transformed into what anthropologists and sociologists sometimes refer to as a *shared ordeal*—that is, an experience that would be debilitating if borne alone but can become exhilarating when shared with others who have the same risks and feelings of uncertainty. Such an experience can build a sense of community and purpose beyond oneself and beyond the immediate milieu in which one is currently operating.

Learning to Think Strategically

Systems cannot be properly apprehended through linear thinking, and just as it would be a mistake for leaders to think of systems in a linear fashion, leaders would be equally mistaken to think of the processes needed to transform systems in a linear fashion. Rather, leaders must employ systems thinking to understand the way that systems are linked to one another, how they interact, and how those qualities affect the process of transformation.

It is also true that some things have to be accomplished before other things. Thus, a clear understanding of sequencing of events is essential. Similarly, some actions produce more widespread results in intended directions than do others, so an understanding of the concept of leverage is important.

Strategic thinking and strategic planning are primarily concerned with decisions about sequence, linkage, and leverage. Such decisions are shaped by the implicit or explicit theory of action the leader embraces as he or she goes about the work on which he or she is embarked.

Building Internal Support

The next step for a leader of transformation is to develop an internal support structure and come to a clear understanding among those who are called on to support that structure of the theories and assumptions to be embraced as the process of transformation unfolds.

The superintendent is necessarily the key leader with regard to inspiring the internal changes that will be required to transform the schools in the district, as well as the operation of the superintendent's office and the central office apparatus on which the superintendent depends. The superintendent will also need the commitment and support of the board of education to carry out this task, for the board is the only entity that can provide the leadership the community needs to support transformation. For school boards to effectively embrace this task, the role of the board must be transformed. For example, local school boards are going to need to reorient their actions so that they become more concerned with leading the community in matters educational than they are with leading the schools. Moreover, they are going to need to lead in ways that make schools the central features in the effort to build communities as well as in the effort to serve them. The superintendent must be prepared to support such a transformation in the role of the school board.

A second group to which the superintendent must personally attend is building-level principals. Among other things, the superintendent must work to ensure that these leaders are committed to the idea of transformation and that they understand what this transformation might mean for their roles.

Finally, superintendents and building-level leaders need to develop teams of thoughtful people to advise them and help them think through the design of the systems and structures they are going to need to create and issues of timing, leverage, and support that must be addressed in this difficult process. In my work as a consultant, I frequently advise the creation of what we at the Schlechty Center call "design teams." These teams are not committees or stakeholder groups. Rather, they are collections of persons whom the formal leaders trust and believe are especially wise, thoughtful, and creative, as well as especially attuned to the way various stakeholders view the world of the schools. These teams should be thought of as the essential learning communities around which other learning communities will eventually come to be organized.

It would, however, be a mistake to think of such a team as a strategic planning group or a problem-solving group. Rather, the team should function as a group of internal consultants who provide advice to those charged with planning and problem solving. It should be an organizational unit expressly charged with worrying about the future of the school and the school district, constantly reviewing and reflecting on progress and limitations, and examining strengths and weaknesses in order to identify and frame opportunities. The primary mission of such a team would be to contribute to the capacity of the school or school district to focus on the future and maintain direction in the difficult times associated with transformation.

Such teams would be developmental in nature and more concerned with strategic thinking than with strategic planning. Because this is so, these teams must be insulated from requests that they take action or solve problems. It is the function of such teams to provide the kind of disciplined thinking required to support those who are called on to act. Because team members will also occupy action roles in the system, it will be necessary for them to learn to compartmentalize their roles as consultants to action and conductors of action. The intent here is to create a habit of reflection and to prevent mindless action informed more by habit than by disciplined thought.

Such teams must be developed rather than appointed. Primary responsibility for developing the district-level team rests with the superintendent; primary responsibility for developing building-level teams rests with the principal.

Among the questions these teams should be prepared to address are the following:

• How can district-level teams and building-level teams work together in mutually supportive ways?

- What is the nature of the new direction to which we are becoming committed, and what kinds of innovations will be needed to pursue that direction?
- Does our school or school district have the capacity to support the necessary innovations?
- If we do not have that capacity, which of the critical systems that shape behavior in our district seem to be the most problematic with regard to these deficiencies? What would it take to transform them?
- How are those who occupy current positions in our school or school district likely to respond to the innovations and the systemic changes needed?
- What might be done to increase positive support for these changes? Who should be responsible for ensuring that the required actions are taken?

Other questions will emerge from consideration of questions like these, and over time, such questions will need to be pursued as well.

Recruiting Advisors and Confidants

In his book *Good to Great,* Jim Collins writes of "getting the right people on the bus."[1] Early on in the transformation process, there is no more critical decision a leader can make than the one regarding those on whom he or she is going to rely for advice and counsel and in whom he or she will be willing to confide when things go awry.

One of the ways such persons might be identified is for the superintendent or the principal to lead discussions regarding the need for transformation and then to reflect on the responses individuals make to the major ideas advanced. Another way is to invite participation in seminars and book study groups, where issues of transformation are discussed. Such activity provides needed information to potential allies and allows the leader to make more refined judgments regarding who should be consulted in the future.

What the leaders should be looking for, in addition to evidence of willingness to support the idea of transformation, are people who are trustworthy self-starters. They should have displayed a history of taking initiative and of willingness to be assertive, even in the face of opposition from superordinates and peers. At the same time, they should be flexible and accommodating to the views of others, as

[1]Jim Collins, *Good to Great* (New York: HarperCollins, 2001).

well as reflective and thoughtful in style and demeanor. They should be known to be readers who are willing to share with others what they glean from their reading. They should be advocates, but they should not be sycophants, which is to say they should be capable of independent judgment and critical thought.

Understanding the variety of opinion and its nuances that emerge from different racial and ethnic groups, as well as other demographic categories, wise and effective leaders will attend to racial and ethnic considerations, as well as other demographic features such as age and experience, that might be important in seeking advisors. It is not enough, however, that a team member be a member of a critical demographic group; he or she must also have a clear understanding of the variety of opinions and perceptions that emanate from that group. Advocacy for group interests is not what is needed; what is needed is an understanding of the nature of those interests and what they might mean for action.

It is therefore crucial to keep in mind that it is more important that the persons on whom leaders rely for advice and council be the right people than that they occupy the right positions or represent the right interest groups. Matters of representation can be handled in the action arena of task forces, committees, and problem-focused learning communities. What transformational leaders need, especially in the early stages, is a local think tank that can serve as a source of advice regarding issues of systems and system design. In their operational roles, these advisors may be doers, but in their role as advisors to transformational leaders, they must be thinkers, inventors, and "imagineers."

TOWARD A THEORY OF ACTION

Theories are sets of propositions that make it possible to describe, explain, and sometimes predict. They are sometimes highly technical and disciplined, and sometimes nothing more than the tacit assumptions an individual makes regarding the way the world works. Leaders of transformations, especially those who assume formal and visible leadership roles, must be explicit about the assumptions they make concerning the key elements of the transformation process, and they must share these understandings. Disciplined conversations are impossible without such shared understandings, and without disciplined conversations, design teams cannot do their work. Therefore, one of the first actions of those who assume leadership roles is to clearly articulate the theories that will guide their work.

Listed below is a set of assumptions consistent with the arguments I have presented in this book that might constitute such a theory of action:

1. Continuous and persistent innovation is essential to school improvement.

2. If the systems that define behavior in the organization cannot accommodate disruptive innovations, then innovation will be disjointed and will involve a great deal of abandonment and wasted resources and energy.

3. Because the introduction of disruptive innovations requires changes in the structure and culture of the school or school district, as well as changes in the systems that are defined by that structure and culture, disruptive innovations introduce much more uncertainty into the system than do sustaining innovations. Therefore, they place many more demands on leaders than do sustaining innovations.

4. Schools that are based on the principles of learning organizations are better equipped to handle disruptive innovations than are schools based on bureaucratic principles.

5. Sustaining innovations can be introduced through programs and projects. Disruptive innovations can be introduced only by leaders who understand systems and how systems work to shape behavior in groups.

6. Six critical systems come into play when disruptive innovations are introduced:

   - The directional system
   - The knowledge development and transmission system
   - The recruitment and induction system
   - The boundary system
   - The evaluation system
   - The power and authority system[2]

7. Each of these systems is defined by sets of norms that apply to each of the functions defined by the system. Together these norms define the normative order of the school or school district.

[2]These systems are defined and discussed in Phillip C. Schlechty, *Creating Great Schools: Six Critical Systems at the Heart of Educational Innovation* (San Francisco: Jossey-Bass, 2005).

8. Implementing disruptive innovations, unlike sustaining innovations, requires changes in the normative order as well as changes in the systems defined by that order.

9. Norms are defined as the range of permissible, expected, or required behaviors and beliefs that apply to members of groups and organizations as a condition of their membership in those groups and organizations.

10. Some norms are prescriptive, defining what must be done. Some are proscriptive, defining what cannot be done and what will not be accepted.

11. Some norms are universal and apply to all members of the group at all times; other norms are situational or specialty norms that apply only at some times or to people who occupy particular roles.

12. Some norms appear in the form of preachments, defining what ought to be done. Some norms appear in the form of practices, defining what it is actually acceptable to do, or what it is required be done. Some norms appear in the form of pretenses and fictions, expressing shared explanations of the reasons for discrepancies between preachments and practices.

13. Leaders who are effective in introducing disruptive change must be alert to and understanding of the normative order, and they must understand how the systems defined by that order interact and affect each other.

14. Schools or school districts that are able to support and sustain the systemic changes needed to introduce disruptive innovations must possess the following capacities:

    • The capacity to focus on the future

    • The capacity to maintain direction

    • The capacity to act strategically

15. The capacity to focus on the future requires leaders to do the following:

    • Clearly identify and articulate the core business of schools and be able to persuade others regarding this matter.

    • Articulate and share with others a set of beliefs that is consistent with the nature of the business as it is defined—and gain consensus on those beliefs.

    • Develop a vision of the school or school district that is based on and congruent with the beliefs that guide the system, and help others to see the meaning of this vision for the positions and roles they occupy.

- Develop a shared understanding of the problems that must be addressed and the changes that must take place if the articulated vision is to be realized.

16. The capacity to maintain direction requires leaders to do the following:

- Center all activity on the pursuit of the core business and make all decisions with an eye toward enhancing the capacity of schools and those who work in them to conduct such business effectively, efficiently, and ethically.

- Use the beliefs and values that guide the organization as standards for assessing the merit and worth of decisions and the consequences of actions that result from those decisions.

- Ensure that those whose support is needed and whose actions are required to install the innovation have sufficient involvement in decisions that affect them and their interests, in order to encourage them to voluntarily support the actions even when their short-term personal interests may appear to be threatened.

- Ensure that systems are in place to support continuity of leadership, including the development of appropriate induction systems and evaluation systems, as well as leadership succession plans.

- Provide consistent leadership to help others prevail in the face of adversity.

17. The capacity to act strategically requires leaders to do the following:

- Ensure that those who support the innovative effort are themselves provided the training and support they need, including political support, resources (time, people, space, information, and technology), and social support (for example, collegial support).

- Encourage a spirit of experimentalism by reducing the risks attached to failure on initial tries and encouraging the expression of contrary and controversial views.

- Ensure that the technologies and skills required to install the innovation are present and accessible to all who need them.

- Identify and develop those partnerships and other collaborative arrangements that will enhance the installation of the innovation and develop strategies to protect the innovative effort from distracting forces both inside and outside the system.

SUBSEQUENT STEPS

Having developed clear commitment among leaders and a support system for them and articulated, at least in a general way, the theory of action that will guide the effort, the following actions need to be considered to move the transformational effort from the realm of ideas to the world of action.

Focused Discussions

The initial stages of school transformation require a great deal of discussion and conversation. Thoughtful discussion and conversation are not valued in bureaucracies, which are designed to direct action, not to encourage reflection and analysis. It is essential, therefore, that the transformational leader develop skill in leading focused discussions and signaling that great value is placed on such activity.

At the outset, these discussions should be topical in nature rather than problem focused. Indeed, effort should be made to ensure that the discussions do not devolve into problem-solving activities that center on the issue of the day or the momentary concern of one of the participants.

The intent of these initial discussions is to encourage a focus on the future. No matter how real and pressing they may be, existing problems have their origins in the past. It should be kept in mind, therefore, that in schools, especially those most like bureaucracies, maintenance needs will always overwhelm developmental needs unless leaders provide substantial protection for developmental resources and activities.

Action Research

Once leaders have a reasonable grasp of the terrain they are about to travel (this process might take six months to a full year, depending on the amount of time and energy available to dedicate to the preliminary work), they might next undertake a careful study of the capacity of the organization to support and sustain transformation. (See the discussion of capacity standards in Chapter Eleven.) Where these capacities are lacking, learning communities should be organized to think strategically about the systems that are involved in these shortcomings. Based on such thinking, these groups should be expected to develop some clear notions regarding what attention needs to be given to strengthening these systems and thereby moving the organization forward in the transformation effort.

Follow-Through and Persistence

Bureaucracies are designed to separate thought from action by routinizing action so that responses become automatic and habitual. Unfortunately, as those who live in bureaucracies come to understand, thought and action are inseparable, and great harm can be done when leaders try to separate them. Learning organizations are designed to make thinking a habit and to connect thinking to a clear course of action.

Leaders in the transformation of schools where bureaucratic thinking is the norm must consistently urge others to think and reflect. At the same time, they should not allow themselves or others to confuse thinking with delay or to let reflection serve as an explanation for lack of progress. This is why the capacity to lead through attention to common beliefs and the results suggested by those beliefs is so critical. Without such a commitment, planning can become a substitute for action and a mechanism for maintaining the status quo rather than a means of ensuring the disciplined introduction of innovations.

This is perhaps why all leaders must be, in a sense, teachers, for one of the roles of the teacher is to help those he or she teaches to make transparent the process of their thinking, and thereby subject their thinking to discipline and control. It is also the reason that every teacher must be a leader, for leaders have a bias for action and a penchant for getting things done.

A THEORY, NOT A PRESCRIPTION

Transformational change is a messy business. Sometimes things must be done sooner when they logically should be done later. Sometimes things that might be done later have to be done sooner, if for no other reason than that there is a compelling opportunity to act at the moment. For example, in an ideal world, much of the initial work needed to transform schools would be done with central office staff and perhaps with principals before undertaking any real or sustained effort to change the way teachers go about their work. The reason this is so is that those who occupy power positions in the existing bureaucracy control the resources needed to bring about transformation, and until they see it in their interest to allocate such resources to transformation, it is unlikely that transformation will occur.

The political realities in which schools exist often make such a logical process untenable. For example, efforts to alter in fundamental ways what teachers do, and the meaning teachers give to what they do, are not likely to be sustained unless significant effort is expended in transforming the structure and culture of the central office, the relationship between the school board and the community, and the relationship between the school board and the superintendent. Most policymakers, however, want quick results, and they see a clear focus on teachers and classrooms as the way to those results. The idea of systemic effects often escapes them, as is the idea that substantial changes in what teachers and students do in school require changes well beyond the classroom door.

Moreover, many legislators, business leaders, pundits, journalists, and others who comment on schools view the commitment of resources to the development of leaders other than classroom teachers and principals as bureaucratic waste. They are wrong. Furthermore, until their thinking is better informed, efforts to transform schools will always be in jeopardy. Therefore, those who would transform schools must take on as well the task of educating the local politicians, legislators, and the members of the media who most affect the context in which they (the local change leaders) work.

Given the messiness of transformational work and the tendency of policymakers to underestimate the complexity of the work, a disciplined approach to school transformation cannot be—or at least should not be—prescriptive. Local contingencies will determine sequence and leverage more than deductive logic and strategic planning.

It is common, for example, for legislators to insist that resources committed to school improvement be focused on the classroom, Thus, it is often necessary to use the classroom as the entry point for the introduction of a new learning technology, even in circumstances when it might be more effective to begin the implementation by making the new technology available first to central office trainers, perhaps to principals, or maybe even to the school board. The result is that teachers are often encouraged to develop new skills or incorporate new technologies well in advance of the time there is a system in place to support their efforts. This often leads to frustration and abandonment.

A useful theory of action therefore will give more attention to linkages than to sequence, because it is recognized that sometimes there are reasons for putting off acting on high-leverage areas, even though it would be preferable to do so. By focusing on linkages rather than sequence, however, leaders are constantly reminded of what remains to be done, and why some of the things they have done have yet to produce the results promised.

It is preferable to take the actions that have the potential for highest leverage, and, to the extent possible, the sequence of actions should be determined by an assessment of leverage. For example, there is good reason for starting with the central office: this office is most likely to serve as a barrier to change, yet it has the greatest potential for enhancing the capacity of the school district to support and sustain transformation efforts. Unfortunately, too few central office personnel understand the potential that central office positions have for enhancing organizational capacity—and too many critics of schools see central office personnel as nothing more than bureaucratic overburden. As a result, central office personnel too often have a vested interest in ensuring that potentially disruptive innovations introduced at the school or classroom level are quickly abandoned or transformed into programs that can be more easily administered and controlled through existing bureaucratic mechanisms.

The leader who is committed to transformation but still feels compelled by local realities to concentrate initial effort on the classroom rather than on the boardroom cannot forget that there is much work yet to be done with other top-level leaders if the work done at the classroom level is not to be abandoned or domesticated, especially if it requires the introduction of disruptive innovations. Furthermore, if such work at the top is not accomplished, or cannot be accomplished, it should be understood that the problem does not necessarily lie with the innovation. Rather, the problem more likely resides in the system in which the innovation is being installed. This point was made abundantly clear by Neal Gross and a group of his graduate students who conducted a careful study of the process of innovation in schools. Among the more profound of their findings was that one of the reasons many innovations did not produce the results intended was that they were never fully implemented, or were implemented in ways at wide variance with the ways they were designed.[3] This conclusion may not seem particularly surprising, but it goes far to explain why so many innovations installed in schools make so little difference.

A CLOSING COMMENT

The arguments and assumptions presented in this chapter are intended as a template against which the reader can contrast his or her own views about the

[3]See Neal Gross, Joseph Giaquinta, and Marilyn Bernstein, *Implementing Organizational Innovations* (New York: Basic Books, 1971).

way transformational change is best accomplished in schools. More important than the specific content of the theory of action I have advanced here is the idea that all leaders should have a theory of action to guide and discipline their work. Without such a theory, and a commitment to that theory, it is likely that in the morass of transformational change transformation will revert to reform and reform to the maintenance of the status quo.

Personal theories are, however, just that—personal. Until their assumptions have been articulated and made public there is little chance that fundamental errors in fact and in logic can be detected. My hope is that by revealing as clearly as I can how I have come to view these matters after a lifetime of experience I might encourage those who are leading our schools to more fully explain to themselves as well as to others the assumptions on which they act and are asking others to act. It is only when the thinking of leaders becomes transparent that potential followers have a basis for making the commitments that must be made to transform our schools.

Engaging the Heart and Recapturing Our Heritage

I hope that this book will encourage local leaders to take the actions necessary to restore to their communities the right to set the direction of their schools. More than that, I hope that in this work, they will discover how attending to their schools might serve as well as a catalyst for building and strengthening their sense of community.

To transform schools and communities, leaders must shape their arguments in ways that others embrace. This means that they must understand the values and needs of those they would persuade. More than that, they must learn to connect these values to the ideas they want others to embrace. Through making these connections, educational leaders can make their most important contributions to the community conversation that is essential to transforming America's schools. Educators must therefore become marketers of ideas about how schools should be organized to achieve the ends we need them to achieve.

DEVELOPING A MARKETING MENTALITY

Selling begins with a product. Marketing begins with the needs and values of the customer. The salesperson query has to do with what he or she can do to persuade the customer to buy whatever it is the salesperson has to offer. The marketer is concerned with designing a product or service that meets the needs and requirements of the customer. If a product is properly designed it should sell itself, or nearly so.

For the most part, the experience of school reformers has been with sales: they are trying to persuade others to buy a program or a strategy they believe will help to improve the schools. Usually, however, many whose support the reformer wants see no pressing need or may even believe it is antithetical to their interests.

To be successful, therefore, leaders of transformation efforts must move from sales to marketing and system design. They must learn to connect to what the authors of *Applebee's America* refer to as the gut values of their audiences.[1] They must learn that transformation is a matter of the heart as well as the mind.

Facts, data, and logic are important elements in the design of change initiatives, but so are matters of taste, tradition, core values, and binding beliefs. Fact-based decision making is not enough to transform schools. Values-based decision making is required as well.

Two of the gut-level values that Americans hold are the value of local control of education and the idea that schools should be central places in the life of the community. Both of these values are threatened by efforts to improve schools through the increasing use of standards promulgated by bureaucrats external to the local community—and through the transformation of schools from community institutions to government agencies. Many citizens suspect that this is so, but to date few educators, other than right-wing critics of public education as a concept, are willing to say that this is so. (Indeed, these critics often use the pathologies of government-run schools to argue against public schools and for privatizing education.)

Educational leaders sympathetic to the cause of public education in America must learn to make these threats clear, and they must do so without resorting to the demagoguery that is so often implicit in some of the rants against public schools.[2] Then they must seek to enlist community leaders in a cause bigger than

[1]Douglas B. Sosnik, Matthew J. Dowd, and Ron Fournier, *Applebee's America: How Successful Political, Business, and Religious Leaders Connect with the New American Community* (New York: Simon and Schuster, 2006).
[2]See Bruce Fuller, Melissa Henne, and Emily Hannum, *Strong States, Weak Schools: The Benefits and Dilemmas of Centralized Accountability* (Bingley, U.K.: Emerald Grove Publishing, 2008), for an excellent example of a line of research that is making this point clear. It is an even-handed treatment of the problems associated with the implementation of centralized accountability systems and clearly documents the tendency of bureaucracies to overwhelm good intentions.

themselves: the cause of restoring public education as central to the life of local communities and under the control of citizens who place the common good above self-interest.[3] They must help the public understand what David Mathews makes so clear: the word *public* is not synonymous with the word *government*.[4] It just may be, furthermore, that the greatest threat to public schools in America is the threat of government control of schools.

Educational leaders must avoid treating community-building work as a public relations effort intended to put the right spin on some of the uncomfortable facts about the performance of their schools. They must operate from the assumption that most citizens understand that problems occur and are willing to share responsibility for solving problems if they trust their leaders.

What most citizens want from their leaders is a commonsense discussion about the nature of the problems that are to be confronted, some ideas regarding what might be done about them, and clear indications of what will be required of the community and individuals if the problems are to be addressed. Most of all, Americans want leaders who can communicate in ways that are authentic—leaders who know how to use stories and metaphors to persuade rather than simply facts and policy discussions to convince. They want leaders who can develop a narrative and a story line rather than simply present a report or an evaluation study.

Educational leaders need to be attuned to those to whom citizens turn for direction when they are confused about civic issues (the authors of *Applebee's America* refer to these persons as *navigators*) and they must make every effort to connect to these people in every way possible, including electronically. For example, a superintendent bent on transforming schools might create an electronically based network of persons who can be identified as navigators and then use this network as a means of receiving ideas and communicating actions and problems.

Educational leaders need to examine critically some of the assumptions they make about parents, senior citizens, nonparent taxpayers, members of minority groups, and others with whom they interact about school matters. Is it the case, for example, that senior citizens are inherently opposed to increases in taxes for

[3]The April 2008 issue of *Phi Delta Kappan* has several articles dealing with the issue of communities and the need to build a public for public education. I am the author of one of these articles, but other views are presented as well. See especially David Mathews "The Public and Public Schools: The Coproduction of Education" *Phi Delta Kappan,* April 2008, pp. 560–571.
[4]See David Mathews, *Reclaiming Public Education by Reclaiming Our Democracy* (Dayton, Ohio: Kettering Foundation Press, 2006).

schools? Or might it be that the lack of connection between schools and senior citizens provides seniors with no reason to support the schools? Do many parents fail to support the schools because they are uninterested in them? Or are the conditions of the interaction between parents and schools off-putting and inconvenient for many parents? Might it be possible to think of ways to use electronic networks as a means of generating more parental involvement in the life of schools and perhaps even in the lives of their own children?

Like all other leaders, educational leaders must not be afraid to admit mistakes and unfortunate efforts. They should not rationalize such occurrences. Rather, they should use mistakes as opportunities to establish and maintain trust by demonstrating that even in times of crisis and personal embarrassment, they are committed to the values of integrity and loyalty to friends—values that most citizens cherish above most other personal qualities. Failure in this regard is almost certain to squander whatever gut-level connections have been made.

Finally, educational leaders must become much more attuned to the possibilities that digital learning can provide for the education of children, and they must recognize that new technologies are a fundamental reality in our lives. Such technologies must be used by schools (as they are in the world of business) to build communities, make connections within communities, more fully engage students in the intellectual and moral life of the school, and bind students to the schools as well as to one another.

SOME ADDITIONAL SUGGESTIONS FOR ACTION

If public schools are to be transformed and communities are to be revitalized, educational leaders need to learn to stand conventional thinking on its head. Rather than ask how schools can gain more support from the community and how school leaders can bring the community into the life of the schools, they need to ask how the schools can be more supportive of community life and how they can more effectively insert the schools into the life of the community.

It will not be enough to invite parents to be connected to the schools. The schools must help parents connect to each other, as well as to citizens who have no school-age children. It will not be enough to invite citizens to support the schools by volunteering to be tutors, participating in the PTA, or voting for bond issues.

They must also be invited to participate in restoring the ability of local communities to run their schools. Indeed, without political action by local leaders, the ability of local citizens to direct their schools will increasingly deteriorate. Lobbying against federal control and bureaucratic domination must become part of the agenda of every local school board. Civic leaders who are concerned about building and sustaining a sense of community where they live must also become concerned with restoring the local communities' control of schools.

To accomplish these ends, there are many possible actions educators might take. For example, volunteers from among parents, senior citizen groups, and other citizens interested in education might be asked to form small discussion groups of no more than eight or ten people. The superintendent, a principal, or a school board member might prepare a short video setting forth a proposition that frames an issue for discussion to serve as the focal point for a group meeting. At a more sophisticated level, a book study might be in order to focus discussion. Provocative articles from popular magazines and opinion pieces from publications like *Education Week* might be used as well.

Such meetings might well occur in homes, in the meeting rooms of senior citizens' housing complexes, the party rooms of condominium complexes, or any of the many other places that citizens might get together for informal conversations. Such discussions should be led by noneducators, though educators might be invited to participate.

The intent of these study groups would be to encourage serious discussion of serious matters, but the meeting would serve as well to build networks of citizens who have at least some common bonds built around consideration of issues that should be of concern to all citizens.

It would not be expected that such meetings would result in consensus or orthodoxy. Rather, the intent would be to encourage informed and disciplined discussion among small groups of citizens. Some citizens may, as a result of these discussions, become activists, but there should be no intent to control the direction that activity would take.

The long-term intent of such activities would be to build a network of informed citizens who have a clearer understanding of the issues that confront local schools and who see the need to organize schools so that they are centers of community life. These discussions should serve as well to reframe the issues of standards, accountability, and the role of local leadership in the governance of schools. In the short run, the intent would be to provide parents and other citizens the opportunity to develop a sense of community and shared concern regarding the future of education in America.

Another strategy might be to build on a practice that is even now common among politically astute school board members: the practice of consulting with influential constituents. With support from school staff, school board members might be encouraged to identify navigators in the community and make personal contact with them for the purpose of soliciting their views of the schools. Their views then provide data to help inform the nature of the conversations school officials might have with the community more generally. For example, if it is discovered that some of these navigators have negative attitudes toward the schools, and that these attitudes are based on faulty information or lack of information, then conversations could center on clarifying the matters of concern.

It would be critical that these navigators be listened to and that they know they are heard even when the messages they bear are unpleasant. Until navigators trust school officials, they will not trust the information school officials provide, and it is the navigators who will determine whether others in the community will trust school leaders.

The most efficacious way to build community and trust is through face-to-face and person-to-person interaction, especially between leaders and navigators. Committee meetings and hearings will not do. Openness and transparency, and the willingness to make oneself vulnerable, are the only avenues to trust. To be trusted, leaders must behave in trustworthy ways.

Another strategy to build community might focus on the idea of developing local graduation standards. This strategy might be embedded in the study group approach. For example, study groups might be encouraged to examine both state graduation standards (assuming that these exist) and the literature on standards more generally. (Of course, I recommend a few chapters from this book, but there are other materials that should be consulted as well.)[5] These groups might then be encouraged to consider proposals from the local board of education or school staff regarding the issues.

These strategies need to be carefully designed and will call on educators to function in new ways. For example, if the study group strategy is undertaken, it will probably be necessary, in the initial stages at least, to provide considerable training and support to the volunteer leaders. Care must be taken that this training and support are not, and are not perceived to be, manipulative. The intent

[5]See, for example, "The Indiana Academic Standards and Resources" mentioned previously. Indiana State Department of Education, "The Indiana Academic Standards and Resources." 2006. http://dc.doe.in.gov/Standards/AcademicStandards/PrintLibrary/docs.

of forming such groups is to cause disciplined discussions of the right subjects rather than to ensure that the conclusions drawn are the "right" conclusions. This requires that school leaders learn to trust the naïve democratic belief that, given adequate information, citizens do not do a bad job of figuring things out for themselves.

Political organizers have engaged in activity much like this for a long time, but it would be a mistake to think of this as a political activity or a public relations effort. The difference is that the intent of what I am proposing is to advance a community conversation rather than to push an agenda. Learning what citizens are hearing is as important as making sure they are hearing the story school officials want to tell. Indeed, what the citizens are hearing might more accurately define the meaning of the school in the community than does the story school officials might want the citizens to hear.

A COMMON CAUSE

As a young man, I did not see the dangers of government control of education that I now see. Had I understood sooner, I would have been more active in opposing much of the federal education legislation that has been passed in recent years, as well as state efforts to centralize definitions of what children should learn.

I am not, however, persuaded that children would be better served if all parents were given vouchers to attend private schools. I work with private schools and find that many of them suffer from the same problems of bureaucratization that beset public schools. As I argued earlier, vouchers are a bad idea, if for no other reason than that over the long run, they are likely to weaken even more the ties that nonparent taxpayers have to public support for the education of children.

Neither am I persuaded by the rhetoric of some of the more conservative members of the academic community regarding the declining quality of American schools. Recent high school graduates are certainly no more ignorant than some graduates were in 1955, but in 1955 (the year I graduated), few of us were expected to know very much—all most of us needed to know was how to follow directives of superiors and do our jobs. Furthermore, the standards of high schools today are certainly not lower than were the standards when I graduated. For example, in 1955, algebra was a gatekeeper course for entry into college, and only the college bound were expected to enroll. Today algebra is a minimum requirement for graduation for all students in at least twenty states. The problem is that expectations have changed dramatically, but the performance capacities of schools have not improved at a similar pace.[6]

We need twenty-first-century schools if we are to provide an education for citizens of the twenty-first century. Schools based on structures created in the nineteenth century will not do what needs to be done. Schools need to be transformed into organizations capable of engaging the hearts as well as the minds of students. It is not enough that schools ensure that students can satisfy the conditions set by external groups and agencies more concerned with the utility of the products of the schools than with the dignity and worth of the human beings the schools ought to nurture, educate, and develop. Schools need to be concerned with supporting the development of young people into the kind of human beings and citizens our democratic culture requires and our shared values dictate. It is time to reclaim our schools from the narrowly instrumental role that has been forced on them and to attend as well to the expressive needs and values of families and communities, values around which our children can establish identity.

It is time to reinvent schools as they should be and are needed to be: vital centers of community life and places around which America's inherent diversity can be united in a common cause bigger than any of us—a cause so grand that it will not only inspire us today but will also "secure the blessings of liberty to ourselves and our posterity."

[6]I present data to support these assertions in an earlier book: *Inventing Better Schools* (San Francisco: Jossey-Bass, 1997).

appendix
A

Organizational Properties and Systemic Qualities

Bureaucracies and learning organizations differ in kind rather than in degree. Schools can and often do reflect characteristics that are similar to both types, but this simply illustrates that the two types are idealized models, "expressing in a pure—and therefore unreal—form, the core characteristics of a pattern of conduct."[1] No organization, including a school or a system of schools, will reflect either type with perfection.

The material presented in this appendix provides a detailed description of the patterns of conduct one might expect to observe in schools organized on bureaucratic principles, in contrast to schools organized on principles suggested by the idea of the learning organization, organized using the framework of the six critical systems outlined in Chapter Two.

These patterns are not descriptions of reality; they are tools that make such descriptions possible. It is intended that these descriptors be used as a framework for assessing current conditions in school districts and for making decisions regarding which systems should receive priority attention in the effort to transform a given school or school district.

[1]Everett Wilson, *Sociology: Rules, Roles, and Relationships* (Homewood, Ill.: Dorsey Press, 1971), p. 644.

Directional System

Bureaucracies	Learning Organizations
Rules and policies rather than beliefs and values define all operations, and compliance with these rules is enforced through the application of sanctions that are more likely to be punishments than rewards.	The beliefs, values, and images that guide operation in the school are clear, well understood, consistent, and embraced by most who participate in the life of the school and school district.
Only top-level officials are expected to understand the direction that has been set for the school district. For most employees, including most teachers, their commitment to the system is largely contractual and carries no obligation beyond that specified in the operating job description.	Teachers, principals, central office staff, the superintendent, and members of the board of education share a common understanding of and commitment to the direction that has been set for the school district. They are expected by those who participate in the life of the school district to behave in ways that are supportive of that direction.
Standards are used as a means of assessing compliance with rules and as a means of distributing rewards and administering punishments.	Standards are used as indicators of direction and benchmarks of progress rather than as expressions of power and indicators of compliance.
Relationships with groups and agencies outside the school or school district are limited, and when such relationships are perceived to be necessary, leaders try to structure them in a way that ensures that control will not be lost to some other agency or group.	The school district has established relationships and structures that promote collaboration and cooperation with other organizations that have an interest in the direction of the school district, such as the teachers' union, parent organizations, civic organizations, and business groups, endeavoring thereby to increase civic capacity and decrease adversarial behavior.
Goals are set with an eye toward the past rather than a focus on the future. For example, what is referred to as a strategic goal often turns out to be nothing more than a tactical solution to a pressing problem and a possible way to relieve some existing tensions created by existing policy or courses of action.	Goals are set with careful attention to the prospect that they will capitalize on emerging opportunities and make optimal contributions to the realization of the vision that guides the district. Moreover, goals are designed to ensure that the means by which they are to be achieved will be consistent with and

Directional System (*Continued*)

Bureaucracies	Learning Organizations
	supportive of the beliefs and values that are intended to guide behavior in the district and in each school.
Establishing strategic direction, to the extent that there is such a direction, is highly centralized, and goals are usually set without much input from employee groups.	Strategic goals are set at the district level, but each school establishes operational goals that take local circumstances into account.
The installation of innovations that require changes in structure or culture seldom occurs, and when it does, the innovations are more likely to be rejected over time or modified to fit the existing system, thereby diminishing their effects.	When the pursuit of goals requires the introduction of innovations, the power and authority system, the evaluation system, and the boundary system are adjusted to accommodate needed changes in the knowledge development and transmission system and the induction and recruitment system.
The maintenance needs of the system typically overwhelm developmental needs, and resources officially committed to improvement and development are usually co-opted in support of maintaining the status quo. Performance goals are often displaced by maintenance goals.	Mechanisms are in place to ensure that resources are allocated in ways that are consistent with official goals and expectations. When resources are not available, goals are adjusted to reflect this fact.
Policies and procedures are more likely to focus on internal matters than issues emerging from changes in the external environment.	Policies and procedures are in place to ensure the continuous assessment of progress toward achieving goals, and clear points of accountability are identified.

(Continued)

Directional System (*Continued*)

Bureaucracies	Learning Organizations
Those who set goals frequently have little contact or interaction with those who are expected to take the actions needed to achieve the goals, and those who are expected to carry the primary responsibility for action often see little relationship between what they are doing and the goals they care about.	Those who have primary responsibility for achieving goals have a voice in shaping these goals, especially in determining the way these goals are to be achieved.

Knowledge Development and Transmission System

Bureaucracies	Learning Organizations
Knowledge regarding practices and procedures is codified in formally adopted programs and policies. These policies often have their origins outside the school or school district to which they are applied. For example, as state and federal bureaucracies have become increasingly intrusive, much that is critical to the operation of schools is determined in bureaucratic offices far removed from the schools affected by these decisions.	In each school and at the district level, there exists one or more teams, organized as learning communities, that center attention on questions such as the following:
	How can schools and classrooms be organized to most effectively support teachers in creating engaging work for students and to encourage students to become engaged in the work they are provided?
	How can engagement be identified, measured, and differentiated from compliance produced by the promise of extrinsic rewards or the threat of unpleasant consequences?
	What are the elements of schoolwork that teachers control, and how can

Knowledge Development and Transmission System
(*Continued*)

Bureaucracies	Learning Organizations
	teachers ensure that these elements are built into the tasks they assign to students or the activities they encourage students to undertake?
	What evidence is there that students who do tasks because they are engaged develop more profound understanding of what they learn than do those who are simply compliant? What evidence is there that engaged students learn more and retain what they learn longer than those who are simply compliant?
	What do teachers and school principals need in order to ensure that they can and will focus effectively on creating engaging work for students and on creating school environments that encourage student engagement in academic tasks?
Central office staff and building principals assume that their primary role is to ensure compliance with programs, policies, and procedures specified by district officials.	Central office staff and building principals assume that part of their role is to provide members of learning communities with opportunities to develop the skills needed to conduct action research, as well as opportunities to gain access to cutting-edge information that might bear on the questions they are pursuing—that is, opportunities to attend conferences, conduct and participate in seminars, and so on.

(*Continued*)

Knowledge Development and Transmission System
(*Continued*)

Bureaucracies	Learning Organizations
Direct supervision of performance, rather than management by results, is typical.	Learning communities are encouraged to network with others inside and outside the school district and to engage in dialogue and conversations regarding what they are learning.
Rules, policies, and procedures, rather than values, commitments, and shared beliefs, serve as standards against which performances are judged. These standards are more likely to be based on the codification of past practice than on research, though this codification process is often called "research."	All the learning communities in the district share a common framework and vocabulary to facilitate discussion and analysis. Members use these frameworks and this language in a disciplined way. (An example of such a framework can be found in the theory of action presented in Chapter Twelve.)
Electronic networks are established primarily to facilitate top-down communication. Management by memo is still the style, though the memo may come by e-mail.	Electronic networks are established to facilitate the communication of information.
State-of-the-art data management systems may have been installed, but their use is more likely to be for management purposes (for example, tracking students) than for instruction or development.	State-of-the-art data management systems have been installed, and the range of data available from these systems is wide and varied. It includes student test score data but is not limited to such data.
It is assumed that the knowledge requirements of higher-level positions are greater than the knowledge requirements of lower-level positions. Therefore it is assumed that the judgment of superordinates is almost always better than the judgment of subordinates. This applies to the relationship between principals and teachers as well as the relationships between teachers and students and between principals and superintendents.	It is assumed that every person employed by the school district, regardless of title, is a teacher and a learner. It is further expected that each teacher-learner has a clear understanding regarding his or her obligations as a teacher. For example, it is assumed that school board members understand that one of their primary obligations is to educate their constituencies about the condition of education generally, as well as to shape the direction of

Knowledge Development and Transmission System
(*Continued*)

Bureaucracies	Learning Organizations
	schooling in the local community. Similarly, it is assumed that the superintendent and central office staff members understand that part of their role is to support the board in carrying out this external educational function as well as to work to ensure that those with whom they work in the school district get the training and support they need to be effective in their roles.
Policies aimed at controlling teaching and learning are based on the assumptions that learning is simple and predictable and that behaviorist psychology should guide classroom practices.[a]	The central office staff works to ensure that all staff members are made aware of literature (books, articles, and so on) relevant to broadening and deepening the understanding staff have of their roles and of the problems and prospects of public education. For example, central office staff members should constantly interact with various learning communities in the district and make sure that others in the district are made aware of what these groups are learning and of the kinds of resources they have found to be most useful.
Knowledge is as likely to be evaluated by its source as it is by its basis in fact and analysis. In a bureaucracy, the research most likely to be valued and adhered to is whatever research superordinates endorse.	The district and the community provide all school employees with rich cultural opportunities, including participation in seminars and classes that deal with art, music, contemporary literature, and so on, as well as educational experiences directly related to the academic disciplines.

(*Continued*)

Knowledge Development and Transmission System
(*Continued*)

Bureaucracies	Learning Organizations
Training and development of employees has a low priority in the district, and the training that is provided is more likely to be concerned with the clarification of policy, the remediation of perceived deficiencies, or the introduction of newly adopted programs than it is with the continuation of the growth and development of individual staff members.	Efforts are made to identify and celebrate creativity among staff members and to celebrate contributions staff members make to the common good and to the common store of knowledge.
Opportunities to make presentations to audiences outside the school and the local community are generally limited to those who occupy higher-level positions, and even then little is done to encourage off-site visits or attendance at conferences. Indeed, conference attendance, especially by teachers and principals, is likely to be discouraged on the basis that such activity is an unwarranted interruption of the "real" work that must go on.	Staff members are encouraged to make presentations to audiences outside the school and the local community, and they are provided support to ensure that these presentations are of the highest caliber.
Most craft knowledge is imported from outside the organization and usually through persons who have considerable bureaucratic authority (for example, curriculum specialists). Locally developed knowledge (for example, information derived from action research) is rare and gets little support from superordinates.	

[a]See Linda Darling-Hammond, *The Right to Learn: A Blueprint for Creating Schools That Work* (San Francisco: Jossey-Bass, 1997).

Recruitment and Induction System

Bureaucracies	Learning Organizations
Job descriptions clearly specify tasks to be carried out, duties assigned, and procedures for accountability.	The individual qualities and characteristics that make it most likely that new employees and future leaders will embrace the values and roles defined by the norms of the district are clearly identified.
Beyond that required by law (for example, the requirement of a teaching license), usually little attention is given to standards of employment for entry-level positions. Frequently employment is as much dependent on insider sponsorship as it is on actual qualifications. This is especially true for noncertified positions.	When new employees are recruited, the qualities and characteristics specified as critical are systematically used in making employment decisions.
The career structure for teachers is flat; the only real promotion opportunities involve promotion out of the ranks of labor into the ranks of management.	The content of early orientation and induction experiences is clearly centered on developing an understanding of and appreciation for ideas like the following: the core business of the schools is providing students with engaging schoolwork; teachers are leaders and designers of schoolwork; principals are leaders of leaders; and students are viewed as volunteers.
Management personnel are more likely to receive opportunities to participate in training opportunities than are members of lower-level employee groups.	Induction experiences are especially attuned to developing among teachers those attitudes and habits of mind needed to ensure a continuing commitment to the cultural ways of the school and to developing the skills needed to continuously improve the quality of the schoolwork they provide to students.
The content of early induction programs tends to place emphasis on classroom discipline and preferred strategies for ensuring student compliance with formal performance expectations. New employees usually have little awareness of what they will be expected to do once employed. Indeed, it is not uncommon for a new teacher to be hired by a central office functionary and informed about placement after the formal commitments have been made.	The recruitment process is used as a means of communicating expectations to new employees and to those seeking advancement, and it is also used as a means of ensuring an adequate supply of new members and persons qualified for promotion.

Recruitment and Induction System (*Continued*)

Bureaucracies	Learning Organizations
Entry into employment requires little evidence of prior commitment, and when the demand for employees exceeds the supply, standards of employment are modified to make entry easier.	Initial employment, advancement, and continuing employment require evidence of commitment to the core values of the school as well as demonstration of skill.
Stages of entry are vague and largely undifferentiated. For the most part, teachers are treated as interchangeable parts of a well-oiled machine.	Entry and full status in the organization are carefully staged, and there are clear patterns of promotion and advancement.
Time in grade and seniority, at least as much as past performance, determine access to the few perquisites available. For example, beginning teachers are more likely to travel from room to room and receive low-status assignments than are experienced teachers.	Identification with entry cohorts (for example, the entry class), collegial support, and team building are encouraged, and initial job assignments and training experiences are designed to support these intentions.
Each new employee is treated as a separate case, and there is little effort to build group cohesion or identity.	Induction experiences are designed in a way that develops awareness of defining events in the life of the school district and the schools, as well as knowledge about the myths, lore, traditions, and rituals that define the culture of the school district.
Little formal attention is given to making new employees aware of the culture of the school, the events that define the style of the organization, and so on. Isolation and segmentation typify the system.	
Training, rather than development, is the key element of the induction system, and on-the-job training is the primary means of training.	Staff development opportunities intended to develop the language and concepts needed to ensure a systematic approach to the design and assessment of schoolwork are made available.
To the extent there is a preferred training model, it is likely to be based on an apprenticeship model, but usually whatever instruction is provided comes from supervisors or specially designated technicians.	Intensive evaluation and feedback are provided during the initial stages of entry into the district or into a new position.

The presence of strong peer support is ensured through the integration |

(*Continued*)

Recruitment and Induction System (*Continued*)

Bureaucracies	Learning Organizations
New employees, like most other employees, are usually isolated from their peers, and to the extent that they have formal work-related conversations, these conversations are more likely to be with superordinates than with peers or colleagues.	of new employees into established learning communities and the assignment of mentors who provide mature models of the performances and attitudes expected.
Punishment rather than reward characterizes the system. For example, gaining tenure is not likely to be celebrated, and the reasons for granting tenure are not likely to be specified, but nonrenewal is likely to be associated with elaborate procedures and processes.	Learning communities are purposefully used as a means of communicating norms, values, commitments, and operating styles.
	New employees and new appointees are provided many opportunities for structured conversations, with a wide range of people positioned to provide feedback on performance. These conversations are supported through the use of protocols and similar activities that ensure disciplined conversations regarding progress and problems.
	Clear milestones are established, and meaningful acknowledgment and celebration are provided when inductees pass each milestone.

Boundary System

Bureaucracies	Learning Organizations
Membership is carefully defined and boundaries are aggressively defended, both within the school and between the school and the external environment.	Decisions regarding membership are situational and dependent on need and willingness to contribute.
External groups and agencies are often perceived as threats to internal control and organizational boundaries. A great deal of energy is invested in boundary maintenance activities.	Leaders at the district level and the building level aggressively seek to develop alliances and formal relationships with groups external to the school, and they work to ensure that these relationships are mutually beneficial and do not distract from the direction that has been set for the district.
Insider status is defined by official status in the school system and the presence of one's name on a payroll. All others, including parents and students, are defined as outsiders, with some being "more outside" than others.	Parents and students are defined as insiders in the school organization and are more likely to be treated as partners and members than as clients and products.
There is typically considerable tension between those operating at the building level (principals and teachers) and central office personnel, who are viewed, for the most part, as extensions of an impersonal bureaucracy with origins far beyond the community served. That is, the central office is perceived as an extension of government bureaucracy.	The local school board, rather than the state or the federal government, is the primary forum in which discussions of issues related to goals and objectives occur.
School board members perceive themselves either as separated from and superordinate to the school district leadership or as community representatives charged with controlling the work of functionaries in the schools.	School board members see themselves as insiders in the district, who are therefore expected to contribute to the pursuit of goals, rather than as outsiders who simply monitor the way others pursue goals. In effect, the school board is central to the learning community around which the larger community is organized and from which the community learns about educational matters.
Policies and procedures are determined by agencies outside the	The local board of education has considerable discretion in the way funds

Boundary System (*Continued*)

Bureaucracies	Learning Organizations
control of local personnel (for example, the state and federal government), and representatives of local constituencies (for example, the board of education) frequently view these external agencies as boundary threats.	are expended, rewards are distributed, and goals are established; the board exercises this discretion in ways that are consistent with the vision that has been set for the school district—that is, the vision of the school district as a learning organization.
Leaders of the district struggle to maintain a monopoly of control over all educational services, and they are constantly seeking ways to expand services into other agencies where educational functions are provided.	Community groups and agencies, as well as families, are invited to provide educational experiences for students, and school leaders allocate resources to support these efforts. In a school organized as a learning organization, the school not only provides educational experiences, but also supports others outside the school who provide such experiences. The tendency to separate "homeschooling" from "school schooling" has no place in the world of the school as a learning organization. Home-based education, conducted cooperatively with the school, is as much a part of the learning organization as is community-based education.

Evaluation System

Bureaucracies	Learning Organizations
Preference is given to operating standards that can be assessed through direct observation and measured in standardized ways.	Operating standards as well as performance standards are clear and derive from the beliefs, values, and vision that are intended to guide life in the school district and the schools.
Standards are usually stated as minimums rather than as expectations of high quality—what will be tolerated rather than what is to be desired, encouraged, and expected.	Assessment of performance and operations is data based, continuous, and rigorous.
The means by which data are collected and used are those that are least susceptible to variability introduced by the "human factor." Thus, objective tests are likely to be preferred over essays and standardized tests over "authentic" evaluations.	The means by which data are collected and used are transparent to those whose performance or programs are involved, and, when the assessments reveal deficiencies, all those involved in the assessment assume responsibility for ensuring that corrective action is taken.
The evaluation system gives emphasis to instrumental values, such as reading, writing, and arithmetic, and is less concerned with and less focused on expressive values, such as those found in the arts, literature, and so on.	The evaluation system takes into account the moral and aesthetic values supported by the schools, as well as the technical norms and instrumental ends that are being pursued.
Evaluations, whether of personnel or programs, are aimed primarily at ensuring conformance with minimum performance standards and properly labeling the performance capability being assessed.	Evaluations, whether of personnel or programs, are aimed at continuous improvement rather than documentation of mastery or inadequacy.
The expectations supported by the evaluation system are generally of more concern to persons outside the school (for example, employers, colleges, and universities) than they are to teachers and students. Indeed, teachers and students may be antagonistic to these standards and comply with them only to the extent necessary to avoid punishment.	The expectations that are supported by the evaluation system are widely known and accepted as legitimate, and the performances or results that are being evaluated are perceived to be performances or results that are important and over which control is possible.
	When performance targets are not met and results are not achieved, the reasons for these shortcomings are presented, and the subsequent analysis leads to corrective action.

Evaluation System (*Continued*)

Bureaucracies	Learning Organizations
When performance targets are not met and when results are not achieved, considerable effort is made to conceal these facts. When concealment fails, effort is expended in placing blame on forces or parties outside the control of individuals who are assigned responsibility for successful completion of the task. Elaborate myths and fictions are created and shared to explain away failures.	The evaluation system makes clear distinctions between what happened and why it happened—that is, a distinction between description and analysis.
Distrust, factionalism, and adversarial relationships abound, including adversarial relationships between labor and management and competitive relationships between and among departments and other subunits (for example, between and among schools in the same district).	There is an attitude of trust, mutualism, and common interest among those conducting evaluations and those people whose performances or programs are being evaluated.
When evaluations are used as a means of exercising formal authority (for example, disciplinary action or the abandonment of a program), the basis for the evaluation is usually couched in highly technical terms and designed as much as to protect the system from legal action as to ensure the quality of the product or service.	When evaluations are used as a means of exercising formal authority (for example, disciplinary action or the abandonment of a program), the basis for the evaluation is transparent and the sources of data are visible to those being evaluated as well as to the evaluator.
Evaluation is used more as a tool for the exercise of authority than as a means of giving direction to improvement efforts.	

Power and Authority System

Bureaucracies	Learning Organizations
Power is treated as a tool for ensuring uniformity and compliance and is likely to be assigned to positions.	Power is treated as a resource for getting work done and is more likely to be assigned to people and tasks than to positions and levels in a hierarchy.
Position-related power is the basis of directing and controlling activity, and the way this power is used is legitimized by elaborate sets of rules and procedures.	The use of position-related power as the basis of directing and controlling activity is limited. For the most part, authority is assigned on an ad hoc basis in response to perceived need rather than on a basis related to formal position.
Decisions regarding how resources will be used (time, people, space, information, and technology) are typically made at the central office, and whatever decision-making autonomy teachers and principals have is clearly specified in job descriptions. The exercise of such autonomy is carefully monitored.	Decisions regarding how resources will be used (time, people, space, information, and technology) are typically made within the context of operating units (schools, departments, and learning communities), though direction and priorities may be set centrally with input from operating units. For example, district policy might require that equity guidelines be followed in making employment decisions, but local school principals and faculties, working within these guidelines, have autonomy regarding who will be hired.
Administrative directives, adopted programs, and threats of punishment for noncompliance serve as the primary means of ensuring direction and control.	
Individuals develop increasing amounts of influence as they demonstrate their willingness to be compliant with directives and supportive of the decisions made by superordinates.	Dialogue and discussion, rather than directives, serve as the primary means of ensuring compliance with intended direction.
Rewards are distributed based on willingness to comply with directives.	Individuals develop increasing amounts of influence as a direct result of the contributions they make to solving important problems and to maintaining the ability of the group and organization to function as a continuously improving organization.
Gaining seniority and tenure and avoiding mistakes are highly valued.	

Power and Authority System (*Continued*)

Bureaucracies	Learning Organizations
Informal relationships between superordinates and subordinates are discouraged, thereby reducing the ability of superordinates to influence the behavior of subordinates without resorting to the threat of formal sanctions. (This results in a tendency to vacillate between inattention or noncompliance and extreme formal sanctions as dismissals and disciplinary furloughs are applied.)	Rewards are distributed based on contributions to the achievement of goals.
Rules aimed at codifying precedents and preventing the worst-case scenario are the norm.	The primary means by which control is maintained is self-control, and from time to time, informal sanctions are applied by peers. The application of formal sanctions is rare, and when it does occur, it is generally seen as a signal that something has gone wrong with the induction and recruitment system or the knowledge development and transmission system.
Bureaucratic scapegoating and strategic deviancy are commonplace, because the rules seldom take human variability into account. Indeed, one of the things that makes bureaucracies viable is the willingness of participants to violate the rules, even when they place themselves at risk for doing so.	The processes and disciplines (that is, the codified means) of arriving at decisions are well articulated and include specific attention to such matters as "what we know about teaching, learning, and schools, and how we know that what we know is so" and to ways to address issues of personal taste and values.
Informal networks frequently emerge that are designed to offset, sabotage, or mitigate the way formal authority is used and to redefine the rules in ways that are more responsive to local conditions.	For the most part, participants in the organization understand, support, and believe in the decisions made. When they do not, they feel they have access to a means of ensuring that their contrary views are heard and taken into account. Furthermore, even when this accounting does not result in a changed decision, critics feel their views have been heard and honored.
Most participants in the organization are ignorant about or do not believe in many of the rules and procedures they must adhere to, and therefore they have little commitment to them. Moreover, rules, once established, are often separated from the results they are intended to produce,	Each member of the group accepts responsibility for the decisions of every other member of the group and

(Continued)

Power and Authority System (*Continued*)

Bureaucracies	Learning Organizations
sometimes to the point that enforcement of a rule becomes more important than the attainment of the intended result.	trusts that these decisions are, or are intended to be, consistent with the values shared by the members of the group and the disciplines they have agreed to apply to their decision-making process.
The results of decisions and actions are often unclear and the locus of authority often ill defined, thereby encouraging more attention to the study of decision making than to the making of decisions, and more attention to fixing blame rather than to fixing the system.	The results of decisions and actions are made transparent through systemic attention to specifying and measuring intended results.
	Processes are in place for evaluating the consequences of decisions. When these consequences do not prove to be those that are expected or needed, a means has been specified for analyzing why this is the case and then taking corrective action.

Images of School

Image	Distinguishing Characteristics
Student	
Volunteers and customers for engaging work	It is assumed that student motives should be the focal point for designing work for students and that the success of a task is best judged by the extent to which students volunteer time and effort, focus their attention on the related tasks, and persist when they have difficulty.
Clients	Students are expected to comply with the directives of teachers, perform prescribed work, and focus attention and exert effort on tasks prescribed by the teacher in exchange for some extrinsic reward they value—for example, good grades, parent approval, admission to college, access to extracurricular activities.
Raw materials	It is assumed that student academic ability and family background, more than any other factor, are the primary determinants of student academic performance.
Inventory	Students are treated as objects to be contained and entertained rather than people to be educated and engaged in meaningful activity.
Inmates	Students are seen as hostile to the ends of the school and are therefore subject to coercive actions by teachers and administrators, including students' being denied access to favored programs, having their mobility limited, and being isolated from others.
Parent	
Partners	Parents are expected to participate in determining both the ends and means of schooling and are treated as equals (with the teacher) in assessing the needs of the student and setting standards for the student's performance.

(Continued)

Image	Distinguishing Characteristics (*Continued*)
Guarantors and questionable allies	Parents are expected to support teacher decisions and directives, ensure students comply with duties and tasks assigned, and encourage respect for the expert- and tradition-based authority of the teacher. Few parents are, however, fully trusted, and their support is always viewed as problematic.
Supply sources and determinants of product quality	The quality and characteristics of parents are a primary explanation for the performance of students: "an apple does not fall far from the tree."
Shippers and receivers	Parents have little direct contact with the schools their children attend, and teachers and other school officials have little direct knowledge about the child's life circumstances.
Distrusted visitors	Parents are viewed as potential antagonists and critics. Their presence in the school or the classroom is looked on with disfavor and is likely to be a source of tension among teachers and office staff.

Teacher

Leaders, designers, and guides to instruction	Teachers are expected to design engaging work for students and lead them to those forms of instruction needed to ensure the successful completion of that work.
Performers, presenters, clinicians, or diagnosticians	Teachers are likely to compare themselves to service delivery professionals such as lawyers and physicians and to base their authority claims on special knowledge and expertise as well as tradition. Some may view themselves as junior members in the professoriate or perhaps as the "sage on the stage."
Skilled workers	The work of the teacher is usually carefully proscribed and prescribed. Moreover, the teacher is subject to tight supervision and likely to be provided incentives similar to those offered for piecework in a factory.
Clerks and record keepers	Teachers spend a great deal of their time doing paperwork to comply with bureaucratic mandates and putting students through busywork tasks that have no purpose other than keeping the students busy and occupied.
Guards	The primary task of the teacher is to maintain order and decorum in the classroom and hallways and on the playground.

Image	Distinguishing Characteristics
Principal	
Leader of leaders	The principal seeks and helps others seek ways to more effectively create engaging work for students. The principal views teachers as leaders and designers and takes the development of these leaders as a primary responsibility.
Chief of staff	The principal sees himself or herself as "first among equals" and sometimes as an instructional leader who facilitates communication between teachers and superintendent and school board entities.
Shop foreman	The principal views teachers as subordinates and assumes primary responsibility for enforcing rules, evaluating teachers' performances, and maintaining order.
Midlevel bureaucrat and keeper of keys	The principal operates more as a functionary than as either a manager or a leader. He or she is likely to be obsessed with completing paperwork and forms, keeping supplies in order and under administrative control, developing schedules, and so on.
Warden	The principal ensures tight supervision and the maintenance of decorum and order. It is common that the principal also spends a great deal of time in the role of disciplinarian.
Central office	
Capacity builders	Staff work in partnership with building-level leaders to procure resources, garner support, and facilitate system-level changes required to support and sustain continuous innovation at the school and classroom levels.
Technicians and support staff	Staff provide technical assistance and support to building-level staff.
Supervisors and program managers	Staff manage budgets and programs, supervise building-level operations, and ensure compliance with district and state mandates and regulations.
Site supervisors and schedulers	Staff provide technical assistance to superintendent and other top-level administrators in the preparation of reports, the placement of students, and the distribution of resources.
Shift supervisors and compliance officers	Staff serve as compliance officers and hearing officers, function as liaison to courts and law enforcement officials, arrange placement of misbehaving students, and oversee the management of special schools and programs.

(Continued)

Image	Distinguishing Characteristics (*Continued*)
Superintendent	
Moral and intellectual leader	The superintendent assumes a central role in the development, articulation, and maintenance of a clear direction for the district and supports this direction with a clear vision of what schools would look like if they were headed in the preferred direction. This superintendent is also likely to be a reader and a storyteller and capable of inspiring others through what he or she says and does.
CEO	The superintendent works with key subordinates and the board of education to make major policy decisions and develop strategies to support those policies. This superintendent is likely to spend a good deal of time with school board members, key central office staff members, and powerful community leaders, but little time with principals and classroom teachers.
Plant manager	This superintendent is likely to be concerned with strategy, systems, and structure and will be hands-on, sometimes to the point of micromanaging key operating units, including school buildings. He or she will likely be adamant about lines of authority, the chain of command, and who reports to whom.
Property manager	This superintendent is likely to be more concerned about things than about people and programs. He or she may, for example, spend a great deal of time building budgets, visiting building sites, and tracking material and material costs. He or she is likely to leave curriculum, instruction, and personnel policy to subordinates.
Bureau chief	The superintendent operates more as an overseer and far-removed manager than a hands-on manager or a moral leader. This superintendent is more likely to be concerned with compliance than with results.
School board	
Community builders and community leaders	The board develops and implements strategies to involve most community members in serious dialogue about the schools, especially about what children should learn in school and how the community will know that they are learning these things.

Image	Distinguishing Characteristics
Board of directors	The board functions much like a well-operating corporate board. This board usually has a committee structure, tightly structured agendas, strong board leadership, and board members who concern themselves more with policy and overall assessment of the performance of the system and top-level leaders than with day-to-day operations.
Owners and advocates	These board members represent special interests of constituencies that elect them and see their primary role as that of ensuring that schools follow the operating directives promulgated by the board. Boards that view themselves as owners and advocates are likely to be more concerned with regulations than with policy and to state policy as directives for action rather than as broad principles that provide direction for action.
Safety inspectors and fire marshals	This type of board is likely to "major in minors" and to be more concerned with the material side of schooling than with the human side.
Hearing officers and parole board	The board sets sessions to resolve disputes and ensure that standards of behavior are consistently applied. Consequently this type of board holds many meetings dealing with student and staff discipline, grievances, and other quasi-judicial matters.

Bibliography

Arendt, Hannah. *Eichmann in Jerusalem: A Report on the Banality of Evil.* New York: Penguin, 1994.

Bitner, Terry Lynn. *Homeschooling with Attitude.* http://homeschoolattitude.blogspot.com/, May 21, 2005.

Blanchard, Ken. *Servant Leader.* Nashville, Tenn.: Countryman, 2003.

Booher-Jennings, Jennifer. "Below the Bubble: Educational Triage and the Texas Accountability System." *American Educational Research Journal,* 2005, *42,* 231–268.

Botstein, Leon. *Jefferson's Children.* New York: Doubleday, 1997.

Bryk, Anthony S., and Schneider, Barbara. *Trust in Schools: A Core Resource for Improvement.* New York: Russell Sage Foundation, 2002.

Callahan, R. E. *Education and the Cult of Efficiency.* Chicago: University of Chicago Press, 1962.

Christensen, Clayton M. *The Innovator's Dilemma.* Boston: Harvard Business School Press, 1997.

Christensen, Clayton M., Horn, Michael B., and Johnson, Curtis W. *Disrupting Class: How Disruptive Innovation Will Change the Way the World Learns.* New York: McGraw-Hill, 2008.

Coleman, James S. *The Adolescent Society: The Social Life of the Teenager and Its Impact on Education.* New York: Free Press, 1961.

Collins, Jim. *Good to Great.* New York: HarperCollins, 2001.

Collins, Jim. *Good to Great and the Social Sectors: A Monograph to Accompany Good to Great.* Boulder, Colo.: Jim Collins, 2005.

Crozier, Michael. *The Bureaucratic Phenomenon.* Chicago: University of Chicago Press, 1964.

Darling-Hammond, Linda. *The Right to Learn: A Blueprint for Creating Schools That Work.* San Francisco: Jossey-Bass, 1997.

de Tocqueville, Alexis. *Democracy in America.* New York: New Library of America, 2004.

Dornbausch, S. M., and Scott, W. R. *Evaluation and the Exercise of Authority: A Theory of Control Applied to Diverse Organizations.* San Francisco: Jossey-Bass, 1975.

Dreeben, Robert S. *On What Is Learned in School.* Reading, Mass.: Addison-Wesley, 1968.

Dreeben, Robert S. *The Nature of Teaching and Schools: Schools and the Work of Teachers.* Upper Saddle River, N.J.: Pearson, 1970.

Drucker, Peter F. *Management: Tasks, Practices, Responsibilities.* New York: HarperCollins, 1974.

Drucker, Peter. "The Age of Social Transformation." *Atlantic,* Nov. 1994. http://www.theatlantic.com/politics/ecbig/soctrans.htm.

Drucker, Peter F. *The Essential Drucker: The Best of Sixty Years of Peter Drucker's Essential Writings on Management.* New York: HarperCollins, 2001.

DuFour, Richard. "Schools as Learning Communities." *Educational Leadership,* 2004, *61*(8), 6.

Durkheim, Emile. *Education and Sociology.* Trans. Sherwood D. Fox. New York: Free Press, 1965.

Etzioni, Amitai. *A Comparative Analysis of Complex Organizations: On Power, Involvement and Their Correlates.* New York: Free Press, 1961.

Finn, Jr., Chester E., Petrelli, Michael J., and Julian, Liam. *To Dream the Impossible Dream: Four Approaches to National Standards and Tests for American Schools.* Washington, D.C.: Thomas Fordham Institute, 2006.

Fishman, Charles. "No Satisfaction." *Fast Company,* Dec. 2006, p. 82.

Foster, Judy. "Anti-Public School Movement Grows." *WorldNetDaily,* Apr. 16, 2002.

French J., and Raven, B. H. "*The Bases of Social Power.*" In D. Cartwright (ed.), *Studies in Social Power.* Ann Arbor, Michigan: Institute for Social Research, 1959.

Friedman, Milton. "The Market Can Transform Our Schools." *New York Times,* July 2, 2002.

Fuller, Bruce, Henne, Melissa, and Hannum, Emily. *Strong States, Weak Schools: The Benefits and Dilemmas of Centralized Accountability.* Bingley U.K.: Emerald Grove Publishing Limited, 2008.

Gerstner, Louis V. Jr. "Lessons from 40 Years of Education 'Reform': Let's Abolish Local School Districts and Finally Adopt National Standards." *Wall Street Journal,* December 1, 2008.

Gross, Neal, Giaquinta, Joseph, and Bernstein, Marilyn. *Implementing Organizational Innovations.* New York: Basic Books, 1971.

Goffman, Erving. *Frame Analysis: An Essay on the Organization of Experience.* New York: HarperCollins, 1974.

Grunwald, Michael. "Billions for an Inside Game on Reading." *Washington Post,* Oct. 1, 2006, p. B1.

Helms, Ann Doss. "CMS May Go Beyond Moving Teachers." *Charlotte Observer,* Jan. 25, 2008.

Herberg, Will. *Protestant—Catholic—Jew: An Essay in American Religious Sociology.* Chicago: University of Chicago Press, 1955.

Hersch, Patricia. *A Tribe Apart: A Journey into the Heart of American Adolescence.* New York: Fawcett-Columbine, 1998.

Hofer, Eric. *The True Believer: Thoughts on the Nature of Mass Movements.* New York: HarperCollins, 2002.

Hofstadter, Richard. *Anti-Intellectualism in American Life.* New York: Knopf, 1963.

House, Ernest. *Evaluating with Validity.* Thousand Oaks, Calif.: Sage, 1980.

Humes, Edward. *School of Dreams: Making the Grade at a Top American High School.* Orlando, Fla.: Harcourt, 2003.

Hutchens, David. *Shadows of the Neanderthal: Illuminating the Beliefs That Limit Our Organizations.* Waltham, Mass.: Pegasus Communications, 1999.

Indiana Department of Education. "Indiana's Academic Standards and Resources," 2006. http://dc.doe.in.gov/Standards/AcademicStandards/PrintLibrary/docs-english/2006-06-ela-grade12.pdf.

James, William. *On the Pluralistic Universe.* Hibbert Lectures at Manchester College, Oxford University, 1908.

Kanter, Rosabeth Moss. *On the Frontiers of Management.* Boston: Harvard Business School Press, 1997.

Kelley, Robert. "In Praise of Followers." *Harvard Business Review,* 1988, 6, 142–148.

Kotter, John, and Rathgeber, Holger. *Our Iceberg Is Melting: Changing and Succeeding Under Any Conditions.* New York: St. Martin's Press, 2005.

Lakoff, George, and Johnson, Mark. *Metaphors We Live By.* (2nd ed.) Chicago: University of Chicago Press, 2003.

Leddick, Susan "Educating the Knowledge Worker," *School Administrator,* Mar. 2001. http://www.aasa.org/publications/saarticledetail.cfm?ItemNumber=3832.

Mathews, David. "The Public and Public Schools: The Coproduction of Education." *Phi Delta Kappan,* April 2008, pp. 560–571.

Mathews, David. *Reclaiming Public Education by Reclaiming Our Democracy.* Dayton, Ohio: Kettering Foundation Press, 2006.

McAdams, Donald. *What School Boards Can Do: Reform Governance for Urban Schools.* New York: Teachers College Press, 2006.

McClure, Stewart E. Oral History Interviews, Senate Historical Office, Washington, D.C., 1983.

McColl, Ann. "Tough Call: Is No Child Left Behind Constitutional?" *Phi Delta Kappan,* Apr. 2005, p. 605.

Merton, Robert K. *Social Theory and Social Structure* Glencoe, Ill.: Glencoe Press, 1957.

Mills, C. Wright. *The Sociological Imagination.* New York: Oxford University Press, 1959.

Mitt Romney in 2012. "Raising the Bar on Education." http://myclob.pbwiki.com/Raising+the+Bar+on+Education.

Montgomery, Kathryn C. *Generation Digital: Politics, Commerce and Childhood in the Age of the Internet* Cambridge, Mass.: MIT Press, 2007.

National Center for Education and the Economy. *Tough Choices for Tough Times: The Report of the New Commission on Skills for the Workforce.* San Francisco: Jossey-Bass, 2006.

National Commission on Excellence in Education. *A Nation at Risk: The Imperative for Educational Reform.* Washington, D.C.: U.S. Department of Education, 1993. http://www.ed.gov/pubs/NatAtRisk/index.html.

Nichols, Sharon L., and Berliner, David C. *Collateral Damage: How High Stakes Testing Corrupts America's Schools.* Boston: Harvard Education Press, 2007.

O'Neil, John. "On Schools as Learning Organizations: A Conversation with Peter Senge." *Educational Leadership,* Apr. 1995, p. 28.

Open to the Public Speaking Out on "No Child Left Behind": A Report from 2004 Public Hearings. Campaign for Fiscal Equity, New Visions for Public Schools, Good Schools for All, and Public Education Network. 2004. http://www.publiceducation.org/ portals/nclb/hearings/national/Open_to_the_Public.pdf.

Packer, Joel. "The NEA Supports Substantial Overhaul, Not Repeal of NCLB." *Phi Delta Kappan,* Dec. 2007, pp. 265–269.

Pascale R. T., and Athos, A. G. *The Art of Japanese Management: Applications for American Executives.* New York: Warner Books, 1982.

Perlstein, Linda. *Not Much Just Chillin': The Hidden Lives of Middle Schoolers.* New York: Ballantine Books, 2003.

Perlstein, Linda. *Tested: One American School Struggles to Make the Grade.* New York: Holt, 2007.

Peters, Tom. *Thriving on Chaos: Handbook for a Management Revolution.* New York: Knopf, 1987.

Prensky, Marc. "Digital Native, Digital Immigrants." 2001, *9*(5). http://www.marcprensky. com/writing/Prensky%20-%20Digital%20Natives,%20Digital%20Immigrants%20- %20Part1.pdf.

Prensky, Marc. "Engage Me or Enrage Me: What Today's Learners Demand." *Educause Review,* Sept.–Oct. 2005. http://net.educause.edu/ir/library/pdf/erm0553.pdf.

Putnam, Robert D. *Bowling Alone: The Collapse and Revival of American Community.* New York: Simon & Schuster, 2000.

Raelan, Joe. *Creating Leaderful Organizations: How to Bring About Leadership from Everyone.* San Francisco: Berrett-Koehler, 2003.

Ravitch, Diane. *The Great School Wars: A History of New York City Public Schools.* Baltimore, Md.: Johns Hopkins University Press, 2000.

Ravitch, Diane. *Left Back: A Century of Failed School Reforms.* New York: Simon & Schuster, 2000.

Records of the Governor and Company of the Massachusetts Bay in New England. 1853.

Reeves, Douglas B. "Power Standards: How Leaders Add Value to State and National Standards." *Educational Leadership: The Jossey-Bass Reader on Educational Leadership.* (2nd ed.). San Francisco: Jossey-Bass, 2007.

Resnik, Lauren, and Williams Hall, Megan. "Learning Organizations for Sustainable Education Reform." *Daedalus,* 1998, *127*(4), 89–118.

Robinson, Ken. *Out of Our Minds: Learning to Be Creative.* Mankato, Minn.: Capstone Publishing, 2001.

Rose, Lowell C., and Gallup, Alec M. "The 39th Annual Phi Delta Kappa/Gallup Poll of the Public's Attitudes Toward the Public Schools." *Phi Delta Kappan,* Sept. 2007, pp. 33–45.

Schlechty, Phillip C. *Teaching and Social Behavior: Toward an Organizational Theory of Instruction.* Needham Heights, Mass.: Allyn and Bacon, 1976.

Schlechty, Phillip C. *Reform in Teacher Education: A Sociological View.* Washington, D.C.: American Association of Colleges for Teacher Education, 1990.

Schlechty, Phillip C. *Schools for the 21st Century.* San Francisco: Jossey-Bass, 1990.

Schlechty, Phillip C. *Inventing Better Schools: An Action Plan for Educational Reform.* San Francisco: Jossey-Bass, 1997.

Schlechty, Phillip C. *Shaking Up the Schoolhouse.* San Francisco: Jossey-Bass, 2001.

Schlechty, Phillip C. *Working on the Work.* San Francisco: Jossey-Bass, 2002.

Schlechty, Phillip C. *Creating Great Schools: Six Critical Systems at the Heart of Educational Innovation.* San Francisco: Jossey-Bass, 2005.

Schlechty, Phillip C., and Joslin, Anne Walker. "Images of School." *Teachers College Record,* 1984, *86*(1), 156–170.

Schlechty Phillip C., and Vance, Victor. "Recruitment, Selection and Retention: The Shape of the Teaching Force." *Elementary School Journal,* 1983, *83*, 469–487.

Schlechty Phillip C., and Whitford B. L. "The Organizational Context of School Systems and the Functions of Staff Development." In G. Griffin (ed.), *Staff Development: Eighty-Second Yearbook of the National Society for the Study of Education, Part II.* Chicago: University of Chicago Press, 1983.

Senge, Peter. *The Fifth Discipline: The Art and Practice of the Learning Organization.* New York: Doubleday, 1990.

Silberman, Charles. *Crisis in the Classroom: The Remaking of American Education.* Hoboken, N.J.: Wiley, 1970.

Sizer, T. *Horace's Compromise: The Dilemma of the American High School.* Boston: Houghton Mifflin, 1984.

Sosnik, Douglas B., Dowd, Matthew J., and Fournier, Ron. *Applebee's America: How Successful Political, Business, and Religious Leaders Connect with the New American Community.* New York: Simon & Schuster, 2006.

Stone, Clarence N., Henig, Jeffrey R., Jones, Brian D., and Pierannunzi, Carol. *Building Civic Capacity: The Politics of Reforming Urban Schools.* Lawrence: University of Kansas Press, 2001.

Swanson, Christopher B., and Barlage, Janelle. *Influence: A Study of the Factors Shaping Education Policy.* Bethesda, Md.: Editorial Projects in Education Research Center, Dec. 2006.

Teaching Interrupted: Do Discipline Policies in Today's Public Schools Foster the Common Good? Washington, D.C.: Public Agenda, May 2004.

Toppo, Gregg. "How Bush Education Law Has Changed Our Schools." *USA Today,* Jan. 8, 2007, p. 2A.

Turtle, Joel. "Parents' Complaints—Arrogant Public Schools Turn a Deaf Ear." 2005. http://www.mykidsdeservebetter.com.

Twain, Mark. *Following the Equator.* http://www.twainquotes.com/Idiots.html.

Twohey, Megan. "Desegregation Is Dead." *National Journal,* Sept. 17, 1998. pp. 2614–2619.

Tyack, David. *The One Best System: A History of American Urban Education.* (New ed.) Cambridge, Mass.: Harvard University Press, 2007.

Tyack, David, and Cuban, Larry. *Tinkering Toward Utopia: A Century of Public School Reform.* Cambridge, Mass.: Harvard University Press, 1995.

U.S. Bureau of Labor Statistics. "Employment Characteristics of Families Summary." May 20, 2008. http://www.bls.gov/news.release/famee.nr0.htm.

Waller, Willard. *The Sociology of Teaching.* Hoboken, N.J.: Wiley, 1967. (Originally published in 1932)

Weber, Max. *Theory of Social and Economic Organization* (ed. Guenther Ross and Claus Wittich). Los Angeles: University of California Press, 1978.

Williams, Robin M. *American Society: A Sociological Interpretation.* (3rd ed.) New York: Knopf, 1972.

Wilson, Everett. *Sociology: Rules, Roles, and Relationships.* Homewood, Ill.: Dorsey Press, 1971.

Wineburg, Sam. "Maintaining the Vitality of Our Irrelevance: Preparing a Future Generation of Education Researchers." *Education Week,* Apr. 6, 2005, p. 35.

INDEX

A

Academic ability: schools' emphasis on, 6–8; standards-based movement's focus on, 178–180

Accountability: education delivery mode to ensure, 261–262; transparency to ensure, 259–261

Action: standards focusing on, 244n, 244–246; strategic, capacity for, 225, 235–238, 274. *See also* Theory of action

Action research, 275

The Adolescent Society (Coleman), 12

Alienation, 60

American Federation of Teachers, 155

Anti-intellectualism, 6, 6n

Arendt, Hannah, 16n

Assessment: of capacity for change, 253–254; of conditions increasing student engagement, 255–258; of current status of school, 228n, 228; of social systems, 254–255, 255n

Athos, A. G., 62

Authority: consensual, 55–57; decision-making, 228n; exercised for social control, 53–57; types of, 53–54, 55

Authority relationships, 18, 51

B

Behavioral psychology, 75, 92, 93

Blanchard, Ken, 131

Block grants, 258–259, 260–261

Boundary systems, 30, 31, 46, 272, 299–300

Bronk, Detlev, 145

Building capacity. *See* Capacity

Bureaucracies: capacity in, 223; characteristics of leaders in, 233–234; vs. community, 136–137; core businesses of, 63–65; government, transformation of schools into, 143–157; lack of trust assumed by, 201; origin of term, 39; professionals in, 97–99; rational, 40; role of standards in, 241; schools as, 42–44, 45, 46; social control in, 51, 52, 53, 55, 58–59, 61; social systems of, 46–48, 49, 50, 289–305; structure of, as barrier to innovations, 23–25; superordinate goals of, 63; transforming, into learning organizations, 138–140. *See also* Images of schools

Bureaucratic ethos, 150–152

Bureaucratic practicality, 34

Business: learning organization model in, 211–212, 217n; profit emphasis in, 162–163. *See also* Core businesses

Business leaders, and school reform, 149–150, 212–213

Busing, 191–192

C

Callahan, Raymond, 74

Capacity: to act strategically, 225, 235–238, 274; in bureaucracies, 223; civic, 187–188, 193–195; defined, 223–224; to focus on future, 225–229, 273–274; to maintain direction and focus, 225, 229–234, 274; and persistence of effort, 238–239; standards for assessing, for change, 253–254

Carnegie unit, 37

Central office: in bureaucratic images of schools, 72, 83–84, 94–95, 107–108, 309; in learning organizations, 131, 309

Charlotte-Mecklenburg Board of Education, Swann v., 191, 192

Children: marketing to, 13–15, 18–19; requiring custodial care, 62; schools' dependence on failure of some, 7–8

Christensen, Clayton M., 27n, 27–28, 38

308; transmission of knowledge work culture in, 123–125

Leddick, Susan, 120

Local control: Americans' desire for, 188; educating citizens for, 189–190; risks with, 262–263; suggestions for building trust in, 202–204

M

Marketing to children, 13–15, 18–19

Mass media, 17

Mathews, David, 160, 283

McClure, Stewart, 144, 145, 146, 196

McColl, Ann, 147

Mental models, 70; exercise on, 219; power to change image, 210–214. *See also* Images of schools; Metaphors

Merit pay, 149, 212–213

Metaphors, 70; lessons about, and school reform, 216–218; as makers of meaning, 214–215; policy as shaping, 215–216; selecting, to aid transformation, 218–219; using, to transform schools, 219–221. *See also* Images of schools; Mental models

Military, 53n

Mills, C. Wright, 150–151

Mission, vs. vision, 229

N

National Board for Professional Teaching Standards, 99

National Business Roundtable, 156

National Chamber of Commerce, 148, 156, 196

National Defense Education Act (NDEA), 146, 258–259

National Education Association (NEA), 144, 149, 155

National Governors Association, 155

National Science Foundation, 32

No Child Left Behind (NCLB): and federal government control of schools, 147, 149, 156; impact on schools, 110; issues recognized but not addressed by, 259; opposition to, 201; and parents, 181; and role of teacher, 74, 81

Norms: defined, 29–30, 273; and social control, 50; and social systems, 272–273; types of, 44

O

O'Neill, "Tip," 154

Operating systems: defined, 26; innovations focused on changing, 27, 31

P

Parents: in bureaucratic images of schools, 72, 78–80, 89–91, 103–105, 307–308; concerns of, about children's schools, 172; in learning organizations, 127–129, 307; satisfaction of, with public schools, 189; and standards-based movement, 164, 167–169, 181

Pascale, R. T., 62

Peer groups: increased influence of, 11–13; influence in workplace, 13n; as threat to traditional authority relationships, 18

Piaget, Jean, 14

Power: defined, 51; exercised for social control, 51; as strategy for introducing disruptive innovations, 38; types of, 51, 54

Power and authority systems, 30, 31, 46, 272, 303–305

Prensky, Marc, 18, 227

Principals: in bureaucratic images of schools, 72, 82–83, 93–94, 106–107, 309; in learning organizations, 129–130, 309; obtaining support of, for transformation, 268

Prisons, image of schools as, 99–110; background on, 70–71, 73, 100; central office in, 72, 107–108; and in-school suspension, 214–215; parents in, 72, 103–105; principals in, 72, 106–107; school boards in, 72, 109–110; students in, 72, 100–103; superintendents in, 72, 108–109; teachers in, 72, 105–106

Private schools, 20, 198, 252–253, 287

Privatization, 28–29, 261

Professional service delivery organizations, image of schools as, 87–99; background on, 70, 73, 87; central office in, 72, 94–95; parents in, 72, 89–91; principals in, 72, 93–94; and professionals in bureaucracies, 97–99; school boards in, 72, 96–97; students in, 72, 87–89, 88n; superintendents in, 72, 95–96; teachers in, 72, 91–93

Profit, business emphasis on, 162–163

Profound learning, 45

Public schools: and common good, 199; high-quality, necessary for democracy, 15n, 15–17, 16n; involvement of government in, 135n, 136n, 136; link between communities and, 4–5; parents' satisfaction with, 189; purpose of, 5–6; threat of government control of, 283, 287

R

Rational bureaucracies, 40

Raven, Bertram, 54

Ravitch, Diane, 78

Reading: to become transformational leader, 266–267; standards on skills in, 181–183, 247–248

Reading First program, 155, 155n

Reclaiming Public Education by Reclaiming Our Democracy (Mathews), 160

Recruitment and induction systems, 30, 31, 46, 272, 296–298

Reeves, Douglas, 244n

Reform, systemic, 27. *See also* School reform

Robinson, Ken, 6–7, 179

Romney, Mitt, 198

S

Sanctions: types of, 51–52; used to establish and maintain social control, 51–53

School boards: in bureaucratic images of schools, 72, 85–86, 96–97, 109–110, 310–311; leadership by, 195–198; in learning organizations, 133–134, 310; local, desire for control by, 188; necessary change by, 205–206; obtaining support of, for transformation, 268; responsibility of, to build civic capacity, 193–195

School consolidation, 190, 191–192, 195–196

School of Dreams (Humes), 88n

School reform: and business leaders, 149–150, 212–213; metaphors and, 216–218; reason for difficulty of, 31–35; threats driving movements for, 4–5; as "tinkering toward utopia," 5n, 5, 19; vs. transformation, 3. *See also* Standards-based movement

School vouchers, 28, 198–201, 287

Schools: as bureaucracies, 42–44, 45, 46; core business of, 63–65; functions of, 61–62, 64; future of, in digital world, 19–21; goal conflict and displacement in, 65–68; inner-city urban, 164n, 164, 204–205; as learning organizations, 41, 42–46; parents' concerns about, 172; private, 20, 198, 252–253, 287; relationship between learning and, 163–164; as small communities or families, 134–138; as social systems, 25–26; superordinate goals of, 63, 64; transformed into government bureaucracies, 143–157; virtual, 261–262. *See also* Images of schools; Public schools; Transformation of schools

Scientific management, 74, 75, 92

Scott, W. R., 243

Self-control, 50

Senge, Peter, 40, 41, 44–45, 70, 115, 119

Separation, as strategy for introducing disruptive innovations, 38

Service delivery organizations. *See* Professional service delivery organizations, image of schools as

Shaking Up the School House (Schlechty), 28

Shanker, Albert, 213

Shook, John, 130

Sizer, Theodore, 15n

Skinner, B. F., 93

Social capital: building, 201–204; defined, 187; importance to installing innovations, 187

Social control: authority exercised for, 51, 53–57; defined, 50; influence exercised for, 51, 57–60; and involvement or alienation, 60–61; power exercised for, 51; sanctions used to establish and maintain, 51–53; types of, 50

Social systems: of bureaucracies vs. learning organizations, 46–50, 289–305; defined, 26; difficulties of changing, 31–35; schools as, 25–26; standards for assessing, 254–255, 255n; types of, 30

The Sociological Imagination (Mills), 150

Sociological Resources for the Social Studies (SRSS) project, 33

Special interest groups, 188, 193–194

Spending clause, U.S. Constitution, 147

Sputnik. See Curriculum m reform of 1960s

Standards, 241–263; absence of tests for, 172–173; changing state government's role in, 242–243; complexity of, 181–184; content vs. performance, 175–176; developmental, 246–248; of different constituencies, 180–181; effects of, 173–180; establishing, 184–186, 190; exceptions to, 251–252; graduation, 242, 244–246; and graduation and dropout rates, 252–253; holding communities accountable for enforcing, 248–251; in learning organizations vs. bureaucracies, 241; multiple, 186; nonacademic, 248; organizational performance, 253–258; in schools as factories, 77; technical vs. market-based, 169–170; tests as, 176–178; trivialization of, 170–172. *See also* Tests, standardized

Standards-based movement: as consistency with bureaucratic mental models, 159–160; difficulties of opposing, 160–161; parents' vs. experts' influence in, 164–169; test scores emphasized by, 161–164

Strategic action, capacity for, 225, 235–238, 274

Strategic thinking, 267–268

Students: in bureaucratic images of schools, 72, 76–78, 87–89, 100–103, 307; in learning organizations, 118–123, 307

Superficial learning, 45

Superintendents: in bureaucratic images of schools, 72, 84–85, 95–96, 108–109, 310; in learning organizations, 132, 310; as transformational leaders, 266–271

Superordinate goals, 62, 63, 64, 73

Suspension, in-school, 214–215

Sustaining innovations, 27

Swann v. Charlotte-Mecklenburg Board of Education, 191, 192

Systemic reform, 27

Systems: defined, 26; operating, 26, 27, 31. *See also* Social systems

T

Taylor, Frederick W., 74

Teachers: in bureaucratic images of schools, 72, 80–82, 91–93, 105–106, 308; conforming to rules, 41, 44; difficulty of task of, 14, 45n; high-quality, attracting and retaining, 81–82, 215–216; in inner-city urban schools, 164n, 164; in learning organizations, 125–127, 308; obsolete expectations of, 92, 227; as professionals, 97–99

Teaching and Learning Centers (TLCs), 217

Technology: defined, 26n; digital, 9–11, 18–19, 20; employing, for strategic action, 238; information, 9

Tenth Amendment, 144–146

Tests, standardized: parents' opinions on, 189; predictive validity of, 173; and quality of instruction, 5–6; and quality of learning, 8; as standards, 176–178

Theory of action, 265–279; action research in, 275; flexible sequencing of steps in, 276–278; focused discussions in, 275; follow-through and persistence in, 276; personal comment on, 278–279; steps in, 272–274; transformational leadership for, 266–271

Thinking, strategic, 267–268

Title I, 147

Tocqueville, Alexis de, 15n

Transformation of schools: changes required for, 209–210; into government bureaucracies, 143–157; government policies to encourage, 258–259; leaders required for, 4; into learning organizations, 138–140, 157–158; need for, 5–19, 287–288; as pre-condition for improving school performance, 24–25; vs. reform, 3; selecting metaphors to aid in, 218–219. *See also* Theory of action

Transformational leaders, development of, 258, 266–271

Transparency, 260–261

Trump, J. Lloyd, 36

Trump plan, 36–37

Trust, building, 201–204

Twain, Mark, 195

Tyack, David, 5n, 19, 144

U

U.S. Constitution: spending clause, 147; Tenth Amendment, 144–146

U.S. Department of Education, 189

V

Vance, Victor, 81

Virtual schools, 261–262

Vision: developing shared, 226–227; leaders carrying out, 134, 197, 233; in learning organizations vs. bureaucracies, 47–48; vs. mission, 229; and use of metaphors, 217

Vouchers, 28, 198–201, 287

W

Waller, Willard, 103, 125

Warehouses, image of schools as, 99–110; background on, 70, 73, 100; central office in, 72, 107–108; parents in, 72, 103–105; principals in, 72, 106–107; school boards in, 72, 109–110; students in, 72, 100–103; superintendents in, 72, 108–109; teachers in, 72, 105–106

Weber, Max, 39, 40, 53–54

Working on the Work (Schlechty), 255

CREATING GREAT SCHOOLS

Six Critical Systems at the
Heart of Educational Innovation

By Phillip C. Schlechty

ISBN: 978-0-7879-7690-3
Hardcover

"Schlechty offers a clear and concise vision of systemic change to address the problems with education." —The School Administrator

In *Creating Great Schools*, Phillip C. Schlechty offers a hands-on primer that shows educational leaders how they can sustain continuous innovation and improvement in order to create truly great schools.

Schlechty outlines the six critical systems that define the norms and expressions of a school's organizational culture—recruitment and induction, knowledge transmission, power and authority, evaluation, direction, and boundaries—and shows what it takes to lead effective systemic change in order to sustain new values and direction.

The book is filled with effective strategies and offers guidelines for introducing the "disruptive innovations" that are necessary to change the fundamental norms of an educational organization and truly revitalize a school. He also offers suggestions for working through the thorny issues that arise from the efforts to introduce new norms and provides school leaders with valuable insights into the critical rules, roles, and relationships in schools.

Creating Great Schools is based on Schlechty's decades of work with schools and districts all over the country. His practical wisdom provides leaders with the information and tools they need to transform their schools into outstanding learning institutions.

SHAKING UP THE SCHOOLHOUSE

How to Support and Sustain Educational Innovation

By Phillip C. Schlechty

ISBN: 978-0-7879-7213-4
Paperback

"Shaking Up the Schoolhouse *is all about empowering leaders so they can improve schools. This book is a must-read for policymakers at any level and for those who think and care about school improvement.*" —Paul D. Houston, executive director, American Association of School Administrators

"*Schlechty shares leading-edge insights and offers practical guidance to anyone who affects student learning. His suggestions are wonderful dialogue starters for educators searching for ways to make dramatic improvement in schools.*" —Dennis Sparks, executive director, National Staff Development Council

In this visionary book, renowned educator Phillip Schlechty argues for change-adept school systems. He not only challenges educational administrators, teachers, teacher leaders, legislators, and policymakers to recognize the need for transformation, but also shows how they can grow into skillful leaders of lasting change.

Shaking Up the Schoolhouse begins with an incisive discussion of the dangers and opportunities in reworking school systems. Drawing from decades of experience and from actual cases, the author describes the essential characteristics of change-adept organizations. He then presents a practical framework for helping teachers to overcome obstacles in the learning experience, from reviewing the competition to improving student engagement through more effective standards. Schlechty also focuses on empowering principals, superintendents, and school board members as they struggle with structural and cultural change in their schools and communities.

WORKING ON THE WORK

An Action Plan for
Teachers, Principals, and Superintendents

By Phillip C. Schlechty

ISBN: 978-0-7879-6165-7
Paperback

"Authentic student engagement in meaningful classroom work is the key to accountability. If teachers work-on-the-work, accountability will take care of itself. Thanks, Phil Schlechty, for illuminating the way for all concerned educators and parents." —Lawrence W. Lezotte, educational consultant and commentator, and author, *Learning for All, The Effective Schools Process*

If student performance is to be improved, there are at least three ways to approach the problem: 1) work on the students, 2) work on the teachers, or 3) work on the work. Unfortunately, the first two have thus far produced unimpressive results. The key to improving education, Schlechty believes, lies in the third alternative: to provide better quality work for students—work that is engaging and that enables students to learn what they need in order to succeed in the world.

In this practical companion to the author's popular books *Shaking Up the Schoolhouse* and *Inventing Better Schools*, Schlechty presents the Working on the Work (WOW) framework—an outline for improving student performance by improving the quality of schoolwork. Field-tested in schools across the country, the WOW framework describes the twelve essential components of a WOW school and suggests ways to improve the quality of content, organization of knowledge, measurement of achievement, nurturance of creativity, and novelty and variety of tasks. Schlechty offers practical guidelines for redesigning classroom activity so that more students are highly engaged in schoolwork, developing clear and compelling standards for assessing student work, and making clear connections between what students are doing and what they are expected to produce. He also discusses the roles of teachers, principals, and superintendents—and how they individually and collectively play a part in the WOW process.

INVENTING BETTER SCHOOLS

An Action Plan for Educational Reform

By Phillip C. Schlechty

ISBN: 978-0-7879-5610-3
Paperback

Winner of the National Staff Development Counsel Book Award

"Schlechty marshals readers through the ideas-to-action labyrinth of improving school.... A worthy successor to his earlier work." —The American School Board Journal

In this powerful wake-up call to educators, Phillip Schlechty argues that schools must change or become obsolete—and that central to this change is a rethinking of old rules, roles, and relationships. *Inventing Better Schools* offers a plan of attack that is thoughtful, practical, and full of step-by-step advice. Schlechty shows both educators and parents how to envision reform and design quality educational systems. He explains how the visioning process must be rooted in real shared beliefs, how mission statements must unpack visions into concrete goals that are connected to action, and how the results of reform can be usefully assessed. He points out that reinventing schools must be looked upon as a continual process—and provides leaders with the tools to negotiate their way through it.

Drawing on the author's vast experience in the day-to-day work of implementing school reform, *Inventing Better Schools* offers new approaches for setting standards and ensuring accountability—and includes samples of actual mission statements and strategic plans of successful school districts.

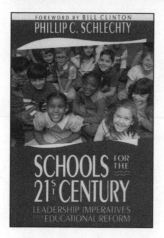

SCHOOLS FOR THE 21ST CENTURY

Leadership Imperatives for Educational Reform

By Phillip C. Schlechty

ISBN: 978-1-55542-366-7
Paperback

"Schlechty's common-sense approach to restructuring is combined with a strategic planner's vision and the translation of beliefs into action. . . . A wide audience, including principals and superintendents, can find in this book practical outlines for restructuring, and a distinctive and focused view of their role in the educational systems of the twenty-first century." —The School Administrator

Schlechty provides an innovative, adaptable framework for helping leaders in all areas of education to identify where change is needed in order to make schools more useful and responsive to children and society.

Contents

Part One: The Purpose of Schools: 1. A Future in Jeopardy: Why the Schools of Today Must Change; 2. How the Past Has Shaped the Present: The Shaky Foundation of School System Structures; 3. New Purposes for a New Era: Reinventing Our Schools

Part Two: The Ingredients of Invention: 4. The Power of Vision: Creating and Sharing the Seeds of Innovation; 5. The Capacity to Respond Quickly: Building Adaptability into the System; 6. The Ability to Rally Support for Change: Managing to Satisfy the Needs of Constituents; 7. The Creation of Change Systems: Tackling Problems at Their Source; 8. A Focus on Results: Evaluating Performers and Performances

Part Three: Leadership for the Twenty-First Century: 9. Leading a School System Through Change: Key Steps for Moving Reform Forward; 10. A Bright Future Secured: Developing Strong Leaders for Our Schools